The Reluctant Defender

The Reluctant Defender

A BIG-CITY ATTORNEY DEFENDS DESPERATE PEOPLE

by David Claerbaut

Tyndale House
Publishers, Inc.
Wheaton, Illinois

Library of Congress
Catalog Card Number
78-55983
ISBN 0-8423-5425-5, paper
Copyright © 1978
by David P. Claerbaut.
All rights reserved.

First printing, October 1978
Printed in the
United States of America

TO ROCHELLE
May she grow in courage and her life be full

CONTENTS

    FOREWORD
    BY CHUCK COLSON | 9
    ACKNOWLEDGEMENTS | 10
1 COLONY OF MISERY | 13
2 THE SYSTEM | 31
3 THE RELUCTANT DEFENDER | 39
4 BIRTH OF A CLINIC | 53
5 LIFE AT THE CLINIC | 67
6 WHAT MAKES CHUCK RUN? | 83
7 THE RULES OF THE GAME | 103
8 THE YOUNG LIFE LINK | 127
9 UNHAPPY ENDINGS | 141
10 THE TRIUMPHS | 161

11	**THE MEN IN BLUE**	179
12	**A MIXED BAG**	201
13	**DREAMS**	221
	APPENDIXES	243

FOREWORD

The Reluctant Defender is a book about justice and community concern. These are vitally important elements in contemporary America. Justice, especially urban justice, is needed to heal the wounds incurred through poverty and discrimination. Community concern is fundamental to the health of any society. In that spirit, I appreciate the efforts of the Cabrini Green Legal Aid Clinic in Chicago, for its ministry of justice is something we here at Prison Fellowship feel strongly about. We are reminded daily of the priceless value of justice and the devastating social problems which emanate from a lack of it.

The book is also about Christians who have seen a reason to get involved in their community, who have become genuinely interested in the well-being of their brothers and sisters, regardless of racial or social differences. As such, their activities provide a demonstration of commitment in action.

It is my hope that people will look at the Cabrini Green Legal Aid Clinic not simply as an interesting and valuable venture into justice and community concern, but rather as a model of what may be possible in other communities throughout America. More importantly, the clinic exemplifies an expanded concept of ministry—one which is characterized by meeting people where they are and attempting to deal with their temporal as well as spiritual needs. This is as it should be. Our Lord is our example here, as we see continually in his earthly ministry a concern for people's physical and spiritual needs.

The Christians involved with the ministry at the Cabrini Green Legal Aid Clinic are to be commended for their dedicated commitment to justice for all people and for their Christlike compassion. I know you will find this book to be both an inspiration and a challenge. I pray that it will have a wide reading.

CHUCK COLSON

ACKNOWLEDGMENTS

Books are rarely individual efforts, and this one is no exception. Although many people were helpful, space limitations necessitate citing but a select few.

Among the most deserving of thanks is Pat Garnaat. Her willing and competent aid, on the shortest possible notice, was of inestimable worth in preparing the manuscript.

I am also indebted to Julie Malloy-Good, the clinic's current secretary, and to her helpers for their tireless efforts in compiling data for the appendixes; and to Mary Klingberg and Dan Malloy-Good for sharing their valuable but difficult-to-gather research on the Cabrini-Green community. John Petersen and Bud Ipema also deserve thanks for their help along the way.

In a somewhat different sense, I would like to extend a personal note of appreciation to Lois Ottaway. Her long-time devotion to the clinic and interest in this book is appreciated by many.

Finally, and most important, a special word of thanks is directed to all those unnamed others whose working, giving, and praying continue to make the Cabrini-Green Legal Aid Clinic a reality.

*. . . for I was hungry and you gave me food,
I was thirsty and you gave me drink,
I was a stranger and you welcomed me,
I was naked and you clothed me,
I was sick and you visited me,
I was in prison and you came to me.*

MATTHEW 25:35, 36

COLONY OF MISERY

1

Driving down Lake Shore Drive toward the heart of Chicago, it is difficult to keep one's eyes on the road. On the left is Lake Michigan. Whether placid, rough, or ice-capped, the lake is always impressive. To the right is the Gold Coast, the Windy City's richest community.

Approximately 70,000 people live in the Gold Coast area. In this spectacular urban oasis, life is free of the usual petty annoyances. There is no grass to cut. No trees to prune. No public transportation to wait for. With average income exceeding $53,000 annually, price tags are nearly irrelevant. Rents averaging $600 or $700 a month for a three-bedroom apartment are easily met by such affluent citizens. Moreover, those in the Gold Coast rarely incur the inconveniences of child care; only 6 percent of the families have children living with them.

Many of Chicago's most famous, powerful, and prestigious figures live here: socialites, an ecclesiastical monarch, political barons, business tycoons, owners of sports franchises. In this community are found the finest art collections, the most exquisite furniture, the most expensive jewelry, the largest number of Mercedes-Benz automobiles in Chicago.

14 | THE RELUCTANT DEFENDER

There are high-rises, town houses, luxurious hotels, and the most exclusive restaurants. Amid all the glamor and wealth there are well-lit streets, physical safety, and first-rate service in the form of security personnel, chauffeurs, and domestic aides.

The most affluent block in the Gold Coast is East Lake Shore Drive. On this block each building has a refined exterior. The families who live here are likely to be listed in the Social Register as members of Chicago's elite. The residents of East Lake Shore Drive have six-figure incomes and a lifestyle to match. The block consists of six high-rise buildings with apartments ranging in size from one and a half to twelve rooms. The people on this street, like those in the rest of the Gold Coast, are philanthropic. The men engage in professional activity, reaping great financial rewards; their wives often donate time and money to enterprises as diverse as health-care charities, operatic productions, live theater, and the symphony.

To the east of the citizens of the Gold Coast are the bright, shimmering waters of Lake Michigan. To the west live their neighbors, the residents of Cabrini-Green.

Cabrini-Green is a colony of misery. Poverty characterizes its black inhabitants. In the winter frostbite is common. In the oppressive summer heat people crack open fire hydrants to get relief.

Depression is everywhere. Drugs are rampant, alcoholism permeates the neighborhood, and crime and violence are a way of life. Murder, robbery, and rape are common occurrences in this crucible of frustration.

Children, often fatherless, grow up among liquor bottles, drug needles, rats, roaches, and shattered glass. Defective schools, angry policemen, and exploitative businesses are integral parts of the environment. Supportive youth services and recreational facilities are lacking. Community pride is in short supply. Before going further, it is vitally important to stress that these conditions are not typical of every black community. To adopt such a stereotype would be patently racist. However, when poverty is mixed with discrimination, Cabrini-Greens are often the result.

Moreover, Cabrini-Green has not always been in this unhappy state. Before 1968, Cabrini-Green was a mixed but rela-

15 | COLONY OF MISERY

tively stable neighborhood. There were Appalachian whites living in the fringe area, with blacks and Japanese of varying economic levels residing in the community. Dr. William H. Leslie, for seventeen years the pastor of LaSalle Street Church, an evangelical church in the community, recalls a time when economic differences among the black families were a source of tension: "Often youth activities with the different income groups had to be held separately to prevent fights from breaking out."

With the assassination of Martin Luther King, Jr., in 1968, black Chicago exploded. Many blacks regarded King as their one remaining hope for peaceful change and justice in America. Seeing that apostle of nonviolence coldly gunned down in Memphis was just too much. The ghettos of the Windy City erupted with a volley of anger, pain, grief, and frustration.

The King riots markedly altered Cabrini-Green. Nonblacks fled out of fear. Older blacks who remained were frequently viewed with disdain by the younger, more militant blacks. The youth saw their elders as Uncle Toms—not the type of people who would be in the vanguard, pressing the city's institutional systems for necessary change. Teen-agers began organizing into gangs. The Black P. Stone Nation came up from the South Side and dominated the rapidly developing local gang structure.

Chuck Hogren, a brown-haired, blue-eyed lawyer, is one of very few whites involved in Cabrini-Green. Since 1973 Hogren has been the primary (and often only) attorney for the Cabrini-Green Legal Aid Clinic. The clinic, located at 1515 North Ogden Avenue in the Isham YMCA building, is a private legal agency dedicated to pursuing justice in the community.

The need for justice and legal representation for the poor was driven home in one of the clinic's earliest cases, that of Arthur Scott. It burns in Hogren's memory.

"Arthur Scott was in his twenties. He was a passenger in a car stopped for running a red light. When the officer pulled up, the driver got out and turned over his license.

"After the officer had written the ticket, he noticed there was a passenger in the car. He told Scott to get out of the car. Scott did. Now, that would never happen in a more affluent area of the city; your passenger is never bothered when you get a ticket. Anyway, the officer asked him, 'What's your name?' 'Arthur Scott' was the reply.

" 'Arthur Scott!' the officer exclaimed. 'Why we've got warrants at the station for Arthur Scott.' So Scott, completely confused, got in the squad car and was taken to the 18th District station. There he found out there were two warrants for Arthur Scott. One warrant indicated that Arthur Scott was six-foot-two and weighed 220 pounds. The other described him as five-nine and about 150 pounds. The Arthur Scott they arrested matched neither description: he was about five-eleven and 175. Nonetheless, they said, 'You're Arthur Scott and you're under arrest.' The court set bail. When Scott told them he didn't have any money to make bail, he was sent to jail to await trial.

"The jail chaplain, Father Santo, called me and said he really felt strongly that a mistake had been made. He asked me to come down and see Scott. Arthur Scott was the first person I visited in jail.

"Scott told me he had committed neither of the crimes. 'I'm not either of those Arthur Scotts,' he claimed. I asked him where he lived, so he gave me his addresses over the last five years. I then went over to the court and found that none of the addresses matched those given in the warrants.

"Two weeks had gone by since Scott was arrested and he was still in jail. So I went to court and explained to the judge that he was not the Arthur Scott in either of the warrants. I presented to the judge the addresses where Scott had lived, his birth date, and his physical description. The judge said, 'I agree with you. I'm going to discharge him.'

"He did. But because he had a common name, Arthur Scott spent two weeks in jail. That was his only crime," says Hogren disgustedly, "having a common name—in addition, of course, to being black and poor."

Chuck went on. "It's just another example of how the system can work against poor people. If Arthur Scott hadn't been so poor, he certainly would have made bail. But then again, if he'd been wealthy the police would have taken the time to verify that he wasn't the Arthur Scott they wanted, instead of just taking him in because of his name."

The Arthur Scott imbroglio is only one of over 600 cases

17 | COLONY OF MISERY

handled by the clinic.* Those experiences of the Cabrini-Green Legal Aid Clinic—sometimes happy, sometimes tragic, almost never predictable—are what this book is about. To understand them better, however, one needs to understand Cabrini-Green, the community from which most of the clinic's clients come.

Technically, Cabrini-Green is the name of a public housing project in this particular near-north-side neighborhood. The oldest parts of the project are fifty-five Francis Cabrini Homes, named after Mother Francis Cabrini. That section consists of what are called "row houses," two-story dwellings lined up next to one another. Completed in 1943, the 581 Cabrini apartments provide lodging for 1,950 people.

In 1958 the fifteen Cabrini Extension buildings were built. Those red-brick structures, ranging in height from seven to nineteen stories, house 6,975 residents.

The Cabrini project was enlarged in 1962 by addition of eight William Green high-rise buildings. Those fifteen- to sixteen-story high-rises, able to accommodate another 5,220 people, are of cheaper, less secure construction.

In all, there are more than eighty buildings (with nearly 3,600 apartments) in Cabrini-Green, twenty-three of which are high-rises. The buildings are crammed into a five-by-eight-block area of 70.5 acres. The Cabrini-Green project is bounded on the north by North Avenue, on the south by Chicago Avenue, on the east by LaSalle Street, and on the west by Halsted Street.

In 1976, the population of the Cabrini-Green area was 26,730. The project population, however, has steadily decreased over the past decade. From a high of nearly 18,000 in 1968, the population dwindled to 14,240 by 1976. About 70 percent of that 14,000 are under twenty-one years of age; more than half are under fifteen. Of the approximately 3,000 families living in the project, about 70 percent are headed by parents under twenty-five years of age.**

Poverty is pervasive. In 1976 the median project family size was about 3.7 with an annual income of $3,895.*** Fully 37

---

*For a statistical presentation of the clinic's case load, see Appendix 1.
**For additional statistics on Cabrini-Green, see Appendix 2.
***This is a rather liberal estimate by the Chicago Housing Authority. Other estimates are as low as $2,800.

18 | THE RELUCTANT DEFENDER

percent of the 5,164 families in the Cabrini-Green area and 53 percent of the 3,058 families in the project were below the federal poverty level. About three-fourths of the residents are on welfare. The poverty is so stark that a three-bedroom project apartment, adjusted to the family income, may be rented for $50 a month.

Unemployment eats away at the community. In 1965, 63 percent of the heads of Cabrini-Green households were employed. By 1974 that percentage had plummeted to 17 percent. It is estimated that the unemployment rate for young males in the neighborhood is between 30 and 50 percent. As a result they are often seen standing on street corners drinking wine and smoking marijuana. The problems contributing to their unemployment are many. A tight economy, poor educational opportunities, and a lack of employable skills are foremost. Some of the unemployed are too proud to work for the minimum wage; most of them desperately want work, but no work is available.

One thing that becomes obvious in looking around the community is the absence of shopping alternatives. A Jet Supermarket on the edge of Cabrini-Green is owned by a couple of community residents. Evidently its proprietors have not always been conscientious in offering high-quality merchandise and service; the store was firebombed during the King riots.

In fact, most of the stores in the area were burned out during the riots, though much of the burning and looting was discriminatory. Rioters especially zeroed in on the stores deemed most exploitative and insensitive to the neighborhood. Stores regarded as reasonable and fair were spared the torch and the pilfering.

Until 1976 there was a large A&P store on the eastern edge of the community, but it also made a practice of gouging the poor. The store would take fruits and vegetables that weren't selling in suburban stores and market them in the neighborhood at inflated prices. In the absence of shopping alternatives, people in the community purchased such produce, often rotten. After some parishioners from nearby LaSalle Street Church began pressing complaints against the store, it closed down rather than mend its ways and serve the community equitably.

19 | COLONY OF MISERY

About the only stores of any size left are on the outer edges of the neighborhood. They are actually Gold Coast establishments. The Treasure Island store rarely carries large economy-size packages of food. Prices are astronomical. Fruit, for example, is of such first-rate quality that two pears may sell for nearly two dollars. For Cabrini-Green families living on about $250 a month, the overall consumer outlook is devastating.

Cooley High School, an aged vocational facility, is the key educational institution in the neighborhood. Ground has now been broken to build a new Cooley High. Chicago's renowned Lane Technical High School actually started in Cabrini-Green but, like so many other institutions that once stabilized and energized urban communities, it has long since moved out.

Hopefully, with the new Cooley building will come improved educational quality. It is badly needed. Several years ago an evaluating team coming to Cooley found that at the end of the ninth grade there wasn't a single student reading at ninth-grade level. The most recent reading survey was taken among twelfth graders. It revealed that the average senior was reading at third-grade level.

With little being learned and many classrooms all but out of control, what academic motivation is there for students? Besides, other alternatives often appear brighter. A Chicago principal tells of a fifteen-year-old student who was amassing $500 a week as a prostitute. The girl rarely came to school. When confronted about her frequent absences, she told the principal that she saw no reason to attend school; it cut into her lucrative enterprise. She was making more money than the principal anyway. Who needed school with a hustle like hers? The principal's reply was a question. "What will happen in twenty years," she asked, "when your flesh will no longer be fresh and marketable?"

For many students, school is just a punishment. Overcrowded classrooms, failing grades, little valuable knowledge, and no real academic future stare them in the face. Lack of a future is especially disheartening; the very finest Chicago inner-city high-school students often have extraordinary difficulty getting passing grades in even the public junior colleges. For many, school amounts to a ten- or twelve-year sentence consisting of six hours' daily encounter with irrelevance.

As one might expect, truancy and "dropping out" are major

20 | THE RELUCTANT DEFENDER

problems. Early on, students develop an erratic pattern of attendance and punctuality. Students often stay home when the weather is bad, when they're feeling out-of-sorts, or when they just want to do something else.

Regrettably, the schools are often less than energetic in their efforts to curb such practices. If the students attend school at all, a school receives much-needed state money. Beyond that, a school benefits little from their attendance. If a youngster presents severe discipline problems the teachers are usually happy to have him remain truant. Hence, a truant officer may not bother to go out looking for him at all.

Cooley High School is the institution upon which the movie *Cooley High* was based. Cooley, however, is not the only mark of distinction for the community. Cabrini-Green is the setting for the popular television show, "Good Times." In addition, quite a few famous people have grown up in the area. Such notables as Walt Disney and Curtis Mayfield (of "Superfly" fame) graduated from Wells High School. A number of successful black singing groups have been spawned at Wells and Cooley.

Recreational facilities are almost nonexistent in Cabrini-Green. For nearly 10,000 youth there is only one swimming pool. Its dimensions are ludicrous: forty feet long, thirty feet wide, and three feet deep. There is no water in it, testifying to the city's awareness of its woeful inadequacy. When it was built, residents of the neighborhood stood near the bulldozer as a way of dramatizing their feelings: such a paltry venture in the direction of community recreation was little more than an insult.

Basketball courts? There is one indoor and one outdoor court. The nearby Lower North Center does provide some recreational outlets, but it has no swimming pool or basketball court.

One resident of Cabrini-Green, Elax Taylor, concerned for neighborhood youth, runs a youth club in his basement, which he has turned into a kind of recreational center. Respected and appreciated for his work, Taylor is rarely bothered with vandalism or other forms of delinquency.

For many kids, the major summer sport is baseball. Other parts of the city have spacious diamonds and parks; in

21 | COLONY OF MISERY

Cabrini-Green, finding a playing field requires a good deal of ingenuity. Youngsters usually solve the problem by using a project building as a backstop, the sidewalk in front of it as the pitching mound, and the street as the outfield.

Less than a mile away on the Gold Coast, where few youngsters live, recreational options abound. The rich kids spend their summers at affluent camps and during the rest of the year have the facilities of their high-rise buildings, such as swimming pools, to enjoy.

The city has instituted a Neighborhood Youth Corps program in which Cabrini-Green teen-agers are supposedly given jobs as a way of earning money. In actuality it operates mainly as a way of paying kids to keep out of trouble; they are often paid whether or not they report to their "jobs."

In the absence of even the most basic recreational amenities, many young people are drawn into gang activity. Though less prevalent now than in the late sixties and early seventies, gangs are still very much a part of life in Cabrini-Green.

The rise of the gang structure occurred after the murder of Martin Luther King. Before 1968 there were no gangs of any consequence on Chicago's north side, although many existed elsewhere in the city. With the tumult of the King riots, however, the Black P. Stone Nation came north and recruited youth from one Cabrini building in particular: the 1150-1160 Sedgwick high-rise. The nineteen-story building had about a thousand kids living in it at the time.

The emerging gang called itself the Cobra Stones, taking the name "Stone" from the P. Stone Nation. It attempted to infiltrate Seward Park, one of the few recreational spaces in the neighborhood. The prevailing code was such that if a gang staked its claim to a bit of property as part of its "turf," no one other than a member of that gang could be on it—even though the area was a city facility or park. Howard Moore, a musician and longtime resident of the community, recalls when gang activity was so intense that a person couldn't walk down Orleans Street without paying twenty-five cents and having a card punched by a gang member to insure freedom of passage.

At the end of the 1960s, gangs all but took over the neighborhood schools. In the Byrd elementary school, a gang came in and equipped third and fourth graders with knives, zip guns, and other weapons. The school was actually closed down for several days. Sexton, a school on Wells Street, was also shut down by the Stones for about a week.

The gangs were able to hold on to the schools for a couple of years. The schools continued to operate but teachers, administrators, and parents would give in to any serious threats or demands posed by the gangs.

Gang turf boundaries are not always obvious. The story is told about a student in a large high school in another low-income area of the city who received high grades in four of his courses but was failing the fifth. The school counselor discovered that four of his courses were taught on the side of the building included in his own gang's turf. The other side of the building belonged to another, rather violent gang. Rather than risk injury or death on that gang's turf, the student simply didn't attend the course that met on that side.

During that era the vicious concept of protection money was in vogue. With no free lunches in the schools, a mother would give her child some lunch money to take to school. Older kids would spot the youngster in the cafeteria and make note of his affluence. Once off the school grounds, they would threaten to beat him up if he didn't give them at least some of his money.

Such extortion would usually bring the child's mother over to the school demanding that the principal put a stop to it. The principal, however, couldn't control activities off the school property, so it was up to the mother to exercise protective vigilance for her youngster's safety elsewhere. Bereft of alternatives, she might give the child some extra money to ward off future difficulties. Of course, if the parasites got wind of the additional money the protection price would rise accordingly. If the child refused to pay up, sooner or later they would jump him on the street. Of course, such hassles had the ultimate effect of inducing the youth to join a gang, if only for insurance. So the delinquency cycle goes on.

The gangs were unabashed in their activities. Once when Howard Moore was in a neighborhood service station, he looked up to see a circle of about 125 Cobra Stones surrounding the station. The circle closed in and robbed everyone trapped within it. Moore was fortunate, however. A gang member who recognized Howard as his piano teacher allowed him to escape. Moore recalls it vividly. "That's the kind of experience that

23 | COLONY OF MISERY

lays a sort of foundation for the feeling that you can handle just about anything. I'm gettin' some gas and I look up and the place is surrounded. I say, 'Man, I can't believe this. This sort of thing's only supposed to happen on television.' Then this kid comes up and says I better get out—fast! So I did."

Moore wasn't content just to escape. He looked for a police car. Finding one about a block away, he told the officers a burglary was in progress. Their response surprised him. "Do you know what he said?" Moore asks incredulously. "He said, 'We're not authorized to go in there.'"

According to Bill Leslie, the violence was incredible. "Fighting would break out in the streets, gunshots would follow, and people would get down in a prone position and inch their way out of the combat zone."

Howard Moore also tells of an incident that occurred one evening in the LaSalle Street Church basement when it was being used as a recreational center for community youth. Everything seemed to be going well when a fight suddenly erupted. Out went the lights and a raging donnybrook ensued. It became so violent that the youngsters began hurling pool balls at each other. Moore could hear the heavy balls caroming and ricocheting off the church walls. Out of sheer survival instinct, Moore and his partner, Chuck Hogren, got down on their stomachs, crawled over to the wall, and reached up to flick the lights back on. Eventually they quelled the disturbance.

Bill Leslie once witnessed seven girls in a now-closed grocery store get sprayed with shotgun fire. The perpetrators just walked out. "Evidently the shooting was in retaliation for something that had occurred earlier."

The absence of recreational outlets, money, or a bright future, coupled with the presence of poverty, deteriorating community life, and gang activity now lead many Cabrini-Green youth into heavy drug involvement. Drugs are everywhere. Marijuana is immediately available. Everyone seems to have it who wants it. According to one community worker, it is as common as tobacco—smoked in the open and accepted as a given in the community. The smoke can get so thick, one person claims, that one can almost get "high" working in a building outside of which a group of youngsters are smoking.

Heroin usage is widespread.* Some drug habits run as high as $90 to $100 a day. Many children get started in elementary school by eating candy laced with a hard drug given to them by a pusher. Drug use gets heavy in the teen-age years. Kids may start at twelve or thirteen, but the habit usually hardens as they approach the later teens.

Much of the dope is passed in school washrooms. Pushers are generally unemployed young people in their twenties. For many pushers—without a job, a decent education, or salable skills—drug pushing is a form of self-employed, albeit illegal, capitalism. (So, for that matter, are pimping and prostitution.) As destructive as it is, a pusher can easily rationalize his activity; if he doesn't push it somebody else will.

Pushers rarely live in physical peril, because to harm or alienate a pusher would cut off the source of supply. Moreover, to stay on the good side of a pusher keeps the price down.

The physical structure of Cabrini-Green seems to invite gang and drug activity. Despite some attempts by the city to improve security, the project buildings remain dangerous. For safety reasons, the top floors of the high-rises have been closed. Those areas, simply boarded up, become havens for gang and drug activity.

Even worse are vacant buildings. Drug abuses, violence, and sex are "going concerns" in such sanctuaries. Consider this dismal incident: A youth purchased drugs from a female pusher in the neighborhood. After injecting the drugs and failing to get the desired high, he returned to the woman's apartment, demanding his money back. The pusher said she didn't have time just then because she had to pick up her daughter at school. The indignant customer said he would accompany her. On the way to the school they passed a vacant building. She suggested that they go into the building, offering to compensate him sexually for the faulty drugs. He agreed, only to find that experience also highly unsatisfactory.

The woman was wily, however. Making no fuss, she told him to continue with her to the school. He did. When they entered the building, she pointed to him and shouted to a nearby security guard, "That man raped me! Arrest him!" The

---

*It is estimated that 10 to 20 percent of the youth are heroin users.

25 | COLONY OF MISERY

young man fled, but was soon apprehended and charged with rape.

Unemployment plus expensive drug habits foster crime, so there is no shortage of illegal activity in Cabrini-Green. Probably the majority of it is performed by young males—often on drugs. Muggings and purse snatchings are especially common. Addicts prey on almost anyone with money. Often violence is absent if the victim offers no resistance; money is the goal.

Many mugging incidents take place in the project's high-rise buildings, especially in the elevators. Most of the buildings have only two elevators, and frequently neither of them is working properly. Thus, unsuspecting victims are often trapped in malfunctioning elevators or in dark stairwells and robbed.

A rather large elderly population lives right next to Cabrini-Green. The fact that the elderly are frequent crime victims is one of the most depressing aspects of the community. Many of the senior citizens are already very poor. They may receive a monthly Social Security check of about $125. With $90 to $100 of that going for rent they may have only about $30 left for utilities, food, and everything else. Hence to lose any of their money places them in inconceivably difficult straits.

The supermarkets won't cash Social Security checks because the elderly seldom spend enough money in the stores to make it profitable. As a result the elderly have to go to neighborhood currency exchanges. There they are easy marks for addicts or gang members who rob them on their way out, often knocking them down and injuring them in the process. The only deterrent many senior citizens have against such marauding is to go in groups to cash their checks.

Stealing welfare and Social Security checks by raiding mailboxes is another common activity. According to Bill Leslie, senior citizens or welfare mothers seldom attend a church event on the third of the month; they stay home, waiting for the mailman to come and put that check in their hand.

It all becomes a tragic, interlocking system. Poverty, poor education, joblessness, and lack of recreational opportunities produce gangs; gang association leads to drug use and abuse; drugs lead to crimes perpetrated on other residents of the community.

Although not all the crimes involve aggression, the level of violence remains high. To those who work in the community, coping with the climate of violence is a difficult but necessary adjustment one must make to survive. Gang fights, shootings, beatings, violent accidents, and rape are so common that a person has to develop a certain air of psychological detachment to be able to function in the neighborhood.

Bill Leslie learned that lesson firsthand. One summer Sunday in 1975, as he was about to leave the church after the morning service, he was confronted by two men. They tied him up and demanded the money from the morning offering. Leslie told them the deacons handle all the money. Because in many black churches in the community the offering goes directly to the pastor, they didn't believe him. Thinking he was lying, they became increasingly enraged. Finally, realizing there was no money to be had, they debated audibly whether or not to kill him. They decided against it, beating him savagely instead. Although Leslie continued his pastoral activities the shock of the experience did not soon wear off.

In an environment such as Cabrini-Green, children are introduced to adult realities early in life. Older children frequently have to stay home to care for younger siblings while their mother works at whatever job she can find. Sometimes a girl or boy of twelve may have to take full responsibility for the younger children. Before having any practical instruction in economics, they have to buy the family's food and clothes.

For many mothers, existence is hellish. Some have to get up at dawn in order to reach the suburbs or an affluent urban area to put in a full day as a domestic. Their day ends in the evening only after they have prepared and served dinner to the rich family in whose home they work. Then they take public transportation home to Cabrini-Green. For such workers there are no paid holidays, no paid vacations, no sick leave. One embittered black girl, whose mother was employed in such a slavish domestic role, vowed to her pastor, "When I get older I'm going to make a lot of money and hire a white maid. I'll make sure she isn't home with her own children on Christmas, but is at my house cooking dinner for my family."

Adding to the strain on a working mother is her constant

27 | COLONY OF MISERY

fear for the health and safety of her children left back in the raging crucible of poverty.

Many children are victimized early. For girls, sexual exploitation is a constant threat. In the absence of other outlets and the danger of going out in the street, sex, by default, becomes one of the few available recreational alternatives. For a girl to reach eighteen without having had a child, in or out of wedlock, is a remarkable achievement. In 1970 for example, 67 percent of the children born in the area were illegitimate. With little knowledge of contraception, little opportunity for an economically or socially stable marriage, females are easily victimized.

For many young women a child represents love and companionship, someone to cling to and nurture. Whereas in the middle class a child may pose a major financial burden and occupational inconvenience, in Cabrini-Green and other depressed areas a child may be the only source of warmth and light in an otherwise cold and dark existence.

Not every child is welcomed, however. With the pressures of poverty and minority status eating away at an individual, mental illness is always a potential result. And when it develops, there is no money for a $40-an-hour psychiatrist. You just learn to cope. Some can't. In a recent incident two children were found dead in a Cabrini-Green apartment. The children, abandoned, had been dead for two weeks.

In a similarly depressed area on the South Side, a fourteen-year-old girl jumped from her fourteenth-floor apartment while one of her children looked on. What violence was done to the sensibilities of that little girl to watch her mother succumb to the tortures of a life of poverty?

For boys, early initiation into drugs, alcohol, and gang activity is the norm. Moreover, with nearly 70 percent of the families headed by females, the community lacks male models. Leadership of almost any kind is absent. A family that reaches an economic level above that of their Cabrini-Green peers, is almost forced to move far away from the community. (The only nearby residential area is the Gold Coast, far out of their economic reach.) Thus Cabrini-Green stays poor and helpless, without power or money, and most of all, without hope.

28 | THE RELUCTANT DEFENDER

Cabrini-Green is often considered one of the last stops, to be avoided at all costs. For many Chicago blacks, the specter of having to move into Cabrini-Green is never far off. Such a move carries with it the stigma of having to leave a West- or South-side community to enter a project area—in addition to the possibility of losing life and limb there. Many doggedly continue to tough out a poverty existence in a South- or Westside "hole in the wall" rather than head north for Cabrini-Green.

Mack Andrews is an example of the human wreckage of Cabrini-Green.* Mack, arrested at least six times for stealing, has often been a client of the legal aid clinic. Only one incident was marked by any aggressiveness or potential violence. All the others were in the form of break-ins.

Not long ago Mack was in LaSalle Street Church. After hearing a sermon by Bill Leslie, Mack said he wanted to invite Christ into his life. Ostensibly he made such a commitment. He has been in church twice since. He has spent more time in jail.

Mack Andrews has an $80-a-day heroin habit. Almost nothing can be done to break it. Mack and his situation are typical. Ordinarily two options are open to a Cabrini-Green addict who wants to be liberated from heroin.

One is to get into a program sponsored by a well-known evangelical organization. That program, successful for some middle-class teen-agers, seldom works for ghetto youth. A typical day begins with an hour and a half worship service, followed by an hour and a half of prayer on one's knees. After lunch there is an hour and a half Bible study before a recreational period. During the evening the young people are sent off to rescue missions to aid evangelistic efforts there. Such a schedule does keep an addict busy. But since few Cabrini-Green kids are Christians in the evangelical sense to begin with, such a regimen is almost unendurable. Moreover, most have a very short attention span. To focus on anything for even thirty minutes is an extraordinarily difficult task. Directing that kind of attention toward a religious activity becomes totally unrealistic. So far, no young person from LaSalle Street Church sent to that organization has lasted through the entire program. It was too much for Mack Andrews.

---

*Some pseudonyms are used in this book.

29 | COLONY OF MISERY

The other alternative requires getting up each morning and walking two miles to a downtown city hospital to get a swallow of methadone. That alternative is also a high-risk venture with many barriers to success.

During the winter, temperatures of ten below zero or even lower make getting to the hospital difficult. In addition an awesome amount of willpower is required; going the methadone route is like going on a crash diet with no one around to offer encouragement. If the addict misses a day because of illness or inclement weather, or for any other reason, he or she is left in an environment virtually surrounded by opportunities to get back on heroin. With most of one's peers addicted to or pushing heroin, any break in one's isolationist existence can bring on a regression.

Heroin is only the beginning of the problems plaguing Mack Andrews and others like him. Mack is not only unemployed, he is very nearly unemployable. All attempts to secure employment for him have been unsuccessful. One reason is his lack of education.

Mack, now twenty, has not attended school since he was thirteen. At that age he dropped out. The school made no serious attempts to find him. A diagnostic test indicated that Mack's reading level was equivalent to that of a first grader in the fifth month of school.

Perhaps Mack Andrews is a genuine Christian, perhaps not. He is a very pleasant, courteous, and agreeable young man when not on drugs. But regardless of his spiritual status, Mack Andrews is an unemployed, illiterate, poverty-stricken, ghetto-dwelling heroin addict.

He is not unusual. Bill Leslie tells of his church's neighborhood follow-up work for call-ins to an evangelical television program. "When we follow up on people who call in, all I have to do is look at the caller's address and I can tell you what the problems are. If the person lives in Cabrini-Green, he or she probably has some legal problems. They may be related to consumer victimization, divorce, unjust arrest, or something else.

"There are also family stresses. If the caller is an adult female, she is probably a single parent. If there are two parents present there are usually communication snags of such proportions that there is almost no ability to give and receive love.

"They are almost certainly unemployed or underemployed. The educational level of the community is so low that people often can't read well enough to fill out a job application. And then there are always financial problems. As a result, although an evangelist may confront them with the gospel of Christ and reach them in one night, it takes us at least two years of intensive follow-up to help them function as whole Christian persons.

"Exploitation is so common that to say 'God loves you' is like saying that God wants to have sex with you. Since love of any genuine sort is in such scarce supply, the only understanding many of the people have of love is selfish and exploitive sex.

"We had one black girl in our church discipleship class who said that the concept of God as Father had absolutely no positive significance for her. Her father was completely negative in her life. So to use even the standard illustrative tools to teach her about God is problematic."

So it goes. As long as society allows the conditions that create Cabrini-Greens to prevail, there will be victims. The entire community functions in part as a malignant system which methodically sucks the energy and lifeblood out of its victims. Children are born into the devastation of poverty, subjected to illness and danger, miseducated, and then turned loose into a community so segregated and walled-in that their frustrations are invariably taken out on their fellow residents.

THE SYSTEM

2

Cabrini-Green residents are preyed on not only by their peers. They are oppressed by outside forces so that they become victims in every sense of the term: victims of neglect by the city and its often insensitive officials, victims of brutality by irresponsible policemen, victims of political disenfranchisement by careless bureaucrats, and victims of economic exploitation by avaricious merchants.

The city of Chicago has seldom shown much interest in protecting the poor and oppressed. The Chicago *Daily News* reported the experience of a nun who visited the late Mayor Daley early in his administration. She told him about her work on the West Side, where the children of the poor were getting lead poisoning from the paint used in rental units. Landlords in the area had been cutting apartments up, converting them into very small units, and charging exorbitant rents, yet failed to keep the buildings in adequate repair.

She wanted the city to send out its inspectors to enforce the building code, and she wanted those cell-like apartments deconverted. The mayor was unmoved by her requests. His response was particularly disillusioning. He reminded the nun of their common Irish heritage, alluding to the efforts of Irish immigrants to "pull themselves up by their own bootstraps." He concluded by saying that the dispossessed and disenfranchised west-siders would have to do the same.

Mayor Daley seemed completely oblivious to the fact that when the Irish came to Chicago they immediately seized control of the then wide-open political arena, dominating the police and fire departments; the blacks, who arrived later, faced segregation and discrimination which made it impossible for them to advance politically or economically in any meaningful way.

That distinction between the Irish and black experience in Chicago is epitomized in the nun's exchange with Daley. The legacy of Irish political brokering was evident right there in the mayor's office in the person of Mayor Daley. The nun represented the concerns of blacks who remained sealed in poverty ghettos.

The city holds awesome political control over residents of Cabrini-Green, especially because of their heavy dependence on city services. In February 1973 a mass community meeting was held in a neighborhood church. Housing was being torn down without new housing being made available for tenants who had been evicted from their apartments. At least two hundred concerned people attended the meeting. City officials were present as well, and were challenged and questioned on the matter by worried Cabrini-Green citizens. The meeting ended with the officials assuring the people that improvements in the housing situation would indeed be forthcoming. Another meeting was scheduled for March 1 to evaluate the city's actions on those pledges.

After much publicity and high expectations concerning the upcoming meeting, only about twenty people showed up on the first of March. Where were the people? They were staying home. Someone from "downtown" had called the tenant council in one of the project buildings to inform them that if the meeting were held as scheduled, welfare checks for those involved would be mysteriously delayed in coming. The threat of losing their only means of livelihood kept the welfare recipients away.

The city was now in the catbird seat. They had a perfect

excuse to continue business as usual. They could publicly claim that poor attendance at the meeting indicated that Cabrini-Green residents were actually quite satisfied with the situation and not interested in further discussion.

Cabrini-Green is an example of a great reversal in big-city machine politics. Politicians once sought to gain the respect and support of the people by attempting to meet their needs. Now the political system, especially through the welfare system, suckers the people into becoming absolutely dependent on it for their survival. As a result people are forced to support the entrenched political figures because they're afraid the power brokers will cut them off if the voting support isn't there.

It is no secret that all it takes in many of Chicago's poor communities to "get out the vote" is to drop the suggestion that if adequate electoral support is not in evidence there may be an unexplainable lag in city services: fire or police protection may be less vigorous, garbage may pile up, buildings may go unrepaired and unmaintained, or some much needed city facility may be forced to close.

The welfare system, however, is downright insidious. Rather than making poor people rich without working (a mythology to which many middle-class and wealthy people seem to cling), it amounts to a method of making its recipients so dependent on the prevailing political system that they become truly powerless.

When genuine equality of opportunity is lacking—so that the urban poor go to the poorest schools; live where industries and businesses (and therefore jobs) no longer exist; have the poorest health-care facilities around; lack any strong political voice or representation (almost every advocate of the nation's poor has been outside the political system, never holding public office); and must rear their children in the most disadvantageous circumstances—what does society do? The usual procedure is to compensate for that opportunity-gap by simply giving money to the poor in amounts barely sufficient for physical survival. Despite all the stereotypes of the "welfare Cadillac" or "welfare queens," one is hard-pressed to think of a single economically successful person whose financial empire was built on a welfare foundation.

Any governmental attempts at improving the quality of life

in Cabrini-Green are actually rather suspect, for much of the pressure for such endeavors has come from, of all quarters, the Gold Coast. Many people in that princely community are open about their fear concerning the proximity of Cabrini-Green. They are terrified of the high crime rates in Cabrini, feeling that at any time an angry coterie from that dispossessed neighborhood may travel the seven-tenths of a mile to the Gold Coast and begin pillaging and looting.

In the minds of many Cabrini-Green youth, the only difference between themselves and their peers in the Gold Coast is that the rich were born among riches rather than rats and roaches. That simple distinction at birth is turned into lifelong status differences: the Gold Coast offspring go to the finest schools, receive private tutoring, and are set up in business or a profession. So, when the summer gets hot and frustrations surge into consciousness, there may be little to deter Cabrini youth from trying to take matters into their own hands and aggressively neutralize some of those differences.

Politics is played for keeps in Chicago. A person who tries to buck the Democratic machine is inviting disaster. Examples of such disasters are legion and John Stevens, a longtime community worker in Cabrini-Green, provides one of them.

Stevens decided to run for ward alderman as an Independent candidate several years ago. Bill Leslie and Chuck Hogren worked for him in his political effort. The campaign was intense. It was a three-man race, with Stevens, along with another aspirant, battling it out with the Democratic machine candidate. To avoid a runoff between the top two vote-getters one candidate had to receive a majority of the ballots cast. As it turned out, the machine candidate escaped with a slim 700-vote majority—a razor-thin margin by Chicago Democratic standards.

For Stevens, however, opposing the machine was not without its consequences. During the campaign he was personally threatened, his car was bombed, and his headquarters was set on fire.

With "the system" oppressing them on one hand and internal crime impinging on the other, citizens of Cabrini-Green have been in desperate need of legal service and counsel. Cabrini-Green residents, especially mothers who work as

35 | THE SYSTEM

domestics in the homes of the affluent, are conscious of the need for justice and legal protection in the community. In their years of working as maids, many of them became aware that whenever the children of the rich got into trouble with the law their parents have had the option of buying them out. For a traffic violation, all it seemed to take was to grease the palm of the right person in the city system and the problem would be quickly disposed of. For a particularly serious matter, a sharp defense attorney would be hired to ace out the state's attorney in the case.

Adults in many well-to-do homes talk openly about their system-beating activities. Often when a maid heard about such maneuvers and mentally compared them with the plight of Cabrini-Green teen-agers who were being arrested for lesser offenses and jailed without adequate legal counsel, their bitterness grew. And whenever a maid passed along such a tale to her own offspring, it fed their anger toward the system.

Chuck Hogren began working with community youth in the LaSalle Street Church recreation center. In 1968 he first became conscious of the pressing legal need in Cabrini-Green. Once it became known that he was a lawyer, the kids would ask his advice whenever they got in trouble. Soon he found himself taking their cases.

In one early case, a fourteen-year-old youth who attended the recreation center was accused of raping a woman in the stairwell of a church basement in Cabrini. Hogren represented him. The judge, feeling that the process by which the victim had identified the teen-ager (in a lineup, alone) was unjustifiably suggestive and bordered on being rigged, acquitted him.

There was little doubt in Hogren's mind that the young man was innocent. The gangs were very strong at the time, and the youth didn't live on the turf of the gang that ruled the area in which the rape had been committed. "If you ventured into the wrong territory at that time, you were in peril of being shot," recalls Hogren. "In fact a brother of one of our clients was actually shot for inadvertently crossing a gang boundary."

Most of the early cases weren't so dramatic. They usually involved kids being picked up off the street and taken to the police station. According to Hogren, "They would be in jail for awhile and then released without even being charged with an offense. Some kids were repeatedly harassed. I became so concerned that at one time I was handling twenty cases in addition to my full-time legal practice."

Poor legal protection breeds unemployment. "A client," says Hogren, "would have a job, be accused of a crime, go to court, and be acquitted. Yet, because he had to leave work for a day each month until the case was disposed of, he would lose his job. Others with cases pending are unable to get jobs simply because no one wants to hire them."

As much as anything, it was problems between the community and the police that got Hogren involved in legal aid activities.

The police are feared in the community. Its citizens are very reluctant to call them even in times of emergency. They fear police brutality in the form of physical beatings, verbal abuse, and generally undignified treatment.

The police have their side of the story too. In July 1970 two officers were assassinated by a sniper while amiably talking with youngsters on the Seward Park playground. That, coupled with the belligerence and open defiance of their authority shown by many of the area youth, has embittered many officers.

Harvey Reines is an example of such an officer. Reines, who attended LaSalle Street Church, said that working in Cabrini-Green literally turned him into a psychologically subhuman species. To work in the area, he claimed, engendered such an irrational reaction within him that he felt he was becoming animalized by it. Feeling that he was losing his humanity, he asked to be transferred.

The sniping incident is sharply etched in the memory of both the community and the police. Tension is still high. When it occurred, the police, understandably incensed, knocked down doors, searched apartments, and beat up innocent citizens in a frenzied effort to apprehend the killer.

Police work in Cabrini-Green can indeed be frustrating. Officers often feel they have to intimidate the people in order to stymie potential assaults against themselves. Hatred for the police is so intense in some parts of the community that shooting a police officer has functioned as an initiation rite into the more violent gangs: a show of manhood or gang status. Challenging and obstructing the police in their efforts is strongly reinforced by alienated youth in the neighborhood. Because they face violence, mental illness, alcoholism, lack of social control, epithets, vulgarity, and tire slashings, the police frequently find themselves engaged in self-protection rather than in serving the community.

As a result, cooperation between the community and the police is minimal. The relationship is mutually destructive. The community is unable to get adequate police protection in an area as badly in need of it as any area in the country. The police are thwarted in their efforts to deter crime, in addition to being vulnerable not only to physical attack but also to the seething effects of hate from the citizens in the community they ostensibly "serve and protect."

In view of these rancorous relations, the police often try to avoid the area. That leaves the many law-abiding citizens of Cabrini-Green vulnerable to victimization by both the preying elements in the neighborhood and by certain vengeful police officers. Complaints of late responses to police calls are legion, reflecting the avoidance tendency.

Fear of the residents, hatred for the community, and the knowledge that the poor have little recourse fosters over-aggressive and brutal police activity. In general, police brutality is so pervasive in urban America that the National Advisory Commission on Civil Disorders listed it as one of three main causes of urban riots.

A rather obvious example of such misconduct occurred in April 1975 when two men driving north on Sedgwick Street came to an intersection and were stopped for a traffic violation. The driver, Ellis Green, got out of the car, admitted that he deserved the traffic ticket, and handed the officer his driver's license. The officer refused to follow the standard procedure of retaining the license in lieu of bail. The driver then showed the officer his bail card, certain that it would be acceptable. The card was also refused.

The officer then informed Green that he was going to take him in to the station. Green balked, knowing that his rights were being abridged. The police then radioed for assistance and, because a Task Force had been assigned to Cabrini-Green that month, it was dispatched to the scene. (A Task Force is a unit sent to aid police in maintaining order when disorder appears to be an imminent danger.) Because they move from place to place, Task Forces have no ties with nor accountability to a given community. Their rootlessness contributes to occasionally reckless behavior.

Soon a Task Force of about ten policemen arrived on the scene. Green was grabbed and pulled into a nearby paddy wagon. The aggressiveness of the incident caught the attention of passersby. A crowd gathered and a minor riot developed, with people being knocked down.

A law student working with Chuck Hogren was in the Urban League building at the time and witnessed the melee. He ran out of the building and up to the officers. Saying nothing, he simply wrote down one of the officer's names. As he was about to write the name of a second officer he was arrested for interfering with a police officer. A photographer then emerged from the Urban League building and began taking pictures of the police scuffling with the people. One showed an officer with a club beating and knocking down a woman who was merely standing and watching the fracas. The photographs were turned over to the Urban League.

The law student asked Hogren to represent him in his case. By the time it came up in court, the student had graduated from law school and moved to New York. He was therefore willing to forego a civil rights action against the police in Federal Court provided they would drop their immediate charges against him. The police refused.

Hogren obtained the pictures of the riotous event from the Urban League, had them enlarged, and took them to court. While sitting in court he perused the photographs. A rather surprised group of police officers noticed the pictures and experienced a sudden change of heart. They decided to drop the case.

As a result of that incident, the Cabrini-Green community called a meeting and demanded that the Task Force be moved out of the area. It was.

THE RELUCTANT DEFENDER

3

Born on the South Side of Chicago on September 24, 1936, Chuck Hogren early developed a sensitivity to blacks. On his first day at school in Roseland, Chuck felt lost and bewildered. At lunch time he didn't know where to go or what to do. He was sitting there befuddled, when an older student noticed his confusion. He was a black eighth grader, likely the only black in the school. That youngster took it upon himself to show Chuck around. The experience made a tremendous impression. None of the white children had shown any concern. To some extent Chuck Hogren feels he may still be trying to repay that student's kindness.

Chuck grew up in the Mission Covenant Church. His father was an advertising executive; his mother, a homemaker. He also had a younger sister, who now teaches at a large midwestern university. When Chuck was seven, the family moved to Western Springs. There they went to the local Village Church.

Chuck's mother was already encouraging him in the direction of law school when he was in sixth grade. His first experience with law occurred that same year. The superintendent of schools in Western Springs was very interested in spelling. Rules in the system for spelling tests were such that a student had only one chance to write down a correct answer. There could be no erasures, nothing crossed out or changed. The word must be spelled right the first time.

On occasion questions arose as to whether a given student had abided by the rules with regard to erasures, cross-outs, or corrections. Chuck took a special interest in those cases. A good speller himself, he felt that some kids weren't assertive enough in their claims to have spelled a word in question correctly the first time. So he embarked on his first venture into legal practice, agreeing to talk to the teacher about any student's spelling paper for a fee of two cents a word. Highly successful, Chuck eventually doubled his fee to four cents.

The family moved to West Chicago when Chuck was thirteen. There they attended the College Church in Wheaton, and Chuck went to high school at Wheaton Academy.

While at Wheaton College, Hogren was in ROTC, then a requirement for all male students during their first two years. Impressed with the quality of instructors in the program, and knowing he would have to go into the army anyway, Hogren decided to continue in ROTC.

It was not to be. In the summer following his junior year, Chuck was dropped from the program because it was determined that he had once suffered from asthma while attending a summer camp. Having served three years in ROTC, Chuck was exempted from military service. Out of ROTC and entering his senior year of college, he had to decide what he was going to do. Realizing that he had always wanted to go to law school, he graduated from Wheaton College and then went on to Northwestern University law school.

Not being the least bit interested in criminal law, Hogren studied international law. During his years in law school he worked in a law firm that specialized in real estate. On graduating, he worked full time for that firm, doing real-estate law in addition to some probate work.

In the early sixties Chuck was living in West Chicago and dating a young woman. When that relationship ended, he decided, in the spring of 1962, to visit LaSalle Street Church and Bill Leslie. Chuck had come to know Leslie during his years in

41 | THE RELUCTANT DEFENDER

law school, when Bill was a youth pastor at Moody Memorial Church and in charge of evening youth activities. At that time, Chuck had gone to Fourth Presbyterian Church in the morning and to Moody at night. Chuck liked LaSalle and began getting involved.

The year 1968 was perhaps the most tumultuous year of the past quarter-century, with the assassinations of Martin Luther King and Robert Kennedy, riots in the black area of large cities, civil disturbances at the Democratic National Convention in Chicago, student revolts, and other signs of rebellion and protest. Sensitized by all that, LaSalle Street Church felt they were not adequately meeting the needs of the community. The Christian Education Board, of which Chuck was chairman, decided to open a recreation center in the church basement for neighborhood youth. It ran throughout the summer with five Wheaton College students staffing it. "The students stayed at a house David Goodson and I rented on Fremont Street," Hogren explains. "I got to know some of the kids very well because they would come over to our house. Many good contacts were made during that summer."

The board decided to open the center three nights a week in the fall. One night was used for study; the other two were recreational. The center was staffed by Chuck, Bill Leslie, and Cameron Webb, along with several Wheaton College students. Life wasn't always tranquil at the center. "Some nights we would have as many as sixty kids, ranging in age from ten to seventeen, packed into that small basement," says Hogren. "Fights and other problems would arise, but somehow we stayed open three nights a week.

"I had worked with many of the neighborhood people in the church tutoring program, and some of the same kids were in the recreation center. I had called on many of the people and been in their homes. I met the kids' parents. Sometimes I picked the kids up in my car and drove them home. As a result of those experiences I developed a love for the Cabrini-Green community.

"What really stood out in those kids' lives was the absence of a cohesive family life. There were no regular meals. People simply made their own food. Home was just a crash pad.

"There was a pressing need for a place to go, a place with a wholesome atmosphere where a kid could feel a sense of belonging. The recreation center became a home away from home. A lot of the kids learned to play checkers and chess there."

Hogren was not eager to do criminal law on a voluntary basis, along with his full-time legal work. However, realizing the intense need people had for legal representation, and having kids at the recreation center constantly ask him for help, Chuck felt he had little choice in the matter. "I felt that because I went to the church and knew the kids, I should defend them. Besides, if I didn't, no one else would. There was a sense of obligation."

For Chuck the legal process would usually begin with his hearing about a problem, either from a youngster or from a mother. If necessary he would go down to the jail to visit the kid in trouble. There he would inquire about the charge and the date of the bond-reduction hearing. Hogren would usually check out the defendant's background: his parents, brothers and sisters, employment, school experience, and prior court record.

Hogren can't remember ever being "turned down" by a prospective client. His quiet, accepting, and unassuming demeanor may be the reason. There is a gentle sincerity in his voice.

"Often the bond-reduction or bail hearing would be held the very next day," says Hogren. "Many times the arresting officer wouldn't even show up to testify, so the case was closed. In such instances it was simply a matter of harassment. The kid would be arrested and charged with disorderly conduct. Because the officer didn't bother to appear in court, the kid would be discharged—but not without having gone through the inconvenience of spending a night in jail."

If the case was pursued further, however, the first concern was representing the accused at the bond hearing. Hogren would attempt to get the bail set low enough for his client to make it. If the client had no money Chuck would attempt to get a personal recognizance or "identification" bond. Called an "I" bond, it requires only the defendant's signature to a pledge that he will be present at all future court sessions. Such a bond can usually be obtained if the defendant is young, has never been in trouble before, and the offense is not particularly serious. If, however, a defendant could not make bail and was not

43 | THE RELUCTANT DEFENDER

granted an "I" bond, he would be detained in jail until the preliminary hearing.

Frequently, if bond was reached, Chuck would meet with his client at church or in the youngster's home to prepare for the preliminary hearing. Doing so much Good Samaritan activity on top of his own legal responsibilities was taxing. "It was difficult, and sometimes I had to let some things slide. The court appearances were always in the morning, so a morning was wiped out of my schedule. Often I would interview clients in jail during the afternoon or evening. Fortunately I could get into the jail until eight p.m."

As the number of cases increased, the pressure began mounting. Time was at a premium. "There might be several cases a week, each taking several hours in addition to preparing them." Hogren was finding it more and more difficult to function in two legal careers at once.

A number of the early cases were rather serious. In one, a group of kids were at a party playing records. They came upon a shotgun owned by one of the people who lived in the apartment. Finding some shells, the youths began playing with the gun. Hogren remembers it well. "One of the kids pulled the trigger and absolutely blew the neck off one of the other kids. He was arrested and taken to the Audy Home. The families involved were neighbors. The judge allowed the youth to plead guilty to involuntary manslaughter and placed him on probation."

Chuck's work cemented his relations with the community. "As I got into the work, I got to know the people better and better. I might represent one person, then his brother, then another brother—all from the same family. Then I'd get the cousins. It was hard to say No. So I became very well acquainted with the people and they became friends of mine. I was representing friends, not clients. I might work with members of the same family in tutoring, the rec center, and then as a lawyer."

Some poignant experiences occurred that made a profound emotional imprint on Hogren. "Once I received a call from a client named Ed who was in a police station on the South Side. Ed asked me if I would come over. I did, talked to the officers, and he was released. I then took him home.

"We had a nice talk in the car and Ed told me how happy he

was that his problems seemed to be clearing up. He had two children, even though he was only seventeen or eighteen. He told me about them and how he was trying to straighten out his life so he could be the kind of father they could respect.

"A week later he was shot and died. That made a deep impression on me, because he died needlessly. Ed was shot in the Robert Taylor Homes project. He was allowed to just lie bleeding on the pavement for forty-five minutes until his family could be contacted. They took him to the hospital where he died from loss of blood.

"The family told me the police let Ed bleed to death in that project because they didn't want to get their car soiled with blood. In fairness, it's possible the police didn't move him because they were afraid of possible violence in the project. In any case, he died unnecessarily.

"I had known that young man over a period of years, from 1962 to 1972. You might say I watched him grow up. He and his family attended Sunday school at LaSalle."

Chuck continued to talk about the family with a quiet intensity. "I'm still representing one of his brothers, Allen, who was stabbed in the same project. Allen was stabbed some years ago, but the wound has never healed properly. Now it has turned cancerous. In cases like that, you really get to know the people and identify with them."

Occasionally Chuck sought help from other lawyers. "I didn't always approve of the methods they used, but they really did help. Once I defended a teen-ager, and a little later one of the kid's relatives was charged with murder in a tavern-killing over on Sedgwick. The family asked me to take the case." That was a tough one, a murder case. So Hogren called another city lawyer requesting aid. He agreed to help, so they co-represented the defendant. At the preliminary hearing the client claimed he did shoot the man, but that the victim had a gun and was about to open fire on him. Hence the plea was self-defense. "The police, of course, were not likely to testify that it was self-defense," says Chuck, "because in their mind it was murder."

Just before the preliminary hearing was about to begin, Chuck went out in the hall. Looking down the corridor, he noticed his colleague talking to a policeman and handing him

45 | THE RELUCTANT DEFENDER

some money. When they went back inside for the hearing and the defendant's plea was entered, the policeman, much to Chuck's surprise, changed his story and corroborated the defendant's claim that it was indeed self-defense. The judge then declared "No probable cause," and the client was free.

Not knowing what had happened, Chuck was in shock. Not until after the hearing did he realize what the money was for. "The money, $75, was actually paid to get the officer to tell the truth. Had he not been paid he would probably have testified to some other version," says Hogren.

The temptation not to tell the truth is often extreme for a policeman. One factor is that an officer's record is brightened by making arrests that stick. In some cases the defendant may have been arrested before and gotten off easily, introducing a rather normal revenge factor.

"That," says Hogren with a chuckle, "was my introduction to the criminal law business."

Early on, some of his clients were guilty. "Many cases," Chuck explains, "involved shoplifting, trespass to a vehicle, or property damage. Sometimes the kid has committed the crime, but was, nonetheless, in need of representation.

"Allen Pendleton, the young man who is now suffering from cancer, probably was guilty of some of the things with which he was charged, like breaking into cars. Although that posed a dilemma, I felt he was still entitled to representation and it should take the form of getting him some help—whether it was a rehabilitative program, psychiatric treatment, or enrollment in a special education curriculum. I did my best to see that all his legal options were explained to him so that he could decide on which was the best course."

Nevertheless, pleading "not guilty" was a difficult issue for Chuck. "I wrestled with that for a long time. And my answer is not always a popular one. I've thought about it, prayed about it, and talked to other lawyers whom I respected. The opinion of those lawyers and the one I share is that, under our system, the state is obligated to prove a person guilty beyond a reasonable doubt. The accused need not say anything. That is his constitutional right and it is there for good reason.

"I told my clients that if they were guilty and yet didn't want to plead guilty, they could enter a plea of not guilty, but that I wouldn't allow them to take the stand and testify in their own defense. If they did, I told them, I would withdraw from the case.

"That's where I draw the line. I'll represent a client as far as making the state prove him guilty—which it has the obligation to do under our system. But I wouldn't permit such a client to take the stand. If they're willing to abide by those guidelines, I'm willing to take their case."

There have been occasional surprises. "Sometimes I felt the defendant was not guilty—yet after being acquitted at the trial, the young man would say, 'I actually did that.' But that's quite rare."

Hogren has learned to be very careful about pre-judging a case. In one case involving Allen Pendleton, Chuck felt certain that the young man was guilty of armed robbery. The victim, a delivery man who had not been seriously injured in the incident, had positively identified Allen. The state made the defendant an offer that was very reasonable and that Chuck strongly felt he should take. It included dropping charges against two other people, Ronald and Richard Oak, who were arrested with Allen and who Hogren felt were innocent.

So Chuck discussed it with Allen, urging him to accept the state's offer. He could plead guilty to a lesser charge, robbery, rather than armed robbery. The difference would be one to three years instead of four years in prison.

Chuck told Allen he had a moral obligation to plead guilty as the evidence was quite strong and such a plea would discharge his two innocent friends. Pendleton refused. He wouldn't plead guilty because, he claimed, he didn't do it.

Chuck was frustrated. "I said, 'If you take this course of action you're going to hang all three of you!' Of course, the Oak brothers were encouraging him to take the offer because they wanted to get off. Still he wouldn't budge."

Shortly thereafter, another person confessed to the crime. The experience shook Hogren. "I've never tried to make a judgment on guilt or innocence since," he says. Although he does, in his interviews, seek to determine whether a client is guilty as charged, Chuck is clear about granting the benefit of the doubt. "If a person says he is not guilty, and there's any chance he's not, I'll take his word for it and defend him."

47 | THE RELUCTANT DEFENDER

From the beginning, Hogren agonized over his involvement in this new legal venture. There is fatigue in his voice as he describes the dilemma. "The work was there all right. Right away, in 1968, I was very impressed with some of the incidents I heard about, illustrating the need for justice and legal defense in the community.

"But I also felt strongly that I wasn't qualified. My legal background was not in criminal law, and I never intended at the time to get into it.

"As the cases became more complex I tried to get other lawyers to help me. However, after a while I had used up all my I.O.U.s with them and so I had to take some of the more serious cases on my own. I remember one murder case especially. Many times later I thought I was the biggest fool in the world to have gotten involved in it.

"It was a murder in a Cabrini-Green building. My client, Carl Winters, a man of about thirty, married, with a rather large family, was a janitor on the night shift at the Isham YMCA. Winters was leaving for work at about four in the afternoon. He came down the elevator and when he got off he was confronted by a kid who asked him for a dollar. Carl told him he didn't have any money.

"Winters walked on, and another kid asked him for a dollar. He gave that one the same answer. Then suddenly a rather burly man, about six-foot-three and 220 pounds, came up to Winters and knocked him down. As he tried to get up, Carl was knocked down again and told to come up with a dollar. Winters reiterated the fact that he had no money. With that, the man was about to jump on top of him. At that instant, Carl pulled a small-caliber gun out of his back pocket and shot his assailant as the attacker was coming down on top of him. That, at least, was Winters's version.

"The police version was that there had been a dice game going on on the first floor of the building. They claimed that my client, upset because he felt someone had cheated him out of fifty cents, went up to his apartment to get his gun. When he returned he said he was going to kill the guy who cheated him. The husky fellow, in a heroic attempt to intervene, got in the way of the bullet which was meant for someone else."

That was the case as presented to Hogren. Winters was in jail and it was the first criminal case Chuck had taken on his own.

48 | THE RELUCTANT DEFENDER

He tried to get other lawyers to take it, but was unable to. "I regretted taking it because as I got into it I became increasingly aware of how high the stakes were. Here was a father who was working, supporting a large family with all the children of school age. He was in peril of spending at least fourteen years in the penitentiary. By that time his wife would have been long gone and his children raised without a father. All that if I didn't come through! Here I was, handling a murder case like that without any experience! I had no business doing it. But no one else would take it. Winters didn't want the public defender and by the time he had made bail he probably wasn't eligible for one anyway.

"I found a woman who claimed to be a witness to the crime. She corroborated my client's version and made it even stronger by claiming that the assailant had a knife. Even Carl did not say he saw a knife. She testified at the bond hearing and, because of her testimony, the judge reduced my client's bail to $10,000. That meant that if his family could raise $1,000 he would be out on bail. They raised it and shortly later he was out.

"The case was then continued for a long time, heightening my anxieties. Fortunately, when we finally went to court at the Civic Center the woman was available to testify.

"A judge heard the case. The woman was our key witness. The state presented four witnesses, all of whom were police officers. The police, however, testified only to a conversation they had with the defendant. They claimed he confessed. Carl denied it. After the state presented its case, the defense rested."

The judge stated that the policemen's claim that the defendant had confessed was not, in and of itself, sufficient to convict. He ruled that the state had not proven the defendant guilty beyond a reasonable doubt. Acquittal!

It had come down to the police's word against the defendant, who, if he hadn't been defended, might have been sent up the river for a very long time. There was a witness who said he saw a crap game, but he didn't come to court to testify at the trial. Other than that, there was never any proof of the existence of the alleged dice game.

"I learned quite a bit from that case, and fortunately it turned out all right," says Hogren with a shudder. "Nonetheless, I'm not at peace about it, because I was in an ocean in which I had

49 | THE RELUCTANT DEFENDER

no experience swimming. One slip and my client could have been sent away. But again, I had no other choice."

Hogren felt like Jonah in the Bible, the reluctant prophet. He had no real desire or intention to get into that type of work, but as he got to know the people in the community there seemed no way his conscience would allow him to avoid defending them on his own time.

"I would have loved to get out," he says. "I would have been delighted if someone would have come along and said, 'Hey, I'll take those cases.' I got the feeling that God was sort of pushing me into this endeavor and I wasn't very happy about it. But it would have been hard to live with myself if I didn't respond to the call and take them.

"If I knew the person I'd feel guilty if I said No. I didn't feel so guilty if I didn't know them. But I don't remember saying No very often. Come to think of it," says Chuck, laughing, "I don't remember ever saying No."

The work was closing in on him from two sides. On the one hand, it was taking time, costing money, and getting him into trouble with his law firm. People were asking, "What are you doing that for, anyway?" On the other, there was his conscience reminding him that if he didn't take the cases, the people would go unrepresented. How could he look them in the face on Sunday, knowing he had abandoned them?

His lack of experience in criminal law bothered him most. "It was nerve-racking, very nerve-racking, to go to court on cases in which I had no experience. I would lose sleep. I was extremely nervous going to court feeling I would soon be called to do something I wasn't qualified to do. I didn't have ample time to prepare the cases exhaustively or to read up on the type of law involved. But even if you read, it's not enough. You also have to *do!* And it was the doing, in the absence of an adequate background, that really unnerved me.

"The first few cases weren't so bad, but then I realized how complex it was: how when you deal with felonies or even a Class A misdemeanor the next stop for your client, if convicted, is the pen.

"I was very happy, for example, whenever the other side didn't show up; it alleviated the necessity of having to defend someone. I was also thankful for continuances, as they gave me more time to prepare.

"I was encouraged when cases turned out successfully, but that only seemed to bring in more cases. I was building a reputation I didn't want, dealing with cases I didn't have the self-confidence to handle." Chuck met most of his clients at church. As the case load grew, he found himself trying to avoid people, ducking out of church quickly to circumvent being confronted with still another potential client.

"It was very stressful, emotionally and physically," Hogren says. "It was also a spiritual strain, doing something I didn't want to do, but feeling I had to do it.

"Even now, after five years, I would get out if I could. There's still the tension of handling serious criminal cases without the necessary experience. I still lack self-confidence. I don't mind working with poor people; it's just the lack of experience."

As a result of these ongoing internal dilemmas, few things bother Chuck Hogren more than the image concocted of him as a plaster saint. Many articles in magazines and newspapers have tended to portray him as a willingly involved, self-giving, male Joan of Arc—the blue-eyed soul brother, the handsome single lawyer in an avant-garde profession. Such portrayals induce guilt in Hogren, making him feel he has to live up to that unrealistic profile. It gnaws at him to know that his fatigue, discouragement, feelings of entrapment, and desire to get out are not in keeping with the image in which he is involuntarily cast.

There is a tremendous desire on his part to appear human— subject to exhaustion, guilt, wrong motivations, and deficiencies—in addition to possessing certain virtues.

He has a big thing about honesty. So much so that any inaccuracy that leans in the direction of glorifying him or the quality of his work bothers him, eating away at his conscience. To be known as an ordinary struggling Christian, working at an incredibly difficult task with all the reluctance likely to be associated with such work, gives him a sense of liberation. It frees him from the PR box that those who write about him and his work often place him in.

Hogren is remarkably unassuming and polite, almost to a fault. He seems to have a genuine humility that doesn't weaken his self-presentation, but does make it almost impossible not to like him. Hence it is easy to sketch a saintly, otherworldly profile of Chuck Hogren: that of a sinless person

51 | THE RELUCTANT DEFENDER

acutely aware of the urban dynamics and grisly experiences associated with inner-city life.

But his psyche cannot tolerate such a portrait. Perhaps his own humility is the force that pricks his conscience so easily and turns effusive compliments into pellets of pain. In any case, Charles Hogren is human and frail as well as likable and strong, and he must have that human duality affirmed and accepted to feel free as a public or private person.

One gets the feeling that Hogren will never feel at ease accepting credit for his accomplishments, since he didn't enter the work willingly or voluntarily. Yet the world is full of people reluctant to undertake tasks of critical importance to life and society, and most will *not* engage in them despite being acutely aware that they are abdicating their moral responsibility. Responsibility and accountability are key motifs in Chuck Hogren's life. To be honorable is to be honest, but to be glorified beyond one's own deserts (based on Hogren's standards) is to be dishonest.

BIRTH OF A CLINIC

4

In July 1970 Chuck Hogren's father died. "He was in Germany on a vacation and died suddenly of a heart attack. It was unexpected and traumatic. He was only sixty-two."

Chuck moved into his mother's home to provide companionship and attend to details requiring attention after his father's death. In the fall his mother moved to Florida for the winter. From time to time that winter Chuck would visit her for a few days or a week and then return.

The following summer his mother returned to Chicago. Chuck intended to move back into his own house but his mother asked if he would stay with her in her Villa Park town house. He consented.

In September 1971 Mrs. Hogren was making plans to move back to Florida for the following winter when she suffered a severe stroke. She was hospitalized for about two and a half months.

"The doctors were amazed that she even survived, much less was able to walk," Hogren states. "For a while she couldn't speak, but after a couple of months her speech returned."

The question was what to do then. Chuck decided that he was fed up with cold Chicago winters and would move to Florida with his mother. "I wanted to take the bar exam there and get a house within a reasonable distance of where my mother lived so I could look in on her."

Hogren gave notice to the law firm and began winding down his work. It wasn't very difficult to sever his connections with the firm because he was already a "tenant" lawyer, paying rent to the firm rather than working directly for them.

"I had become a tenant lawyer late in 1970," he says. "I wanted to take cases I wanted to take, and I also wanted to be free to do my legal aid work if necessary. I liked being my own boss, of course, doing work for the firm on a free-lance basis."

It required several months after taking his mother to Florida for Chuck to phase out his work. With his sister married and living in Seattle at the time, it had fallen to Chuck to look after their mother. She progressed, improving slowly. Chuck visited her about once a month while finishing things up in Chicago.

Chuck spent the winter of 1971-72 in Florida. Gardening had been a hobby of his, so he was glad to exchange the snow for a rather sizable garden. His mother returned to Chicago with him the following July, stayed a few days, then went on to Seattle to visit her daughter.

In October 1974 Mrs. Hogren was back in Chicago to prepare with Chuck for their final and permanent move to Florida. Just four days before their scheduled departure she suffered another stroke and died the next day.

"I asked Bill Leslie to handle the funeral services," says Chuck. "On the way to the cemetery I told him I was uncertain about the future. I had severed my ties with the law firm in preparation for the move to Florida. Now I had no reason to go. I told him, 'If there's any work that needs to be done—he had often talked about the need for a business manager for the church—I'd be glad to help.' "

Bill was interested in Chuck's offer to work, but not as business manager. "Bill turned to me and said, 'How about a legal aid clinic?' I hadn't ever thought of that. Feeling I didn't have the proper legal qualifications, I would much rather have been the business person or administrator. But I said, 'Well, if the money could be found . . .' "

55 | BIRTH OF A CLINIC

That was all the encouragement Leslie needed. The seed was planted and his dream of a legal aid clinic in Cabrini-Green took root.

Despite his mother's death, Chuck found Florida hard to pass up. "I had felt a sense of relief over the prospect of moving and starting something new. I had planned to pick oranges and do some physical labor while I studied for the Florida bar exam," he recalls. "I wasn't thinking of practicing law all that much. What I was really interested in was getting into prison administration."

Chuck was somewhat apprehensive about the idea of a legal aid clinic. He felt he should put in an apprenticeship somewhere before directing such an enterprise.

Working with the poor can be trying; there is often little or nothing in the way of legal fees; frustrations abound in dealing with clients who neither understand nor appreciate law; and of course, there is the thankless nature of much of the work. None of that bothered Hogren. It was his obsession about his "lack of proper training" that deterred him.

The irrepressible Leslie was undaunted. "Let's see what we can do," Bill told him. With neither of them having any idea of where the money for a clinic would come from, Chuck said he would work for $100 a week. That small stipend in addition to some legal work on the side would pay the bills.

Leslie, who has ten units of confidence for every one Chuck possesses, went right to work scrounging up the money. In about two weeks he had it. A Christian foundation had agreed to provide $10,000 for the first year of operation and $5,000 for the second. Out of that would come Chuck's modest salary, money for a secretary, and other expenses.

"I couldn't believe the speed," says Chuck, still a bit stunned by the memory. "I thought it was much too fast! In November, Bill started looking around for the money. By the end of the month he had it. He said we could start January 1st. I couldn't imagine being ready to open by then. I still had to handle my mother's estate. Besides, everything was already in Florida, leaving hardly any furniture at all in the house."

Chuck had been secretly hoping that Bill would be unable to raise the money. The specter of being thrown into the directorship of a legal aid clinic on two or three weeks' notice frightened him. With the word "No" scarcely a part of his vocabulary, Hogren reluctantly consented to opening the clinic.

After spending Christmas 1972 in Seattle with his sister and her family, Chuck began work the day after New Year's. He recalls the first day as less than auspicious. "On January 2nd I went to the church, got to the front door, and found it locked. Nobody was around. I had no office—nothing. I went wandering around the neighborhood looking for office space. I couldn't find any storefronts. At that point, I had no idea where the clinic was going to be. All I knew was that we had $10,000 and I was committed for one year."

Finding office space became a discouraging problem: Once again, however, ready with a solution was none other than Bill Leslie. At a church staff meeting in January Bill announced that he had talked to Father Mark Santo, then at nearby St. Dominic's Catholic Church. Father Santo had a vacant convent with three rooms on Hudson Avenue which he was willing to rent for $100 a month. Chuck could use one, Joe White (Young Life director) another, and Regina Berg, secretary for both of them, could occupy the remaining room.

January was hectic. "Besides the time I spent looking for office space," Hogren says, "I had to do a lot of reading in the major criminal cases of the sixties and seventies, the ones that changed the law so much with regard to the rights of individuals."

On February 1, 1973, the Cabrini-Green Legal Aid Clinic opened.

"Very shortly after we opened the clinic we got the armed robbery case involving Allen Pendleton and the Oak brothers. It put me right in the middle of a major criminal case." That was the case in which Chuck felt convinced of Pendleton's culpability only to have someone else confess to the crime later. The experience did nothing to buoy the new clinic director's confidence.

If the Pendleton case was the frying pan, the Roy Harris fiasco was the fire. It all began in March 1973, when two fifteen-year-old boys were playing basketball across the street from the clinic in the parking lot of Montgomery Ward. Montgomery Ward had installed basketball equipment in their parking lot so that after hours, when their employees were gone for the day, the neighborhood kids could play basketball.

57 | BIRTH OF A CLINIC

After the boys had finished playing they headed home toward the row-house area in Cabrini-Green. They were walking west on Chicago Avenue. As they were crossing Cambridge Avenue they met a white man headed east. As they were about to pass the man in the middle of the street, one of the youngsters, Jackie Irvin, said something to him. Irvin then proceeded to pull out a gun, and shot and killed the man right on the spot. There was, according to Chuck, "absolutely no provocation whatsoever." Both of the young men fled the scene but were caught by the police shortly after.

The police interrogated the two and found that the crime had been committed by Irvin. They felt that the other youth, Roy Harris, probably wasn't directly involved in the act, but nevertheless they charged both of the teen-agers with murder.

Shortly after the incident, Roy Harris's aunt came to Hogren's office asking him to take Roy's case. Chuck said he would. By that time Chuck had already built, albeit unintentionally, a considerable legal reputation in Cabrini-Green. It was not greatly surprising, therefore, that the very next day Jackie Irvin's mother also came in, requesting Chuck's services. But a lawyer may not handle two clients involved in the same case if there is any likelihood that their defenses might conflict, so Hogren had to turn Mrs. Irvin down. Disappointed, she told him she would have to get the public defender.

Although Roy did not do the shooting, he was in trouble because of what is termed the "theory of accountability." That doctrine holds that if a person is in the company of someone who commits a crime he is equivalently guilty unless he can show he had no foreknowledge of it. If one has foreknowledge of a criminal act he must either not be in the presence of its commission or be actively seeking to prevent its occurrence.

Before Hogren's involvement in the case, the state's attorney discussed the matter with the public defender who initially represented both youths. They decided that Harris probably had nothing to do with the murder and didn't know that Irvin had a gun.

The state's attorney then asked Roy, since there were no other witnesses, if he would testify against Jackie Irvin. The state's attorney told him that all he had to do was to come to court when called and they would drop the murder charges pending against him. Harris said he would. At that point,

58 | THE RELUCTANT DEFENDER

Chuck began representing Roy Harris. Harris was released from custody and Jackie Irvin decided to plead guilty instead of going to trial. Although the guilty plea made Roy's testimony unnecessary, because of the prior agreement charges against him were dropped.

Exactly one month later, on Good Friday evening, a cab driver was murdered on Hudson about a block north of the law clinic's office. At that time Jackie Irvin was in a state institution and Roy was out on the street. The police went right after Harris. "They said to him," Hogren states, " 'You were involved in a murder a month ago and got off; we're going to get you on this one.' " The police took Roy to the Audy Home where he was held in custody.

Chuck was again retained by Roy's aunt. This, however, was a much more serious case, since Roy was the only defendant facing a murder charge. Hogren then filed a "discovery motion."*

A discovery motion consists of a list of questions presented to each other by the state and the defense. For the defense, it might request such items as the names of the witnesses to the crime, any physical evidence the state intends to offer, the time of the offense, and where it happened. The objective of the discovery motion is to discover as much as possible about the opposition's case before the trial. Under state law, each side must respond to the motion. From a legal standpoint, the purpose of such motions is to prevent what is called "trial by surprise." (See Appendix 4.)

One of Chuck's questions was whether there was any evidence in the hands of the state that might be deemed helpful in establishing the innocence of the defendant. The state had to answer that, under a Supreme Court decision called the Brady Rule which prohibits the state from concealing any evidence favorable to the defense.

There had been three witnesses to the crime, two young men in their early teens and a fourteen-year-old girl. The state answered that one of the witnesses, the girl, Valerie Adams, was refusing to testify for them at the trial.

Time was running short. The trial was to begin the following day. Chuck hurried to the girl's home and talked to her

---

*A copy of a Discovery Motion is provided in Appendix 3.

59 | BIRTH OF A CLINIC

mother. She told Hogren that her daughter did see the crime, and that it was not Roy Harris who had done the shooting.

Mrs. Adams then told Chuck what had happened at the police station. "All three witnesses, the two boys and Valerie, had been taken to the police station together. One of the boys was taken into the Interrogation Room first. I was sitting out in the hall with Valerie. Suddenly I heard the boy screaming; he was hysterical. When he came out I asked him what happened. He said, 'The police had a statement for me to sign that said Roy shot the cab driver. I told them he didn't do it and I wasn't going to sign it. Then they took a shotgun out of the closet, held it over my head, and started dropping the shells out of the gun onto my head. I was so scared I signed it.' I said, 'That's terrible, but you're going to tell the truth at the trial, aren't you?' He said, 'No, I can't. I'm afraid.'"

According to Hogren, Mrs. Adams was very upset as she told about the bizarre event. She went on, saying that the other young man was taken into the Interrogation Room with his father. Evidently the father told him, "Sign whatever they give you, just sign it, and let's get out of here." No strong-arm tactics were used on the second witness. Then it was Valerie's turn and Mrs. Adams told the officers she didn't want her daughter to sign any statement. The police said that was okay; they had gotten enough.

"She told me all this when I talked to her," states Chuck. "The state's attorney had called Valerie into his office earlier, hoping she would cooperate by identifying Roy as the one who performed the shooting. She refused, so they couldn't use her and had to list her in the discovery motion."

While talking with Mrs. Adams, Chuck wondered how in the world all this could come out at the trial. In court, the young man who signed the statement under duress was the first to testify. He testified that he knew Roy, had seen him before in the community, and that he had seen him shoot the cab driver.

"Then I cross-examined him," recalls Chuck. "I asked him about the identification: where he was, how far away from the taxi he was, what the light conditions were, and so forth. Then I asked him about what happened at the police station.

"He was just as prepared as he could be! He hung tough with every answer. 'I know Roy, I have seen him before in the community' and on and on. He must have been briefed. It all seemed too pat, because he was hardly the world's greatest genius."

"Knowing the truth," Chuck continues, "I went through all the possible questions I could to shake him, to get him to talk about the gun. I asked him about the incident at the police station. He denied it. I said, 'Were you asked to sign a statement there?' 'Yes I was,' he replied. 'Did you sign it voluntarily?' 'Yes I did.' 'Did the police coerce you or threaten you?' 'No they didn't.' 'Didn't they, in fact, take a shotgun out of the closet, hold it over your head, and eject the shells?' 'No, they didn't.' 'Didn't you see a shotgun in that room?' 'No, I didn't.' Thinking maybe he had gotten the guns mixed up, I asked him if he saw a gun there. He said he didn't. I asked him about the room, who was there, everything. I was extremely frustrated. I couldn't do anything in cross-examination. I couldn't jar anything loose. He was as firm as a rock." Chuck sat down, defeated.

The state's attorney then got up. Since Hogren had talked about the shotgun he asked him about it on redirect examination. "Now, there was no shotgun in that room, was there?" the state's attorney asked.

"Yes, there was," replied the youth. "They held it over my head and emptied the shells onto my head."

"I just couldn't believe it," says Hogren. "The judge couldn't believe it either. It was the most dramatic scene of a witness changing his testimony I've ever seen.

"Once it was out, the witness was consistent about the shotgun incident. Then it struck him that he had made a mistake, blown it. He wasn't exactly sure what he had done wrong, but after finishing his testimony he took off out of that courtroom like a tornado. I never saw him again," Hogren says, laughing.

The state's attorney was Casper Arden. Now in private practice, he has since become a good friend of Chuck's. Although not certain, Chuck doesn't think Arden knew of the shotgun shell shakedown before the trial. Hogren theorizes that Arden told the young witness to stick to the story (a story Arden believed to be the truth) when under the searchlight of cross-examination, but to relax when he, Arden, questioned him.

"When I started asking about the gun," Chuck suggests,

61 | BIRTH OF A CLINIC

"Arden most likely thought I was grasping at straws. But he probably feared that my raising the question might lead the judge to think that instead of just fishing I was actually in possession of some important information. So he tried to shoot it down hard. To reaffirm that there was no shotgun, no coercion whatsoever, he asked the question about the shotgun."

After the bombshell, the state's attorney requested a recess for lunch. After lunch the state brought in the second witness, questioning him in such a way that there was no opportunity to raise the question of what transpired at the police station. "They were very careful," Chuck says, "to keep all the testimony out on the street. They didn't mention anything about a statement, or for that matter, the police station." Because cross-examination has to remain within the scope of direct examination, Chuck was blocked.

Nonetheless, he forged ahead. "When I got up I questioned him about how the police had obtained his signature on the report. The state objected. But the judge gave me some latitude. I knew in advance that this kid had not been coerced by the police, that his father had told him to sign, so I asked him, 'Didn't your father tell you to sign this? You didn't do this voluntarily, your father demanded you sign it!' He denied it. I couldn't shake him on it. It didn't make much difference, however. The cat was long out of the bag."

The state then put on the investigating officer. He told how he had arrested Roy Harris and charged him with the murder. Knowing how the identification occurred, on cross-examination Chuck asked him what his investigation consisted of. Did he conduct an objective inquiry? The officer admitted that they had shown the witness a photograph of a lineup in which Roy was one of four or five individuals pictured. "I think it was a reasonably fair picture as lineup photographs go," concedes Chuck, "but it was inadequate. They hadn't followed the normal procedure: taking a book of hundreds of pictures and having the witnesses spend hours flipping through the pages looking at them. It was transparently obvious that they had just been waiting for the next murder to occur in order to pin it on Roy. The officer acknowledged that the single photograph constituted the total investigation of the felony."

62 | THE RELUCTANT DEFENDER

The state concluded its case with the officer's testimony. Hogren then called Roy to testify and he denied any participation in the crime.

The judge then rendered his decision. Chuck remembers it well. "He said, 'I must follow the law; I must find the defendant not guilty.' The judge's statement really upset me, for it was clear he thought Roy was guilty and was reluctant about releasing him."

About two weeks later Chuck was in court and saw the judge in the hallway. Still upset, he went over and engaged him in conversation. The judge said he was very distressed about the Harris case. He felt that Roy was guilty, but on the basis of the evidence he had no alternative but to enter a "not guilty" verdict. Chuck took issue with the judge. "I didn't feel Roy was guilty," says Hogren, "and I was disturbed that the judge thought he was. The judge said Roy was cold, unremorseful. I said of course he was not remorseful; he didn't do anything to be remorseful about."

Chuck steadfastly maintains that Harris was innocent. "There are several reasons why I don't believe Roy was guilty. For one, I talked to Valerie Adams who was an eyewitness and she told me two people were involved. She said she was not a friend of Roy's but knew who he was and would recognize him. She said neither of the two assailants was Roy and that she told her mother that right away.

"I also have the hearsay testimony of the young man who was coerced to identify Roy, telling Mrs. Adams that Roy was not involved.

"In addition, we have Roy's alibi. But it's a family alibi." According to Hogren, in the gallows humor of criminal lawyers a family alibi is called a "slow plea of guilty." That is, nobody is likely to believe it. Obviously Chuck doesn't press that kind of alibi very often.

With regard to the fateful statement signed by the two young men in the police station, Hogren believes that the question-and-answer document was prepared before they ever got into the Interrogation Room.* "I'm sure," asserts Hogren, "that the kids didn't dictate any part of that statement, because when I cross-examined the second witness his answers as to how

---

*The major parts of the statement are provided in Appendix 4.

63 | BIRTH OF A CLINIC

many times he had seen Roy were completely different from what was in the statement."

Chuck's conversation with Mrs. Adams provided additional support for that notion. "She said her daughter told her that two men had committed the crime, and that when Valerie confronted the first witness with that fact after he had left the Interrogation Room having signed the statement, he agreed that there were two assailants. He claimed that the statement didn't indicate that two people had been involved. That, in addition to the fact that Roy was not involved, was why he initially refused to sign the statement. After the shotgun confrontation, however, he caved in."

As if the case hadn't presented Hogren with enough headaches, several other vexing problems arose before he even went to trial. For one, Chuck felt he had been double-crossed by the state's attorney. At the time of the Irvin murder, Roy Harris had been on probation from a robbery charge dating back to the previous summer. When Harris consented to testify against Irvin, the state's attorney not only agreed to drop the murder charges against Roy but also agreed not to "violate" Roy's probation—provided Roy stayed out of further trouble. (Violation of probation means reopening the original case and having the defendant sentenced on it.)

When the second murder occurred, the state's attorney decided that instead of prosecuting Harris on it, where the standard of proof for conviction is "beyond a reasonable doubt" (about 95 percent surety of the commission of the crime), he would seek a violation of probation. In such a situation, the state must demonstrate "by preponderance" that the defendant has committed the new crime. The same facts and evidence are used, but the standard of proof is much lower: 51 percent (the preponderance of the evidence).

Chuck was very upset when he heard of the state's strategy, feeling that the state's attorney had breached his agreement. The state's attorney argued that his agreement held that a violation of probation would result if Roy got into further trouble. Therefore he had every right to seek such a verdict in view of Roy's being arrested on a murder charge. Chuck protested, asserting that simply being arrested does not constitute "getting into trouble"; after all, people are arrested every day for things they didn't do.

64 | THE RELUCTANT DEFENDER

The state wouldn't budge, so Hogren prepared an affidavit that outlined his understanding of the agreement. The state's attorney read it over and, satisfied that it was an accurate representation of the agreement, signed it. They then took the affidavit to a judge who handled violation of probation cases. Fortunately, the judge ruled that "getting into trouble" means a conviction; being arrested isn't enough. Chuck feels that the decision was critical to the whole case because "when you consider how the judge who actually tried the murder case felt about Roy's innocence, you can bet your life the state would have had no trouble getting a violation of probation verdict."

Another major problem cropped up at the preliminary hearing. When Chuck went to the hearing, the purpose of which is to establish "probable cause" or the likelihood that the accused may have committed the crime, he found himself before a judge "who acted as though it were a foregone conclusion that Roy was guilty." Chuck was alarmed, just on the basis of some of the judge's statements during the hearing. "I felt that we simply couldn't have a trial before that judge because of what he said, in addition to the fact that he had heard a case involving Roy earlier, possibly prejudicing him. I got the impression that if we went to trial before him it would be just a matter of going through the legal motions because the result would be certain conviction."

Chuck talked to the Chief Public Defender, a court veteran, about the dilemma. "He told me the judge had a nickname, 'white death.' He said there was a black judge whose nickname was 'black death,' and that the two along with another judge had a contest each month to see who put more people away in a state institution, with the loser buying lunch for the others." Although realizing the story might be part of courthouse mythology, Hogren nonetheless was taking no chances.

Within ten days of a case being assigned to a judge, a lawyer has the right automatically, without any stated reason, to get another judge. The practice, much used, is called a substitution of judges.* Chuck took advantage of that regulation, naming both "white" and "black death" as unacceptable. (A lawyer can object to two judges in such an action, after which the Chief Judge assigns a new judge to the case.)

---

*A copy of a Motion for a Substitution of Judges is provided in Appendix 5.

BIRTH OF A CLINIC

"That," says Hogren, "is how we got the judge who ultimately handled the case. Since that time, 'black death' has been transferred out, but 'white death' is still there. However, I've never heard that nickname used in reference to him since. In fact, I've heard many positive things about him, have appeared before him many times, and have always been satisfied with the fairness of his decisions whether I won or lost."

Whether or not the public defender was accurate in his assessments of those particular judges is difficult to determine. What is beyond dispute is that people in the legal profession are acutely aware that the judge before whom one appears can have a profound impact on the disposition of a case. The fulcrum on which the scales of justice are balanced is not always in the center.

Despite so many snags, the case turned out all right. Roy Harris was acquitted and has been doing well ever since. "I've talked to his probation officer on several occasions," says Chuck, "and I understand he has finished high school.

"It was a satisfying experience for me because if the clinic hadn't been there Roy would have probably been convicted. That would have made him a very bitter young man and probably propelled him into crime on a heavy scale."

Hogren's sensitivity shows through in his final reflections on the Harris experience. "What was so sad about that case was that a cab driver had to die for all those injustices to come to light."

LIFE AT THE CLINIC

5

Gina Berg, a young woman in her middle twenties, was the legal aid clinic's first secretary. When it opened, Regina had just gotten married and was looking for a job. Although she had a degree in education from Trinity College, she didn't want to teach. A member of LaSalle Street Church, Gina heard that Joe White, the Young Life director, wanted a black secretary because he was going to be located in Cabrini-Green. In addition, Chuck Hogren was going to be in the small office building with White and also needed secretarial help. They told her that the job, serving as secretary for both programs, wouldn't pay much but it was hers if she wanted it. She accepted.

"My earliest memory," Gina says, "is of getting off the 'el' (the elevated train) at the Chicago Avenue stop and having to walk past all those high-rise projects on Chicago Avenue on the way to Hudson Avenue; then walking down Hudson past the row houses to an old, dilapidated-looking building. I thought, 'What in the world am I doing here?'

"For a long time I was scared out of my tree! I had never been in Cabrini before but I had heard a lot of terrifying things about it. By the time I would leave at the end of the day it was starting to get dark. That made me very nervous, so Joe White often walked me over to the el."

Gina eventually became acclimated to the clinic's location. "It wasn't quite as dangerous as I imagined when I first started. Fortunately, we were right off Chicago Avenue and only about a block from Montgomery Ward's. Once on Chicago Avenue, it wasn't too bad. Walking to work didn't make me too fearful in the daylight."

Gina recalls the rather ominous physical characteristics of the Hudson structure. "The small yard in front of the little building was surrounded by a wire fence with bushes about five feet tall behind it. There was a little walk with three or four steps up to the door. Inside the front door were three or four more steps. At the top of those steps were two offices. The one to the left was mine and the one to the right was Joe's. Then you walked through another doorway and there to the right was a very tiny office. That was Chuck's."

One day when she came to work early, Gina was just coming through the gate when she saw a large animal creeping across the sidewalk. "At first I thought it was a squirrel. But it wasn't. It was a rat! It had a body about fifteen inches long. I froze. I stood there while it just kept moving along. I guess it didn't want anything to do with me either. It had something in its mouth but that's all I remember. Then I ran for the door and let myself into the office. I just stood there trembling," she recalls, laughing. Pest control was as lacking on Hudson Avenue as it is throughout Cabrini-Green. "There were also roaches but they didn't bother me much compared to rats."

The building itself was a security guard's nightmare. "It was terribly dangerous. I couldn't believe how bad it was! There was a basement with windows all around. There were no bars on the windows or anything like that, making it very insecure. The entire yard was surrounded by bushes so that an intruder could be down at those windows and no one outside of the yard would notice him. There were also about twenty windows around the first and second floors. The first floor had three entrances. One of them was all boarded up with a grate on it so it couldn't be used. The back entrance also had a grate on it but it had been broken.

"The rear of the building was by far the worst part. The back

69 | LIFE AT THE CLINIC

room on the first floor, Chuck's office, had about six windows in it and not one of them was secure. All you had to do was break one, open the lock, and you were in. For awhile somebody was occupying the building next door, but later it was vacated. To make matters worse, I was the only person in the clinic building most of the day because Chuck was usually in court."

There were incidents. Once, while Gina was gone, someone broke into the building and took all the ten-speed bikes Joe had stored in his office for the Young Life kids. Another break-in occurred at night. The burglars broke the lock and stole the clinic's tape recorder in addition to several other office items.

"Then one day," says Gina, "while Chuck and I were both there, I thought I heard glass breaking. I went to Chuck's office and asked him whether he'd dropped something. I didn't think he had, but I thought I'd feel greatly relieved if he said Yes. He said he hadn't and asked me if I had heard anything. I told him about the breaking glass."

Chuck and Gina checked out the first floor but didn't see anything. Chuck decided to go to the basement and look around down there. Gina offered to go along but he told her to stay upstaris. "So I stayed where I was," she says. "Only about five minutes elapsed before he came back up, but it seemed like an eternity to me.

"I asked him if he had seen anything. He said rather casually, 'Oh, some boys broke out one of the windows, but it's okay. I chased them away.' Just like that, that's how he said it! He told me three teen-age guys coming into the basement took off when they saw him."

One evening Chuck was alone working late. He thought he heard something in the back so he went to see what it was. "He told me about it," says Gina. "There was this guy coming in the window. Chuck confronted him in the hallway. When the guy saw Chuck he must have thought someone else was in the building because certainly no white guy is going to be down in the Green alone at night. Anyway, Chuck said, 'Get out of here!' and the guy turned tail and ran."

Gina had a hard time believing Chuck's courage. "Can you imagine that! It's incredible! Chuck could just say to this guy, 'Get out of here!' and the guy would run."

Fear of being in the building by herself preyed on Gina's

nerves. She knew she would be trapped if the front door was blocked, because the back door was locked. Her fear accumulated.

"I certainly prayed about it," she recalls. "I mean if you have any kind of faith in God at all, man, and you're in a situation like that, you pray a lot!"

Gina tried not to think about the danger while she was there. "I'm the kind of person who usually does what she has to do and then gets scared afterward. I knew what I had to do and did it; and I stayed out of as many dangerous situations as I could."

Something had to give. It got to the point where Gina asked Chuck if they could close before dark during the winter. Although a lot of times Chuck would take her to the el in his car, other times she had to walk through Cabrini alone in the dark. Closing early would at least solve that problem.

The situation continued to deteriorate. "Day and night people would break in if they thought no one was there," says Gina. "It never happened while I was there alone, but several times while Chuck and I were both in the building, there were near break-ins. You could see the would-be intruders out there."

Finally they decided to move the clinic north to the Isham YMCA on Ogden. There seemed to be no choice. The lack of safety on Hudson was making it hard to do an adequate job. "As I look back I can see that we were protected," reflects Gina. "There's no way, in view of the kinds of things that happened, that both of us could have walked out of that place unscathed without the Lord's protection."

Lynette Surbaugh succeeded Gina Berg as clinic secretary. Raised in Wheaton, Illinois, by Christian parents, Lynette spent her first year of college at Trinity. There she met her husband, David, who operated the Logos bookstore on Clark Street in Chicago's New Town area.

Lynette got interested in the clinic through reading about prisons and prison conditions. She became so interested in the subject that in 1973 she returned to college, enrolling at the University of Illinois at Chicago Circle, and finished a bachelor of arts degree in criminal justice. Facing graduation she wasn't sure what she was going to do. According to Lynette, some of her fellow students became social workers or went to law

71 | LIFE AT THE CLINIC

school and others became policemen or policewomen, but she found herself eyeing the clinic. About two weeks before she graduated, she received a call from Gina telling her that there would soon be an opening at the clinic as she and her husband Rod were expecting their first child. "I took that as a sign from the Lord," says Lynette, "because the timing was so perfect. I started training about a week after graduation and it became an ideal situation for me."

Despite the relative safety of the Isham YMCA, every time Chuck or Lynette would leave the office, even to go to the washroom, they would lock the door. Moreover, the violent nature of many of the crimes the clinic dealt with had its effect on Lynette. But eventually she got used to it.

"I don't think I've ever been really afraid here," she says. "The reason, although I hate to sound so pious, is that I felt God wanted me in this job. I believed that strongly. I sensed I was maybe the right person for this work, in spite of all the problems. When you're dealing with crime, however, your mind is often on it and you do take it home with you. Occasionally I wake up at night having terrible dreams. They aren't dreams in which I wake up screaming but when they happen I'm in a sweat and can't get back to sleep. It's almost as if Satan himself is in the room with me, making me imagine the most terrifying events, like guys coming into the bedroom and stabbing David and me while we're sleeping. I also live with the fear of my husband David getting held up at the bookstore.

"I usually pray a lot when such nightmares occur," says Lynette with a chuckle, "because I need a kind of deliverance from them. I feel that Satan uses fear as a real weapon against me, against my peace of mind or whatever." Her prayers must have been answered because the nightmares began subsiding the longer she worked. Nonetheless, the potential remained.

Chuck and his secretary are the only whites who work in the building. The rest of the Isham personnel are very protective of them. "I have a little phone here," says Lynette pointing to a small telephone on the corner of her desk, "that's connected straight to the front office of the building. All I have to do is lift the receiver—not even dial it—and they call me back immediately on my other phone to see if something's wrong. I bumped it off one time by accident and they called me right away."

72 | THE RELUCTANT DEFENDER

Nevertheless there are anxious moments. "Our office is at the corner of the building. A lot of times my door is open and young teen-agers walk in. They're usually casing the place. My first response is to stand up, walk briskly around my desk right up to them, and ask them what they want. The best defense, I figure, is a good offense. I'm not going to let them come in and make me quake in my boots—but sometimes it does make me a bit queasy."

Lynette, in her twenties, is a highly aware, urban woman. "I do have my scissors next to the phone and my letter opener inside my desk. I don't keep that on top of the desk because an assailant could grab it before I did." She seems rather philosophical about the need for self-protection. "It's all a part of city living; it makes sense to take precautions. I've got a whistle on my key chain that I can use and I carry my keys on my fingers like a set of brass knuckles. Once I heard a man talk about preventing rape who said if you become confident and alert, and if you make yourself fairly strong in the way you come on to people, you can intimidate them. You never let them intimidate you. That's the point. You have to carry around an aura of confidence.

"I carry the key chain on my knuckles with my gloves on and I don't talk to people. If they say 'Hi,' I don't even answer. I never get friendly. I don't even maintain any eye contact with anybody on the street, because as soon as your eyes meet, they say something to you and it's openers for getting more involved. You just can't allow that to happen. The kind of culture here prohibits it.

"We have a group of fellows out there who like to drink their Richard's Wild Irish Rose at the bar across the street," says Lynette. "Those men really don't bother me. They sit out there and have their little community together. They laugh and use coarse "Navy" language, the kind I hear every day. Some of those fellows across the street were the same guys who broke into this office one time and took my typewriter, so they do have designs on the place. One thing I don't do is stand by the window and gaze at them, because the less you supposedly know in this neighborhood, the safer you are. They don't like white folks watching them."

Working with Cabrini-Green people has obviously sensitized Lynette to their plight. There's a knock on the door and

73 | LIFE AT THE CLINIC

in come two little four-year-old black girls. Lynette, radiating warmth, rushes up to them and asks kiddingly, "What are you doing, selling something?" The kids look at one another, grin shyly, and nod their heads. Everybody enjoys the teasing. Lynette tells them gently that she can't talk with them right now, gives each of them a kiss, and tells them to come back later when she will have time to talk. Shutting the door, she says, "Those poor kids, all they want is attention. If you're one of twelve kids you need attention."

Although having grown up in a middle-class black background and never having experienced the kinds of life situations Cabrini-Green residents encounter daily, Gina Berg had a special empathy for the clients. "I guess because I'm black it hurt me to see the problems. It's kind of like relatives, you know. You hate to see a distant relative or friend go through something hard. Somehow you feel such a bond with them that when they're oppressed you feel that oppression. What hurt most was that there wasn't always a lot we could do about the problems. A lot of it was institutional stuff—like, a company had given them bad furniture and told them it was good and then didn't want to stand behind the warranty. The people have no recourse when they don't have a lawyer."

The clinic secretaries often involve themselves directly in the clinic's legal efforts. Gina would occasionally sit in on initial interviews with clients to assess their credibility. "Two pairs of ears are better than one, so I would sit in while Chuck asked the pertinent questions," she says. "If Chuck thought someone was lying, he would ask the same question of the client in different ways. If he trapped them, he would just confront them and say, 'Look, you told me two stories; now which one is the truth?' He'd tell them, 'If I'm going to be your lawyer you're going to trust me, or you're going to find another lawyer. And if I'm going to be your lawyer then I have to trust you for what you say.' Sometimes Chuck would be writing things down while I would watch the guy's face to check him out. There would be times when I told Chuck, 'Look, this guy's lying to you. I can't tell you why, but I really don't think he's telling the truth.' Sure enough, Chuck would go back and double-check with some other questions and the guy would come up telling two stories."

74 | THE RELUCTANT DEFENDER

Lynette reflected on her interaction with the clients. "Working in the clinic really enriched my knowledge. I can go to a lot of places and feel confident that I can get around in the city system fairly well. When a person called on the phone, many times they'd talk to me even more than to Chuck, since Chuck is often out. When they had a problem I had to be able to tell them what to do. Although I shouldn't really have given legal advice on the phone I often did. I just knew if they had a certain kind of landlord problem where to send them. I learned where to go for different things in Chicago."

Involvement in a client's plight can sometimes become a plunge into frustration. Lynette recalls the case of Lisa Thompson, one of a number of white, non-Cabrini-Green people Chuck helped out. "Lisa Thompson is a white girl who used to go to LaSalle Street Church. She was locked up because she hadn't been paying her parking tickets. Although she is a rather intelligent person and has a job, she is mentally unstable. Lisa Thompson is an example of a person who has more than legal problems. The legal problem is only a reflection of her psychological condition. She believes that the FBI and the CIA maintain surveillance over her apartment. She even paid a guy a lot of money to find evidence of the surveillance, but of course there was nothing, so she fired him.

"Anyway, while she was in jail we got a call from her asking us to take care of her cats. Well, Bill Lipscomb, an intern at LaSalle, and I did it. It was a half a day's work to get into her apartment because we had to drive out to a mental facility where they had her tied down, in order to get her keys. When we got there she wouldn't release the keys to me because, since she was locked up, she couldn't see me face-to-face. Later Chuck had to break into her apartment to help us.

"When we finally got into her apartment it took about two hours just to get the cats into the car. As soon as you got one in, another would slip out. It was a real comedy. Finally we got all eight or ten cats into my car and took them over to a veterinarian for a few days until we raised the $500 for her bail. Once Lisa was out, we took her to the vet to get her cats and transported them all back to her apartment. With a sigh of relief we left, believing our troubles were behind us.

"Lisa had her court dates and Chuck urged her to let him accompany her to court as her attorney. She is a very inflam-

75 | LIFE AT THE CLINIC

matory person, so Chuck wanted to be sure that things went smoothly. She refused.

"Then we got another phone call. I couldn't believe it. 'Hello, this is Lisa. I'm in the House of Correction and my cats are at home. The judge set bond at $1,000.' Evidently something went awry in court. Now she wanted Chuck to bail her out, which I might add, he went off to do. He was afraid they 'might have railroaded her a bit.' Old 'Never-say-No' Chuck couldn't bear to let a woman remain briefly in the House of Correction over a matter that was clearly her own fault.

"So he took off," said Lynette with fatigue in her voice, "running around trying to find the judge. Lisa had failed to find out enough information to determine what was going on. She didn't even know what the charges were. So Chuck had to do all the footwork to find out the basic information. If only she had let Chuck go with her, all that probably could have been avoided, but she was too obstinate. I kept wondering what we were going to do with all those cats!

"Lisa had a bad relationship with her father. Now he's willing to come and start to heal it, but she's too stubborn and doesn't want to forgive him. Chuck told her to call him but she wouldn't do it. Her dad would have bailed her out and she could have been home with her cats. In fact, because of her refusal to go to him we had to borrow the $500 bail money from two churches in the area with the stipulation that she would go to the Near North Counseling Center of our church to enter therapy. There was no pressure, so she took the money and has yet to go to the center. And as long as she knows she can call on Chuck and he'll run over to help her, there's little motivation on her part to become more responsible."

Lynette picks up the story: "Charlene Gilbert is another rather unstable person. She's had two children taken from her because she was adjudged to be an unfit mother. She had been going to the counseling center but Dave Bryen didn't feel she was making any progress dealing with her problems. She's an expert at justifying everything she does. When her children are living at a foster home she will tell them to do things that will sabotage the arrangement. She encourages them to do clever things that are clearly against the rules.

"She will call me up and tell me why the foster parents are so awful. She goes on and on. Charlene seems to have a pattern of marrying alcoholics, in addition to having a drinking problem of her own. She has tried to commit suicide as well. She talks about the pills she has been taking, telling me they make her feel funny. You can tell she's about to fall off her chair while she's talking. It's pathetic, but she's unwilling to confront her real problems in counseling or anywhere else."

Lynette, Gina, and Chuck have obviously found it difficult to remain objective when confronting human tragedies day after day. Doris Billings stands out in Lynette's mind. "Doris is white, about twenty-five. The Billings girls are poor but attractive southern girls, all of whom have had illegitimate children. The girls are carrying around tremendous burdens and Doris is a heroin addict on top of it.

"One of Doris's sisters occasionally calls me and tells me about what Doris is doing to her child. Her child is not being fed. He's being neglected. It's painful to picture in my mind that little baby being malnourished because her mother is an addict. You wonder what you can do about it. You can't help taking the tragedy home with you so it continues to plague you. That's the problem. You meet these people and you can kind of identify with them. You want to give them advice but often there's so little you can do. Doris was sent to Wisconsin to a home for unwed mothers. She escaped, I guess, and she's now back on the streets, apparently killing herself off gradually."

Perhaps more painful still is the plight of Keith Moran. An eighteen-year-old white boy from a broken home, Keith was involved in three or four armed robberies within a three-month period. His mother, a recovered alcoholic, is very concerned about Keith. According to Lynette, Mrs. Moran is very frail and quiet of voice. "Her voice quivers when she talks about Keith. She doesn't feel Keith is an angel but she has taken this whole thing really hard. Keith's father will have nothing to do with the situation so his mother has all the burden of her son's being in prison. He'll be there for a long time. Keith doesn't have a high school education, has no skills, and has just been turned down in a parole request."

On the phone, Lynette helps Mrs. Moran bear her pain. "I have a brother about the same age as Keith and he's gone through some rough things himself—but nothing like this.

77 | LIFE AT THE CLINIC

You get excited when a parole hearing comes up and you hope maybe something will go through. Keith was right here in this office when he first got into trouble and I know him."

The telephone can be maddening. Roger Henderson's brother was convicted of murder. Roger, also white, is an invalid and will call several times a day. "He'll complain," says Lynette, "about what a lousy job his lawyers are doing. He and his brother are both hypochondriacs, and both highly paranoid. Roger thinks the telephone company bugs his phone." On a typical day, Roger Henderson will call and begin engaging Lynette in a rather lengthy conversation. She tries to converse in some reasonable fashion, making small talk, knowing all along that it's going to amount to nothing. The conversation eventually moves to Roger's concern over his self-diagnosed constipation. Just then Chuck comes in and rescues Lynette from the phone call. "I'm also a doctor," says Lynette, smiling, referring to Henderson's latest bout with irregularity.

Gina had her telephone tribulations as well. "Alice Maxwell about drove me nuts," she says with a sigh. "She had hard times, but almost every day she would call; sometimes more than once a day." According to Chuck, the clinic dealt with a myriad of cases for Alice Maxwell.

Alice, in her middle forties, was divorced. One of her big problems was trying to get additional child support. Chuck finally did succeed in getting some added support, but it was a bitter situation.

"Her ex-husband," explains Chuck, "had visitation rights and wanted to take their thirteen-year-old daughter to Europe to visit relatives. He did, but they did more than visit relatives. He locked the girl in a hotel room, had intercourse with her, and left her in the room while he went galavanting around the country. She was severely damaged psychologically by that experience and hasn't recovered yet. She's getting psychiatric treatment at the present time."

Another Maxwell case concerned an attempt by the mortgage company to foreclose on her home. Chuck talked to the company and they agreed to delay the foreclosure. Then they went to a realtor to sell the home. However, when people came to look at the house, Alice's sons would drive them away—

almost physically. The real estate agent began complaining vociferously to Chuck: "How can I sell the house when her sons drive prospective buyers away? And she herself is so hostile to anyone looking at the house that they're afraid of her, too."

Finally the mortgage company could wait no longer. Alice was about to be thrown out, and lose the house. She then rented an apartment but when the movers arrived at the apartment, the would-be landlady said, "I'm not going to rent the apartment to Mrs. Maxwell." So Alice was left with all her furniture on the truck and no place to go.

The next step was to stall off the foreclosure—have the sheriff delay putting her out—so she could return to her own house for a while. Later she rented another house only to be put out after a month. "She would call up, no place to go," says Chuck. "It was just one aggravation after another. Nothing ever seemed to go right! I've never dealt with any other person where so many things went wrong in such a short period of time. Alice Maxwell's file in the clinic office is an inch thick with problem after problem after problem.

"It began in 1973 and we were still active with her legally in October 1977. She would always call Gina, Lynette, or me about her latest crisis. You wonder if it will ever end."

The telephone has led the frustration derby for Lynette and Gina. They realize that many people call just to make contact with another human being. They see such conversations as functions of their service to troubled souls. But sometimes it is just too much. "Those phone calls last a minimum of fifteen minutes," says Lynette. "I know from picking up the phone that there's nothing I can do but endure another deluge of frustration. At the fifteen-minute point I know I can't help them but from there it may go to an hour. Chuck is on the phone more than an hour with some people.

"I usually listen, but at some point it can get so heavy for me that I'll actually hold the phone away from my ear and do other things. I know what the person is saying. I've heard it so many times before that I won't be missing anything. That way I may get something else done and I also get a breather. When they start getting too redundant, when what they said three minutes ago is exactly what they're saying now, I break in and say, I really can't help you on this. You'll have to talk to

79 | LIFE AT THE CLINIC

Chuck or to another lawyer. For us to continue talking is just wasting our time. You get worked up and I get worked up. Besides, I have other things I have to do here.' That's about the most direct I ever get. I've never hung up or screamed—but I've surely screamed many times on the inside."

Thinking about some of the truly pathetic people the clinic has dealt with, Lynette offers this observation: "In general, these people seem unable to get outside themselves and take some corrective steps. They lack creative energy and are unaware of their options. They've built such a pattern of feeding off their own particular pathologies that it becomes cyclical."

The "repeaters" are another source of discouragement. "A number of young men would constantly be in trouble," says Gina. I became sick from seeing it. Chuck would say, 'I'm going to court.' I would look and discover I had nothing on the books for him that day and would ask who he was going for. Usually it was Richard Thacker. I would remind him that he had gone to court for Richard yesterday. He would say, 'No, this is another case.' Invariably it would be shoplifting. That merry-go-round would really frustrate me. That guy was just using Chuck to get him out on bail so that he could go back to shoplifting in order to support his drug habit."

A tragic figure, Richard Thacker is in his early twenties. He is an attractive, personable, intelligent young man. According to Chuck, his potential is nearly unlimited: he would be able to do almost anything he set his mind to. Although he may have suffered some neglect in his family, Richard lives in a nice home and, compared to other Cabrini-Green youth, has a great deal going for him. Yet Richard is an addict who is either unable or unwilling to kick the habit. To support his habit he has become a professional thief, with nearly twenty offenses against him over the past several years. The clinic handled all his cases. They kept on until they realized that by taking his cases they might be encouraging him to continue stealing.

Richard's mother would put up the bail money to get him out of jail, but Richard was irresponsible about showing up for court dates. He'd either be asleep or involved in something else. Although he never tried to get Chuck to make up reasons to keep the judiciary off his back, Richard would often find a loophole, have his doctor make up a reason, etc., to cover his absences. According to Chuck, when Richard did show up he would, if his addiction were part of the case, con the judge by using halfway measures, such as going through the motions with methadone, to dupe the judge into thinking that he was trying to break his drug habit. But he wouldn't put himself in a full-time in-patient program, demonstrating a genuine effort.

Richard's court truancy placed his mother in dire financial straits, because when a client fails to show, his bond is forfeited and he becomes liable for the full bail amount. For example, instead of paying $200 on a $2,000 bond, he becomes responsible for the entire $2,000. The clinic went to great lengths to help Mrs. Thacker. Lynette spent several days running down all of Richard's bond slips. Dan Van Ness, a lawyer who spent a year working with Chuck and who now operates a legal aid agency on the city's poor West Side,* dealt legally with the avalanche of bond forfeitures. He succeeded in getting them all set aside for Thacker.

Nevertheless, because of his many offenses, Richard owes thousands of dollars to the state and may well die before they are paid. "We spent so much time on all his cases and finally we had to tell him we just couldn't take any more of them," Chuck says sadly. "What is especially tragic is that his mother was hoping so much that Richard's younger brother would escape the same cycle. But now he's going in the same direction."

The accumulation of frustrating events took its toll on both Gina and Lynette. "Getting cussed out two or three times a day is not conducive to lowering your frustration level," Gina says. "Many of the people who were inconsiderate and impolite were other lawyers, or people whose cases we took but who didn't live in Cabrini-Green. They gave us the hardest time and were the people Chuck ran all over creation for, even though they didn't appreciate anything he did.

*While a law student at De Paul University in Chicago, Dan Van Ness heard of the Cabrini-Green Legal Aid Clinic through his association with Circle Church. He got in touch with Chuck Hogren who recommended that he get experience working with the Preventive Legal Services, a legal aid clinic resulting from the efforts of black law students at De Paul. Dan did that, and then after graduation worked with the Cabrini-Green clinic in 1975-76. Since then he has founded the Central Austin Legal Clinic which operates in conjunction with Circle Church on a low-fee, sliding scale. Another volunteer law student, Mary Turck, also worked with Chuck Hogren and has since founded a legal aid clinic which is housed in Association House, located in a *latino* area of the city.

81 | LIFE AT THE CLINIC

"A lot of times I would come home frustrated over my inability to handle the situations that came to me. I'd just be a wreck. I'd have a cup of coffee and my husband, Rod, would give me a rubdown around the shoulders and I'd go to bed early. I would do practically nothing those evenings and I'd especially try not to think about the problems. There's nothing else you can do. If you think about it, it can make you angry at the people who bug you. I tried not to get angry because, although I can't say their problems justified their behavior, I could understand why they were so mean."

Lynette has often felt like quitting because "life is too short to be worked up all the time. The problems are deep enough and the frustrations in such abundance that you can become immobilized by them. To work in a pressure-packed situation like this you really need more than two people, because with only two you can begin feeding off one another's woes."

Lynette believes strongly in the legal aid concept. "There need to be professional, well-financed clinics of this type established in different places all over the country," she asserts. "But you need a larger staff. With a small one you become investigator, counselor, attorney, doctor, and friend. With a larger staff you could go beyond the legal dimension and deal with the whole person because you have more resources available to you. Also, a larger group creates a lighter atmosphere and provides more insights into each problem.

"So many problems make me take the job home; I talk to my husband, cry, and pray about them. I get home and just collapse. It's difficult to develop other parts of my life, yet a person needs that balance: sitting down and reading as well as constantly being involved. Instead I sit down and maybe try to read but soon my mind floats back to some of the problems I see people encounter during the day and I feel bad. I try not to talk to Chuck about some of the more depressing aspects of the work because I'm sure he gets just as frustrated as I do. I know he does. He even gets some of the phone calls at home."

Despite the many agonies, the work brings a profound sense of satisfaction. For Lynette there is the feeling of having ministered to people in need. The rewards, however, often have to come from within. "We don't get a lot of Thank you's," says Lynette. "The black mothers in Cabrini-Green are the most appreciative and I have had some very good conversations with them. But for others, especially those from outside the community, it's different. You're dealing with a problem group, people who are down and live on very little hope. Like the police, every time you encounter such people it's because they're in trouble, not because they want to talk about their successes. You're like the staff in the emergency room of a hospital and you take care of their broken arm. Then they just disappear until the next time. Appreciation is not really built into the system."

There are some light moments, however. "Our laughingest times," Lynette continues, "are not necessarily our happiest. We try to make fun of certain situations. We create a certain degree of joviality in the job. And there are times of fulfillment—usually in closing cases and getting good settlements, but Chuck tends to be closer to the settlements than I am." am."

Gina also recalled times when Chuck would tell her that things went well in court and the client was very happy. She, too, felt she was performing a ministry. "One of the really satisfying things was that we were providing a service that wouldn't be here if we weren't. There was no other law office in Cabrini. There were no other lawyers even near Cabrini that those people could afford to go to. We were right there in the community doing something that was desperately needed. Of course, there are a lot of agencies, lots of bureaucracy in a place like Cabrini, but we weren't just adding another agency to the list. Some agencies seem no longer concerned about what's happening to the people, but rather exist largely for their own benefit.

"I'm sure we accomplished a lot. When you think of Roy Harris, who was charged with murder at age fifteen—he'd be in jail right now if it weren't for the clinic. But Chuck was there. He did his job, and he did his job well, and that young man is not in jail."

WHAT MAKES CHUCK RUN?

6

Gina is unequivocal in her praise of Chuck. "He's very unassuming, even self-abasing, but he's also one mighty good lawyer! He has a dignity about him to which judges react positively."

Gina remembers an incident in court during which Chuck and another lawyer had a special conference with the judge. "This big-time lawyer spoke first. He was very flamboyant, really pushing his case home, arguing this and that with the judge. I thought, 'Oh, man, this is going to be a bad one for Chuck.' When the lawyer finished, the judge turned quietly to Chuck, looked at him with respect, and said, 'Counselor, what do you have to say?' Chuck was very calm and spoke his piece. He undercut the other lawyer's position smoothly, not by putting on a three-ring circus, but simply by being himself. While Chuck was talking, the other lawyer was looking very uncomfortable because the judge was nodding attentively to what Chuck said. You could just see the rapport he had with that judge.

"Chuck's commitment is incredible to me. To see a guy like that turn his back on huge legal fees and walk into something that pays a hundred bucks a week to start! He did it because he believes in the work. He really believes that those people deserve a break, that they deserve fair representation in court. I agree with him. Everyone deserves not just to have his day in court, but to have his say in court. That's where Chuck is at, and that's heavy.

"Yet he doesn't think he's done anything. Just his going to court, his being there, says to the judge, 'Somebody cares about this young man.' It's going to make that judge think twice before throwing the kid in jail at a bail higher than he can afford. And Chuck has often negotiated bail."

Gina drew a sharp distinction between treatment of the rich and of the poor in the legal system. "You can go to the suburbs, and if a kid gets in trouble, do they put him in jail on a high bail? No! They release him on personal recognizance. When they pick up a kid in Cabrini, they ask for bail. So for Chuck to go down there and get these guys out on a small bail, or even an 'I' bond, is really something."

Chuck's rather unassuming exterior belies his firmness. "He can deliver those characters on court day," Gina says with an admiring chuckle. "He says, 'You show up!' and they do.

"The first time they come in to the office, a lot of them will jive. They pull as much bull as they can. They try to convince Chuck they're poor innocent victims of 'the establishment,' especially the younger clients. But it doesn't take long during that first interview for them to realize that Chuck isn't taking any stuff."

How does the community feel about Chuck? "I think they feel he's the greatest," Gina says. "Everybody I've ever talked to who knows him seems to feel he can do no wrong. He's one of the few whites who could walk through Cabrini after dark and nobody would bother him. I don't know if he feels that way, but he's earned that reputation and acceptance."

According to Gina, a number of things keep Chuck going. One of them is "his concern for the people he works with. He feels for those people and what they go through."

Chuck's love for the community was evident in an incident involving Carol Reed, a thirty-year-old woman whom Chuck represented on three occasions. The first case involved a di-

85 | WHAT MAKES CHUCK RUN?

vorce; the other two were criminal offenses in which Carol was guilty: in one she was charged with forging checks and in the other she was arrested for shoplifting. According to Hogren, Carol lacked money but lived high because she liked "nice things."

"At about four p.m. on New Year's Eve, 1975, I was at home preparing for a get-together to be held at my home after church that night," recalls Hogren. "The phone rang and it was Carol Reed. She was at the 18th District police station charged with shoplifting. They were about to take her to the women's lock-up. She had her two-year-old son with her and they were going to take him to the Audy Home. Her seven-year-old daughter was at home alone and there was no way for Carol to contact her."

The daughter would be panicky if her mother didn't return shortly. So Carol asked Chuck if he would come down to the police station, pick up her son, go to her Cabrini-Green home and tell her little girl what had happened, and then try to find babysitters for the children while Carol was in jail. Hogren consented.

Chuck went to the station and then over to Carol's home and explained to the child what had happened to her mother. "Carol didn't give me a key to her apartment so there was no way of locking it up after the children went to the babysitter's," says Hogren. "The daughter said the key was in a sugar bowl somewhere so we turned the whole apartment upside down, the three of us, looking for the key. We got some neighbors over and they helped us look. One of the neighbors finally found the key. The neighbor agreed to take the children and I went back home to continue getting ready for the party."

Although Carol Reed sensed that Chuck could be trusted with the care of her two children in that emergency, he came to realize that she was mentally unstable. So, after taking a series of cases for her, he told her he would not take another unless she would go to the church's counseling center. She did, and apparently has not needed legal assistance since.

Gina also believes that Hogren's devotion to justice fuels his commitment. "He's the type of person who, when he sees something wrong, has to do something about it. That's just the way he is. He knows there's a lot of wrong going on in Cabrini-Green. A lot of crazy and unjust things are done by the people themselves to one another, as well as by outside institutional forces. Chuck feels that somebody's got to do something, and for him, that means he has to do it."

Sometimes that feeling gets Chuck in trouble. "Although his love for the community has grown," Gina continues, "I believe he realizes that you can care too much sometimes. You have to back off and care for yourself too. Chuck's inability to back off has produced long periods of relative stagnancy, loss of energy, and depression. It causes inefficiency on the job, making him less effective as a lawyer for the very people he's trying to serve."

Chuck has his own view of what keeps him going. "I have enough successes to see that this type of work is worthwhile; if you look over the long span you see enough successes.

"By successes I mean situations in which people have been adequately defended and then go on to get jobs so that they never get in trouble again. And successfully dealing with a difficult case, even in plea bargaining, can be very satisfying. That's especially true in a plea bargain that deals with a client's underlying problem like alcoholism or drug addiction.

"Also I read books about the critical importance of Christians becoming involved in social action. I feel strongly that it's a very necessary part of the gospel and I'm happy to participate, to have a role in it.

"And of course, money will occasionally come in when we don't anticipate it, or from people from whom we don't expect it. That provides a sense of encouragement and a feeling of being cared about. This is what keeps me going. I can see God's direction quite clearly from time to time."

Chuck's commitment to the clinic has not been without financial cost. But it is extremely difficult to get Hogren to talk about the economic sacrifices he has made in working there. "He definitely has sacrificed," asserts Gina. "He's just bought a house. Now there's no way a person can have a house and live on a hundred dollars a week, before taxes. He lives largely on the cash reserves from his inheritance. There were times when his mortgage payment was late because he didn't have the money. The church was unable to pay him because it was short and no money had come in for the clinic."

Keeping the clinic above water financially was a task that frequently fell to Chuck. After the initial grant ran out, money

87 | WHAT MAKES CHUCK RUN?

became scarce. So, in addition to taking cases by day, Chuck ended up on the fund-raising circuit at night.

"He didn't like to do it," says Gina, "because he's a very quiet and private person. It's very difficult for him to hustle money. It's one thing for him to get up in court for someone else, dealing with something he knows: the law. It's quite another for him to stand before an audience, trying to sell them on what he's doing and to get them to support him in it."

Chuck's stagnancy and depression became more pronounced after Gina left. Lynette, very protective toward him, is much concerned with the toll the work takes on him. "Although I'm more extroverted in expressing my feelings," she says, "we're pretty close. Chuck is an extremely giving person, often to the point where we're concerned that he could become the king of the doormats. Right now I don't think he has much creative energy. It's not his fault. He gets so sapped by the job, with little encouragement from people except for an occasional pat on the back on Sunday morning.

"Chuck is just too nice! He gives me a great deal of responsibility and yet he'll rarely tell me I made a mistake. He's too accommodating to people's opinions. Sometimes I think he is so accommodating, he gives so much, that he creates dependencies. People aren't sufficiently motivated to get on their own two feet and take control of their lives. With some people it's obvious that they need to have someone lay it on the line with them, for their own benefit. Chuck has a hard time doing that."

Chuck's inability to say No has nearly brought him an additional career. According to Gina, a Young Life clinic on the West Side asked Chuck to work one Tuesday night a month. They pledged to come up with a plentiful supply of lawyers. It didn't seem like much of an obligation, taking a few cases one Tuesday a month. Unfortunately that was only the beginning. It wasn't very long before Chuck was there every Tuesday night, alone. Further, he wound up going out and recruiting the lawyers the organization said they'd provide.

"Chuck didn't have that kind of time," says Gina. "Here he was, going to court full time for Cabrini-Green clients, researching cases at night—he would spend at least one night a week at the law library downtown—plus lecturing at different places in order to raise enough money to keep the clinic going.

Then he had to spend one night a week or more out on the West Side getting more cases than we could handle."

"Chuck is also very self-giving in his personal life. He does extra things for people, which drains off his energy," says Lynette. Of that, there is little doubt. Chuck's relationship with Peter Klein is a notable example.

Peter Klein has been diagnosed as a paranoid schizophrenic. Klein believes that he is the genius who originated all the ideas behind the construction and architecture of the skyscrapers in Chicago's Loop. However, he says, while walking down a city street one day he was hit over the head and, while in at best a semiconscious state, spewed forth all of his engineering gems. With that the assailant took the ideas and marketed them for himself. Consequently, Peter feels he has a right to great riches but will never realize them because of that tragic event.

Peter has requested that Chuck go to court and seek redress for him, but apparently that is one petition to which Chuck has been able to say No. Nonetheless, Chuck has a soft spot in his heart for his long-time acquaintance. The result is that whenever Peter Klein is down and out he calls upon Chuck and Chuck helps him. "Chuck has taken care of him, given him food, gotten him jobs, given him money, and even let him live with him," says Gina.

Peter lived with Chuck throughout the past winter, almost totally at Hogren's expense. During that time there was never any certitude as to Peter's emotional state. The arrangement may even have been dangerous; Klein has threatened Chuck physically on several occasions. Hogren, however, has two very large and rather antisocial dogs Peter is afraid of, so Chuck feels relatively safe.

Peter is not the only boarder Chuck has taken in. Roger Henderson, a paranoid paraplegic whose brother was facing a murder charge, was another beneficiary of Chuck's hospitality. Henderson's paranoia drew the harassment of some of the teen-agers in his neighborhood, and that, in combination with his inability to care for himself, motivated Chuck to take him in.

"I know it was a hardship on Chuck," says Gina. "He would come to work tired, worn down. He would enjoy getting away from the house, eagerly accepting dinner invitations with

89 | WHAT MAKES CHUCK RUN?

friends. That was his only way to escape spending his evenings listening to insoluble problems. But he took care of them."

Chuck believes strongly that Christians need to be prophetically reminded of their obligations if they are to live in obedience to God.

"Christians should identify with the poor," he says. "I attended the Francis Schaeffer meetings in Chicago, where Schaeffer discussed the two greatest weaknesses of today's society. First, people seek personal comfort. In other words, they just want to be left alone. They don't care if their neighbor is suffering as long as they are OK. The second weakness, he said, was the misuse of affluence, the noncompassionate use of wealth.

"I really feel," Chuck goes on, "that people should become aware of how human beings are suffering. Here, they suffer through police brutality; through neglect, as in the case of Jerome Stevens—when someone failed to follow up on a court clerk's work he could have spent four days in jail needlessly, had Chuck not intervened; and through disregard for human rights. We need to be aware of the real problems the poor face, and that they don't bring their problems on themselves; that the poor person is not somebody refusing to work, with his hand out for the dole. That's not what's going on with the poor. They are real victims of a system which almost seems designed to keep them down."

The more Hogren talks on this subject the more exercised he can become. Shyness gives way to eloquence. "They know full well they're turning down something that wouldn't net them enough money to live anyway, a menial job. Why should they always be the ones to push a broom? Why can't they get a union job? Why should they be excluded from the union? Why can't their sons go to the vocational high school which puts you in the union automatically? Why have the unions, rather than the board of education, controlled the enrollment in those high schools? Who will undo all the human damage that such a system has brought on over the decades, all those things that just perpetuate injustice?

"I also believe that to identify with the poor calls for a reduced lifestyle. If you have more than you need and you know someone else who has less than he or she needs, that calls for some reduction of lifestyle so that part of your money and part of your time can be used to alleviate suffering.

"I just finished a book by John Stott, *Christian Mission in the Modern World.* I was so impressed with it that I underlined passage after passage. Stott emphasized that the Bible, and Jesus in particular, stressed social action. Social action is not just bait to get people into church; it is an end itself. Yet although social action and evangelism go side by side, they are also independent of one another.

"The Bible makes a plea for justice in and of itself. So if not one soul gets saved but justice is done, the Lord's work is being carried on. People must understand that we don't have to slip our clients a tract to justify this work. We don't want to neglect evangelism, because it is of crucial import, but there are certain times for certain things, and as Paul says, people do have different gifts. People shouldn't be made to feel guilty because they are not saving souls. What is important is that people use their gifts to further God's kingdom."

Getting that message across to Christians is not always easy for Chuck. Many Christians have a less than enthusiastic interest in social problems in general. They believe that their primary earthly objective should be to communicate the gospel of salvation and win souls. Issues like racism, oppression, poverty, and poor education are often viewed as temporal concerns, and any efforts Christian ministries pour into alleviating such problems are seen as done at the expense of spreading the gospel. Moreover, those who do evince a genuine concern over social injustice are often accused of being "social gospelists," more concerned about human conditions in this life than about the transcendent dimension of the Christian faith.

Chuck's concern is for wholeness. Much of the driving force behind the clinic's effort is a dedication to justice, social concern, and whole personhood.

Regrettably, the Christian church has been divided over the "social concern" issue for ages. Yet Scripture presents consistent evidence of God's interest in the whole person: body, mind, and spirit. Christ not only presented himself as the divine Son of God but also exorcised demons and healed the sick. Bill Leslie, deeply committed to the whole-person concept, is fond of saying that "concern for the soul without the body leaves only a corpse, while concern for the body at the expense of the soul produces a ghost." To create a dichotomy, making one dimension the object of the church's ministry while leaving the other to the often insensitive institutions of the day is to attempt to dichotomize humankind itself.

Moreover, there is an interrelatedness to the human makeup. Mental illness, for example, can often invade one's physical well-being as the multiplicity of psychosomatic disorders indicates. Physiological psychologists, on the other hand, regularly find evidence of how physical well-being can impact on mental health. Poor health can bring on depression, frustration, alienation, and despair. Spiritual well-being can be adversely affected—even deadened—by such negative, depressive emotions. Further, a stagnant spiritual life can lead to emotional deterioration, while spiritual rebirth has led to marked improvements in the mental and physical health and energy of many people. So, although God can work for good through a person's various maladies, there is no doubt that the constituent parts of human beings are interlocked and interactive.

In view of that, a strong case can be built for a comprehensive, whole-person concept of ministry. Social problems that rob their victims of whole personhood and efficient functioning must be a concern of the church. Grappling with such dilemmas is not a merely humanistic effort; it is an effort to "redeem the time," to minister to the whole person as well as to society, to help individuals function as perfectly as God would have them function.

What makes such efforts so difficult, especially those of the Cabrini-Green Legal Aid Clinic, is that they are never fully successful. The task is enormous. People doing Chuck's kind of work always weigh what they can do against what needs to be done. That brings on a feeling of being completely defeated by it all. It's very hard not to "burn out." And when, like Chuck, you're the sole lawyer, you get to feeling that you have to carry the entire burden. It becomes hard to keep in mind that Christians are not enjoined to be successful; Christians are rather to be faithful stewards of their bodies, minds, and spirits—while also being their brother or sister's "keeper."

At the core of almost every social problem is a lack of justice. But a barrier to seeking justice is that many Christians feel that pursuit of justice is valid only if it serves the ultimate goal of

92 | THE RELUCTANT DEFENDER

religious conversion. Yet the Bible makes justice and its pursuit a central issue. Chuck is quick to point out that at least eighty-five Bible passages demonstrate God's interest in social justice in and of itself. Here are thirteen examples (from *The Living Bible*):

> For the Lord loves justice and fairness; he will never abandon his people (Psalm 37:28a).
>
> God blesses those who are kind to the poor (Psalm 41:1a).
>
> He gives justice to all who are treated unfairly (Psalm 103:6).
>
> Happiness comes to those who are fair to others and are always just and good (Psalm 106:3).
>
> Anyone who oppresses the poor is insulting God who made them. To help the poor is to honor God (Proverbs 14:31).
>
> He who shuts his ears to the cries of the poor will be ignored in his own time of need (Proverbs 21:13).
>
> Evil men don't understand the importance of justice, but those who follow the Lord are much concerned about it (Proverbs 28:5).
>
> If you give to the poor, your needs will be supplied! But a curse upon those who close their eyes to poverty (Proverbs 28:27).
>
> The good man knows the poor man's rights; the godless don't care (Proverbs 29:7).
>
> You should defend those who cannot help themselves. Yes, speak up for the poor and needy and see that they get justice (Proverbs 31:8, 9).
>
> If you see some poor man being oppressed by the rich, with miscarriage of justice anywhere throughout the land, don't be surprised! For every official is under orders from higher up, and the higher officials look up to their superiors. And so the matter is lost in red tape and bureaucracy (Ecclesiastes 5:8).
>
> He saw to it that justice and help were given the poor and the needy and all went well for him. This is how a man lives close to God (Jeremiah 22:16).
>
> [God] has told you what he wants, and this is all it is: to be fair and just and merciful, and to walk humbly with your God (Micah 6:8).*

---

*Some other verses pertaining to justice and the poor are Exodus 23:6, 7; 2 Samuel 15:4; Job 29:12, 16; 37:23; Psalm 9:18; 10:18; 12:5; 14:6; 15:5; 25:3; 36:6; 37:3, 30, 31; 67:4; 68:5; 71:24; 72:2, 4, 12; 74:21; 82:3, 4; 89:14; 107:41; 109:31; 119:121; 140:11; 146:6-8; Proverbs 1:3; 8:15; 14:21; 22:9, 16, 22, 23; 28:8; 29:14; Isaiah 9:7; 10:1, 2; 11:3-5; 47:1-8; 56:1; 59:4, 14; Ezekiel 18:16, 17; 45:9; Amos 5:12, 24; Matthew 23:23; Luke 1:51-53; 4:19; 6:35, 36; 11:42; 14:14; 1 Corinthians 13:6; 1 John 3:17-19.

93 | WHAT MAKES CHUCK RUN?

The evidence is unimpeachable that justice, especially as it pertains to the poor and oppressed, is a matter of high divine priority. Those without sufficient social and personal power to insure their receipt of just treatment are objects of God's concern. To leave the ministry of justice for the poor to contemporary institutions is to be certain that justice will not be done.

Day by day in its work, the legal aid clinic faces the pervasiveness of institutional wrongdoing. Among evangelical Christians, institutional sin is rarely viewed as important in comparison with personal or individual wrong. Before the development of large national governments, multinational corporations, and ever-expanding educational systems, evil and its insidious effects found expression largely in individual activities such as murder, rape, larceny, adultery, cheating, and so on. In an institutional society, however, the potential for oppression increases: wrongdoing by a major institution can wreak havoc with the lives of millions. Pollution by a large company jeopardizes the health of thousands of people. To market a harmful product is to endanger the well-being of every consumer. So also, discrimination, political corruption, and denial of equal opportunity as it issues out of large institutions can keep a whole race down.

Often, Christians are faced with the dilemma of working for a large institution involved in corrupt activities. To leave it may place the livelihood of oneself and one's family in peril. To continue is to serve the forces of evil. The situation becomes exceedingly complex for those who care.

With regard to crime—the focus of the legal aid clinic—most Americans seem to think there are basically two kinds of people: criminals and noncriminals. The primary distinction between the two groups is that criminals break the law whereas noncriminals keep the laws and uphold them. In reality, the primary difference is that those who are labeled noncriminals don't get caught breaking laws considered important by society, whereas criminals do.

If the position is taken that one becomes a criminal by breaking a law, then the vast majority of the American population is criminal. William Ryan, in his book *Blaming the Victim*, discussed a study of a largely middle-class group which indicated that fully 90 percent of the subjects admitted to having committed at least one of a list of crimes. Those defined by our society as criminals are actually those who commit what is termed "street crime." Such a definition overlooks "white-collar crime."

The pervasiveness of white-collar crime is evidenced in a survey conducted among seventy of the nation's largest corporations. That survey showed that the corporations had an average of 7.8 court decisions against them for illegal activities. Every corporation had at least one decision rendered against it.

There is also "organized crime," with its complex systems of gambling, prostitution, drug dealing, political payoffs, etc. Such activities take in about twice as much money as all other criminal activities combined. Yet organized crime is not merely ignored; it is actually glorified by such productions as *The Godfather, Honor Thy Father,* and other stories lionizing gangsters like Al Capone.

In spite of the pernicious and all-encompassing effects of white-collar and organized crime, America suffers from a definitional distortion. Our composite picture of the typical criminal seems to be that of a poor, minority person.

An important distinction between street and white-color crime is that the white-color variety, though illegal, usually doesn't disrupt order. Most white-collar crime is carried out within the larger institutional systems of America and seldom keeps the wheels of business from grinding on.

In that sense, it is obvious that the cry for "law and order" is really backwards. We place much greater emphasis on order than on law. Street crime, much less frequent and not nearly so costly to society as other types of crime, is set in the limelight by politicians and the media. Yet the major objectionable characteristic of much street crime is that it disrupts order. (Indeed, even peaceful protest marchers are often treated rudely simply because they become a barrier to the orderly process of American institutional life.)

It isn't surprising that this is so. In a mass society, the convenience and even the lives of millions of people depend on the ongoing operation of major institutions. Hence, what is felt as most threatening and upsetting is behavior that in some way impedes the progress of those networks. The result is that street crime is prosecuted and cracked down upon, while white-collar crime is often ignored or in some cases even viewed as positive (that is, as an effort to "cut through red tape" in bureaucracies).

Thus, the criminality of white-collar crime is often blurred. For example, political corruption may be winked at because politics is a rough-and-tumble business and should not be subject to the same strict sanctions as other behavior. White-collar crime such as income tax cheating has an "everyone is doing it" quality behind it—and that "everyone" includes even many upstanding, good citizens of the society.

As a result, the operational definition of crime lies in the hands of the dominant power groups in the society. They possess the authority to arrest, prosecute, and punish what they will.

An example of prosecution distinction can be found in comparing the situation of an executive of a large company whose business has been found to be in violation of pollution-control standards and a youngster arrested for purse snatching. The executive who has knowingly jeopardized the health of many thousands of people is usually given from thirty to ninety days to bring his plant up to standard; the young mugger is taken to jail that very evening. Moreover, the executive will be certain to hire a first-rate legal-defense team to prevent further difficulty; the youngster will probably be left with an able but overworked public defender.

Laying the entire blame on the police for concentrating on street crime is unjust. The police are often merely doing the job that society and the political structure want them to do. Nevertheless, the street criminal living in poverty has his own notion of justice in America. He often realizes that the only difference between him and those in the large businesses nearby is money and power. He knows that the law is differentially enforced, that the justice system, as measured by representation in court, works to the advantage of the rich and powerful, while the prison system is reserved almost exclusively for the likes of him. The police are only middlemen in that much larger system.

As a famous lawyer once said, referring to the poor, "Some people have a different idea of who the criminals and who the victims are." Awareness of inequality of opportunity and of selectivity of law enforcement breeds bitterness and hostility of a type that only encourages further crime, all in a cycle of self-destruction.

For Chuck Hogren, going out and "getting this message across" was not something he looked forward to with enthusiasm. Rather shy by nature, Hogren had no experience in public speaking. Moreover, his speeches were often, by necessity, related to the ever-present money crisis. That soured his stomach; he felt as if he were panhandling rather than informing. There is little that makes Chuck more uneasy than to have to ask for money.

Speaking also stirs up his old fear of appearing to be a "blue-eyed soul brother" or super Christian, false images Hogren feels trapped by. He tends to feel he owes people a near-perfect job if they contribute financially. He feels he must be everything his backers fancy him to be.

"My general speech format," says Chuck, "consists of talking about the makeup of the neighborhood, and the need in the neighborhood for our type of service. I tell them that the people came to church seeking legal help because I was working there in the tutoring program and recreation center. I usually go from there to the biblical basis for pursuing justice—using some of the pertinent Bible verses. Then I ask the question: Is there actually injustice in the Cabrini-Green neighborhood which we should be concerned about? I give the examples of cases like Roy Harris, Allen Pendleton and the Oak brothers, and Arthur Scott, cases that provide extreme but accurate examples of injustice in the community."

Chuck usually deals with the problem of defending people who are guilty, and then turns to "what a Christian's role might be in some other situations. For example, although there may not be actual injustice as far as the person's being wrongfully accused of a crime, in some situations there is no possibility of rehabilitation unless Christians get involved. I stress the need to get those in trouble into programs like Young Life, counseling, etc. There is a tremendous role available there for anyone who takes an interest."

Chuck has given variations of that speech many times, primarily in suburban churches. He is often invited as a "home missionary" and has participated in church conferences with a home missions emphasis. He is on the budget of two suburban

97 | WHAT MAKES CHUCK RUN?

churches as a home missionary. He finds church people generally quite courteous and attentive listeners.

But there are questions. "The most frequent question," he says, "concerns representing people who are guilty. I go into my explanation that many times I don't really know if a person is guilty or not; and that I will not represent somebody who I know is guilty if he intends to take the stand and deny it. That is perjury and I would withdraw under those circumstances. I remind them that under our system a defendant has the right to remain silent and that the state must prove him guilty. That is his constitutional right and there is every reason to follow that procedure."

A prime reason why Hogren will defend clients under those conditions is that he would rather be able to refer them to a drug rehabilitation center as an in-patient, to Young Life, or to the counseling center than to see them carted off to prison where the outcome of their tenure will almost certainly be a further hardening in crime.

Reactions to his speeches are not always predictable. One suburban woman, who was a close relative of a lawyer and who Chuck anticipated would be greatly in support of his work, was the only one in opposition to Hogren's receiving money from a group to which he was speaking. Her reason was that a Christian in Chuck's role should support himself financially in addition to doing his legal aid work. She cited as an example the Apostle Paul's labors as a tentmaker. Her view did not prevail, but she has neither reiterated her position to Chuck nor opposed the clinic's work in any way.

Chuck's response to her concern was that the clinic itself is more than full-time work if done properly. There are 13,000 people in Cabrini-Green without legal representation. "What town of that size in America wouldn't have a lawyer?" asks Chuck. "In addition, they have other problems we cannot begin to deal with, but yet attempt to." Nonetheless Chuck, ever willing to accommodate any concern, says that "perhaps that woman's view should be explored further. Maybe we could get a number of lawyers to support themselves in part-time work and spend part of their time in legal aid efforts."

On another occasion Chuck spoke at the annual Christmas function of a suburban women's group. They even had a local high-school choir present to make it a truly festive event. Although appreciating the opportunity, Chuck thought it rather bizarre that he should be invited to speak at such an event. As he was reading through a list of Bible verses pertaining to justice, he noticed he was driving his would-be listeners into a deep sound sleep. So, quite spontaneously, he discarded his notes and began describing some of the cases he'd handled. He couldn't believe the reaction. "The people just came to life. They were sitting on the edge of their chairs!" When the group was finally dismissed, many of them came up and talked further with him. A little later, one woman sent a check to the clinic for $1,000. "I couldn't believe it!" says Chuck with a look of wonder. "It was the largest single contribution we ever received from a speech. It shows that people are interested in what's happening to others."

Other groups are really impressed with the Bible verses. In one church, Chuck was invited to dinner in one of the parishioner's homes after speaking. They were so taken with the biblical foundation for the clinic's work that they asked Chuck to go through all the passages again.

Generally, however, people prefer to hear about his experiences. In early 1977 Chuck spoke to a combined medical and seminary group. Their reaction was so favorable that they detained him with their questions for two hours after his presentation. Two checks emanated from the group as well. One professor, after hearing Chuck, suggested putting together a joint seminar of law students and seminarians.

Despite his low-key manner, Hogren is an effective speaker. He prepares carefully for such events in order to give a well-organized presentation. He talks about his experiences with a surprisingly dramatic flair, and that, in combination with the strength of his commitment to justice, holds the listeners' attention.

He is not always at ease, however. In February 1977 he was invited to speak to a "Black Achievers" group, a collection of inner-city youngsters who were being introduced to career possibilities. The movie *Roots* had just been aired on television and Chuck was apprehensive about how he would be received. It seemed to him that it was the "wrong time for a white person to be speaking about justice, or anything else for that matter." But much to his surprise the group's reaction was very favorable and questions abounded. Chuck had expected to be there for little more than ten minutes, telling them how one gets into law school, along with stressing the importance of studying hard and getting good grades in high school in preparation for legal study. He stayed more than an hour.

Chuck's presentation even won over a rather hostile director of the group. Initially, she wouldn't even sit with the rest of the group, but remained across the hall—perhaps as a way of expressing her disdain for a middle-class white professional telling poor black students about justice. Eventually she picked up her chair and moved in among the rest of the audience. The session continued until the leader had to get up and halt proceedings because time had run out.

Hogren even gets invited to Cabrini-Green community functions, highly unusual for a white person. Occasionally he speaks to "building clubs." The clubs consist of an organized group of teen-agers who live in a given high-rise building. Chuck usually discusses their civil rights with them, finding the youths very receptive to his presentations.

Rather early in his tenure at the clinic Chuck was asked to speak in Cabrini-Green's St. Matthew's Methodist Church at a combined observance of Mother's Day and Law Day. "I was very nervous about the speech, initially," he says. "There were two other speakers, both of whom were black. In fact, I was the only white in the whole church." As a result he spent extra time preparing for the speech, writing it over several times.

Chuck was additionally unnerved by the fact that "it was Mother's Day in a black community, where mothers are so central to community life and here I was, a white lawyer, coming in to talk about the law." Hogren contacted the minister to ask if it might not be wiser to celebrate Law Day at another time. The pastor replied they hadn't noticed that it was also Mother's Day until well after the event had been planned, so they preferred that Chuck go through with it.

The more Chuck worked on the speech, the more the seeming incongruity between Law Day and Mother's Day disappeared. For one thing, most of the calls Chuck had received over the years had come from mothers saying their sons were in jail. Chuck worked that in, in addition to describing how his own mother, who had died just before the event, had disciplined him and promoted Christianity in the family. By the

100 | THE RELUCTANT DEFENDER

time he actually rose to give the speech, Chuck was excited about what he had to say.

For the first time in a public speech, Chuck used Tyndale's *The Living Bible.* "The people were extremely taken with the language in the verses about bringing up sons in the way they should go, and how if they are not properly reared they may turn into a lawless gang," says Chuck. "The language was very effective and appropriate because there was a great deal of gang activity in Cabrini-Green at the time. A lot of people came up afterward, shook my hand, and asked about the version of the Bible I had used. It was a very gratifying experience."

Reactions are not always favorable, of course. In November 1976 Chuck spoke at a men's and boy's breakfast at a suburban church during missions week. Chuck had previously spoken at an adult Sunday school class in the church and was well received.

Chuck discussed the police and how they were viewed by the Cabrini-Green community. He related the incidents of Roy Harris, Pendleton and the Oak brothers, along with Arthur Scott as examples. Afterward, a man came charging up to Hogren, livid with rage. He claimed that Chuck's speech was an outrage. "It's terrible to influence these young boys against the police! What will they think?" he shouted. Chuck, quite taken aback by the onslaught, quietly replied, "But the stories are true; they should know the truth."

Fortunately for Chuck, a public defender was within earshot of the exchange. He quickly came up and assured the irate gentleman that the incidents about which Chuck had spoken were actually mild and that "you should hear some of my experiences with the police!" The man went away unconvinced. He felt it had been a terrible morning.

Chuck is frequently asked to verify some of the more spectacular stories he tells of his legal aid experiences. A striking example of such a request occurred when Chuck, in hope of gaining a contribution for the clinic, spoke to the local Kiwanis Club. To illustrate the need for justice in Cabrini-Green, Hogren decided to tell the story of Roy Harris and his near-escape from being unjustly convicted of murder. Chuck described the entire grisly event, including how the police shook down one witness with shotgun shells in order to get his signature on a police statement. Upon completing his speech, Chuck discov-

101 | WHAT MAKES CHUCK RUN?

ered, much to his chagrin, that the president of the Kiwanis Club was none other than the sergeant in charge of public relations for the 18th District police station—the district in which Cabrini-Green is located.

The sergeant was electrified with anger. He raced over to Chuck and in a very agitated state demanded verification of Chuck's anecdotes. Fortunately, Chuck had brought a file with him, from which he pulled out all the background facts and evidence to substantiate the story. He showed the sergeant the police statement in question and provided the names of the officers involved in the coercion. The sergeant wrote down the officers' names and assured Chuck he would check into it.

Since that day, although Hogren has seen the sergeant in his office a number of times, the sergeant has never resurrected the subject or sought to rebut it. On the contrary, his relations with Chuck have been very cordial. The experience at the Kiwanis Club had a happy ending, for the group later gave the clinic a $700 electric typewriter.

Chuck loves to tell another story—but no more than Bill Leslie does—about one of Bill's good friends who happens to be a well-to-do lawyer. When Bill first told his friend about Chuck's legal aid ventures the man was unimpressed. He couldn't see any excuse for indulging in the seamy business of defending ghetto dwellers, who might or might not be guilty, simply on the grounds that they needed legal protection. He saw no reason for a clinic and had little sympathy for the whole concept of justice in Cabrini-Green. He felt that the appeals system, the availability of public defenders for indigent clients, and other legal safeguards assure any citizen, regardless of social status, adequate legal protection.

Not long after the lawyer had expressed those feelings, a young member of the Jesus People movement was arrested for passing out tracts on Rush Street. The youth hadn't really breached the peace or broken a law, but he was regarded as a nuisance and the police's way of dealing with the matter was to pick him up and put him in jail. On hearing of the outrage, Bill's lawyer friend scurried to the aid of the young man. Once at the police station and finding out that all the youth had done was to pass out tracts, the lawyer was indignant. He demanded that the police tell him on what charge the youth had been held. There was no official charge, he was told. "Well, then he shouldn't be locked up," the incredulous lawyer retorted. "You can't lock a person up if he isn't charged with having committed a crime."

"We did, though, didn't we?" the officer replied.

After that experience, Bill's friend required no further convincing of the necessity of legal protection for the poor. He has been one of the clinic's most faithful contributors ever since.

THE RULES OF THE GAME

7

A misdemeanor is a crime for which the sentence cannot be in excess of one year of confinement. Misdemeanors are classified A, B, or C, in descending order of severity. The legal aid clinic deals almost exclusively with Class A misdemeanors. Among the most common are theft of up to $150, possession of marijuana, assault (threatening someone), and aggravated assault (threatening someone with a weapon).*

The usual judicial procedure in a misdemeanor case is for the defendant first to be arrested and taken to jail. On the following day is what is called a bail hearing. It amounts to a court appearance in which the defendant's background is presented to the judge. The background information may include such items as how long he has lived in the community, whether he is employed, his school record, whether he is married and has children, any previous police record, and whether he has ever jumped bail. The purpose of the bail hearing is to show the

---

*Further information concerning classifications of misdemeanors and felonies is provided in Appendix 6.

defendant's ties to the community in order to assess the likelihood of his returning to court for his trial after he is released on bail. Bail is then set, and if he is able to raise the money, a trial date is set for about thirty days later.

For a misdemeanor, bail is customarily set at about $1,000, meaning that the defendant must post $100. The lowest bail is usually $250 for which one must post $25. If the individual has no money at all and the charge is not too serious, the judge may issue a personal recognizance bond ("I" bond). In such a case, a person must simply sign a bond indicating that he is responsible for paying the total bond amount if he fails to appear in court on the stipulated day. If he appears, nothing is paid.

Theoretically, the 10 percent payment is refundable when the person appears in court. However, 10 percent of that amount is not returned but is retained for administrative expenses. Hence the innocent defendant is still getting "ripped off," since he is paying for the judicial process in a procedure in which he (hopefully) is found not guilty.

Some families, especially those on public assistance, cannot make bail. If no "I" bond is issued, the defendant will wait in jail on the misdemeanor charge until his trial is held. That amounts to an obvious discrimination against the poor, as the rich can always make bail and so never have to endure the indignities of spending time in jail.

Bond may be set very high in the rather serious offenses, such as battery (striking someone), aggravated assault, or possession of a weapon—cases commonly handled by Hogren. Judge's discretion is the basis for bond setting or the issuance of an "I" bond, and judges vary tremendously in their mercy in that regard.

The most common reason why bail is jumped in cases handled by the clinic is that the defendant is in jail on another charge. However, if it can be proved that a client has been detained for that reason, the bail-jumping allegation is dropped.

The frustrations are endless. "In one situation I went to court and the client wasn't there," says Hogren. "I called the jail and they said he was in jail. They gave me the client's number and the tier he was on. So a date was set for what is termed a 'status report,' to be sure that the defendant was in jail. In addition, the entire case was sent from the Civic Center

105 | THE RULES OF THE GAME

back to the criminal court building where trials are held for people in custody. Prior to the status report date, I went to the jail and my client wasn't there. He had been released the previous weekend. So then I had to go back and explain why he wasn't in court."

Another reason for failing to show is simply getting to court too late. Clients may come, but instead of appearing at the appointed time, say nine-thirty, they may show up at eleven or even noon. Hogren must then enter a special motion permitting him to bring the individual in a few days later to make good on the appearance.

Time is a constant problem. As often as not, people will make office appointments with Hogren and appear hours after the appointed time or not at all. In two days' time, only one out of four appointments may be kept. Punctuality is a middle-class commodity, important when people have jobs to go to and a future for which to plan. For the poor, one day is as depressing and aimless as the next. The clock is almost irrelevant, as there are no appointments to keep. There is nothing to get up for, no reason to stay up or go to bed at a given time. Hence nine a.m. means "sometime in the morning" and one-thirty means "in the afternoon." Having few if any relationships with middle-class people, the poor are hardly aware of middle-class slavery to the clock. Moreover, many feel rather insignificant as persons and feel that whether they show up or not is of little consequence to a middle-class professional, even one who is their legal advocate.

The most common felony is armed robbery, which means the use of a weapon to hold someone up, no matter how little or much money is taken. It is a Class 1 felony among four classes. The sentence for armed robbery is a minimum of four years and a maximum of life. Robbery, a Class 2 felony, refers to the taking of something from someone by force but without the use of a weapon. The sentence is from one to twenty years. Burglary, a very common Class 2 felony, means entering into property belonging to another or remaining on someone's property without his permission and with the intent to commit a theft. Theft, by distinction, means being in a place one has a right to be, such as a store, and stealing something.

Aggravated battery is a felony in which serious bodily harm or disfigurement occurs through the use of a weapon as in the case of a shooting or stabbing. Striking a policeman, fireman, nurse, teacher, or other public official can move the offense from battery up to aggravated battery.

A common felony with which Chuck deals is possession of drugs such as heroin. The amount of heroin determines its felony class. The highest class is reserved for those instances in which the quantity indicates that the defendant is a dealer. The statute covering drug possession is directed primarily at dealers and sellers of hard drugs.

Murder constitutes a separate class, with the sentence ranging from fourteen years to life. Ranking below murder is voluntary manslaughter. There are two types of voluntary manslaughter. The first is a condition in which a person shoots or kills someone, thinking, without a reasonable basis, that he is in danger of being harmed himself. The other type is defined as killing someone under intense provocation such as in a fight, or when one has been harassed and becomes extremely upset. The sentence for voluntary manslaughter is from one to twenty years.

Involuntary manslaughter is a Class 3 homicide with a sentence of one to ten years. Usually negligence is involved. For example, a person playing with a gun might be deemed negligent for he should have known that his action might harm someone. An example of a Class 4 involuntary manslaughter would be reckless homicide by the driver of a car.

As in a misdemeanor, the day after a felony arrest a bond hearing takes place. Bail usually ranges from around $3,000 for burglary to $5,000 for robbery, and $10,000 for armed robbery. Hogren had one murder case in which bail was set at $75,000. The bail hearing can be a very complex procedure. In one of Chuck's cases, the written record for a bond hearing was more than 100 pages long. The lengthy ordeal was necessary because some evidence of self-defense existed, and that was the basis upon which the judge reduced the bail to $10,000.

Whenever bail exceeds $3,000 there is little chance that a client of the legal aid clinic will be able to raise it soon if at all. That means, whether guilty or innocent, the defendant will have to wait in jail until his case has been completed.

Usually within thirty days of the bond hearing, a preliminary hearing is held. If the victim of the crime does not come to the

107 | THE RULES OF THE GAME

preliminary hearing, the state is customarily granted a continuance. At the preliminary hearing (sometimes called a probable cause hearing), the state is charged with demonstrating to a judge that the preponderance of the evidence (51 percent) indicates that *(a)* a crime was committed, and *(b)* that it is more likely than not that the defendant committed it.

"It's very easy to get probable cause," says Hogren. One notable exception, however, was a case of a grand theft in which five leather coats were stolen. The defendant was the infamous Richard Thacker. The witness, who was an employee of the burglarized store, claimed he saw Thacker driving a car in the alley behind the building. The judge ruled that the state had not proved enough to establish probable cause and the charge was dropped. Normally the state's attorney is not bound by the judge's decision in a preliminary hearing; he can pursue an indictment with a grand jury if he chooses.

At the preliminary hearing the judge is not cognizant of the defendant's previous record; he reviews that only when bail is set. Although the preliminary hearing is held later, the judge, who may have heard over 3,000 cases since the bail hearing, usually does not remember anything about the defendant.

Some judges will not find probable cause if they think the defendant will not be found guilty at a trial. Others will go strictly by preponderance. In one of Chuck's cases the judge said, "If this were a trial I would find the defendant not guilty. However, since this is a preliminary hearing and the standard of proof is much less, I must find probable cause."

The state will usually present only as much evidence as they need to establish probable cause. It is self-defeating to present more, because the preliminary hearing can function as an excellent discovery process for the defense. The defendant rarely testifies at a preliminary hearing, so only the state puts on its witnesses. The defense can cross-examine the state's witnesses and lock them into a story which will be a part of the typed record. That record can later be used for impeachment if their story changes.

Impeachment refers to showing that on some prior occasion a witness has made a statement, either in oral or written form, that is contrary to the statement he is now making under oath in court. Such a discrepancy goes against the credibility of the witness before the judge or jury. A striking example of the effect of such an impeachment occurred in the case involving Allen Pendleton and the Oak brothers.*

The three were charged with the armed robbery of a laundry delivery man in an incident on the corner of Oak and Franklin Streets. At the preliminary hearing a police officer testified that he had talked to the witness and had been told that there were three assailants: Allen Pendleton, Ronald Oak, and Richard Oak.

About thirty days later at a grand jury inquest, the witness himself came in and claimed that three people were involved in the crime. That testimony did not become an issue until the trial, which, due to a lengthy backup in the court docket, was not held until two years later.

In the meantime the defendants were released on bail. (The release from jail took several months; their families, because of their indigent status, had to contact relatives all over the South in order to gather the necessary bond money.) Once back on the street, the defendants began associating with their friends again. Through those associations they came upon a rumor that a youth named Conrad Holmes had actually robbed the delivery man, and that this was a widely known fact in certain sectors of the community.

The clients came to Chuck with that startling bit of news. They told Chuck where Conrad Holmes lived and one of them went with Hogren to point the youth out. Chuck went over to Conrad's building and found him standing in front of it. He introduced himself and said he was representing Pendleton and the Oak brothers on an armed robbery rap involving a laundry delivery man. He also informed Conrad that his clients told him that he, Conrad, might know something about the incident.

Much to Chuck's amazement Conrad said, "Yes, I do. I did it. But I didn't rob him. I just knocked him down because he scared me at night coming up behind me. I knocked him down because I thought he was going to hurt me."

Chuck then asked Conrad if he would accompany him to the state's attorney's office and tell that story to them. To Chuck's

---

* The impeachment process is further detailed in Appendix 7.

109 | THE RULES OF THE GAME

astonishment, the youth consented. They got in Hogren's car and drove down to the state's attorney's office immediately.

It was about four o'clock and both attorneys were in the office. According to Hogren, they told the youth to sit down and proceeded to get out their file with their notes on the case. Conrad Holmes told them the whole story. He explained that he was on the street corner that night with two of his friends when the truck driver came up behind him. Conrad claimed the delivery man put an arm on his shoulder. That startled Conrad, who turned around and knocked the man down. The man got up and Conrad knocked him down again, this time down a stairwell. Conrad warned the man not to get up or he'd hit him again. Then he fled. Conrad reiterated his claim that he'd stolen nothing from the man.

"Amazingly enough," says Chuck, "the notes of the state's attorneys, which I of course hadn't read at that time, quoted the truck driver to the effect that he thought he had recognized Conrad on the corner, came up behind him, and put his arm on the youth's shoulder. That was exactly the same thing that Conrad said, so they knew he was telling the truth. Besides, under the circumstances there was no way in which I could have coached him."

Conrad's story was substantiated when it was revealed that the laundryman had lost nothing. "Even his receipt book which fell out during the scuffle was later found on the pavement," says Hogren. "That corroborated the fact that Conrad was startled and knocked the man down for that reason. That was a pretty strong part of our case, since the man said his billfold was intact and nothing had been taken. There was no robbery!"

After hearing Conrad's story in their office, the attorneys said, "We believe you're telling the truth based on our notes, but we will arrange a lie detector test and if you pass it, the three others will be discharged."

Thirty days passed, and nothing happened, so Chuck reminded the attorneys of the arrangement. They replied, "Oh, we're not handling that case anymore, it's in the hands of someone else." When Chuck went to their office, the new state's attorneys said they knew nothing about the interview with Holmes, and, furthermore, there were no notes in their file. They invited Chuck to look through the file himself, if he didn't believe them. He did. "They obviously had removed from the file all the notes they had taken from Conrad's interview," says Hogren. "When Conrad came in to see them, I distinctly remember that they had at least written down his name, address, and phone number."

In the meantime, it occurred to Conrad that if he kept talking he might be arrested for the misdeed. He refused to cooperate any further. A subpoena was issued for Conrad to come in and testify at the trial and Chuck went over to Conrad's house to serve him with the subpoena. "I gave him the subpoena," says Hogren, "but he said he wouldn't come. He said he was lucky he didn't get locked up the last time and he certainly wasn't going to risk it again. I could understand his position. He had done enough for me, much more than people ordinarily will ever do. He said he just couldn't go again.

"So I said, 'Well, you know it would be very helpful if you would. And I'm giving you this subpoena which means you have to come.' I told him that although he was not going to be granted immunity, if he did go he would not have to incriminate himself since he could plead the Fifth Amendment. All he really had to do was show up and state his name. He didn't have to say a word about the facts of the case. Nevertheless, I was hoping, once on the stand, he might tell the story all over again. In any case, if he continually took the Fifth I might create a 'reasonable doubt' in the judge's mind with regard to the defendants and that was all I needed anyway.

"He just wouldn't come. The next step is a rule to show cause why a person should not be held in contempt of court for disobeying a court order. So I served Conrad with a rule to show cause. His response? 'My mother won't let me come.'"

Chuck then went to see Conrad's mother. She was very hostile. She became so incensed that she picked up the telephone and was about to hit Chuck with it as he was backing out the door. Hogren simply said to her, "Well, I served this on Conrad and he has to come to court."

"I won't let him come. He's not going to come," she answered resolutely.

It was now time for an arrest warrant and Chuck reluctantly had one issued. The police claimed they could never find Con-

111 | THE RULES OF THE GAME

rad. Their claim was badly lacking in credibility, since there was a police substation located on the first floor in the very high-rise in which Holmes lived. "However, in fairness to the police department," Chuck dutifully adds, "it should be pointed out that normally the sheriff's office is charged with serving such warrants."

Nonetheless, nobody seemed to be looking very hard for Conrad and Chuck was disgusted. He almost always could find Conrad at home whenever he looked for him. Exasperated, Hogren then obtained authority from the court to serve the arrest warrant himself. Accompanied by two officers, he went to Conrad's building but this time Holmes wasn't there. Bereft of alternatives, Chuck then explained to the judge why he was having difficulty delivering Conrad—that his mother was blocking the passage.

When the judge heard that Conrad's mother was the fly in the ointment, he was enraged. "I want that woman in here," he demanded. The judge issued a subpoena requiring the mother to explain why she should not be held in contempt of court for preventing a witness from testifying in a felony case.

Never-say-die, Hogren went to her apartment and courageously served Conrad's mother with the subpoena. An angry judge didn't scare her. She refused to appear. She was then served with a rule to show cause. She balked again. Now totally out of patience, the infuriated judge had the woman arrested. The police found her, but not Conrad.

"There was some confusion there, for which I am partly responsible," says Hogren, ever tender of conscience. "I told Mrs. Holmes she would have to come to court when I served her with the subpoena, but I didn't tell her that she could be arrested if she refused. I don't think I explained to her, as fully as I should have, what the consequences for failing to comply with the order were."

Mrs. Holmes was arrested and came to court to testify concerning Conrad's whereabouts. She was charged with hiding a witness and spent a week in jail for it. The publicity was horrible. "It made the Chicago *Tribune*," laments Hogren. "There was the bold headline: 'Mother Jailed . . .' followed by a very derogatory article in which I was named. I talked to her lawyer and explained to him why I did what I did. The problem was, however, that it was illegal for her to be jailed for hiding a close relative. I wasn't aware of that statute and neither was the judge. We both learned the hard way."

Mrs. Holmes' lawyer appealed the case and the appellate court released her. After that, Chuck had to finish the case without Conrad, since his mother testified that she didn't know where he could be found.

Without Conrad, Hogren was left no alternative but to subpoena the state's attorneys on a declaration vs. a penal interest. (The declaration vs. interest constitutes an exception to what is termed the "hearsay rule." Ordinarily a statement made by someone not directly involved about what another person said out of court is inadmissible, because the person who ostensibly made the statement or statements in question is not in court to be cross-examined. However, in a situation like this one, where Conrad was heard by the state's attorneys to have made a statement which was obviously against his own legal interests, namely, that he committed the crime involved, the hearsay rule is waived on the basis of what is called a declaration vs. penal interest.) So Chuck subpoenaed the state's attorneys in order to have them testify to the interview with Conrad held in their office.

Chuck remembers well the bizarre experience of questioning the state's attorneys. "They got on the stand, one after the other, on separate days and one said, 'I remember that you brought someone in and I remember that he was in our office, but I don't remember his name. I don't remember a word he said, and I don't remember whether it was related to this case.' I said, 'Well, I was present.' He replied, 'Yes, I remember you were present.' I asked him, 'Did you make any notes?' His response was astounding, 'Nope, I have a very good memory and I never make notes.' It's just unbelievable for a state's attorney to make a statement like that! He absolutely refused to acknowledge that Conrad had been in his office or had made any statement that would tend to fix the blame for the incident on himself. It was obvious to the judge that the state's attorney was lying because state's attorneys do not proceed in such a careless fashion."

That was only the beginning of the state's problems in the case. The eyewitness, who had testified before the grand jury that three assailants were involved in the offense, was called.

113 | THE RULES OF THE GAME

When he took the stand, he said there were four people who had knocked the delivery man down.

"The reason he changed from three to four," explains Chuck, "was that somehow the state had to account for Conrad Holmes. They were aware that the judge knew about our attempts to find Conrad and the reason why we were looking for him. They accounted for him by saying, 'Certainly Conrad was there, but he was only one of four who participated; and since all participated, all are guilty. Now it's unfortunate that we don't have Conrad before us in court today, but we do have the other three and we are going to proceed against them.' So that provided me with an opportunity to impeach the witness by referring to his prior statement, which was in direct contradiction to his testimony at the trial. It was, however, very obvious to the judge why the witness had changed his story and the state watched its case slip away." As if that were not enough, the screw was tightened further when the laundryman himself said three youths were involved.

"The judge was irate about this case," Chuck recalls. "He was exasperated by the finagling by the state's attorneys and the police." At one point Hogren even had the police records subpoenaed. "They gave me a hard time and the judge was going to hold them in contempt too. At one point, he was even about to jail one of the police officials. He came storming into court and we had quite a scene there, but we did get it straightened out.

"The grounds against the officer were that he did not obey the subpoena ordering him to bring in certain records. I wanted those records to corroborate Conrad's story. Besides, they provided information about other crimes Holmes had been involved in. As it turned out, he had been arrested for a number of things and had actually done some time."

With the state's attorneys caught in a lie, the eyewitness's testimony impeached, and Conrad's mother dispatched, the two sides made their final arguments and the judge declared, "I find the defendants not guilty." It had been a long siege. After years of waiting to go to court, the trial had lasted two months.

Looking back, Chuck remarked that the state had gone "to extreme lengths to convict the defendants; despite the fact that another person had actually confessed and there had been no robbery. In fact, to justify the robbery charge they claimed the man had lost his penknife. That was the robbery," says Hogren with amusement, "he lost his penknife."

Chuck suspects that the impetus for such intense efforts came from the police. "The police officers had known the defendants for a long time and I think they were pushing it. In fact, I noticed that just before the eyewitness testified he was in a conference room, not with the state's attorney, but with one of the detectives. When he came out of that room, he took the stand and said there were four, and that was the ball game."

The apparent collusion between the police and the state's attorneys in that case was not particularly unusual. There is often a rather close relationship between the two, since the state's attorney prosecutes the people whom the police arrest. There are mutual pressures because the police officers want to justify their arrests by getting convictions and the state's attorney wants to get as many convictions as possible in hopes of obtaining a promotion. Bad relations with the police severely impair a state's attorney's ability to obtain convictions, since the police are best equipped to deliver witnesses for the prosecution.

Moreover, the state's attorneys are under pressure not to make mistakes. A case involving Joe Jackson illustrates this.

For Chuck, the case began as if it would test a critical legal point. Jackson, just after being released from the penitentiary, was arrested and charged with armed robbery. The incident revolved around the parking attendant at the Greyhound bus station. The attendant claimed Jackson had threatened him with a gun and robbed him of $50. Jackson was apprehended about a week later at the same bus station. According to Hogren, he was probably loitering there and, matching the attendant's description of his assailant, the police arrest him.

Jackson had a rather intriguing version of the robbery. He claimed that the victim and he were acquainted. They had been drinking together in a tavern and thought it would be a good idea to supplement their incomes. They then decided to stage the robbery and divide the money afterward. Jackson claimed he had failed to give the victim his share of the $50 and that's why the attendant went to the police.

The story didn't ring true to Hogren. "Nobody's going to stage a robbery for $50," he asserts. "They'd wait until the parking till had risen to about $500 and then make their move."

115 | THE RULES OF THE GAME

In any case, between the preliminary hearing and the trial, the victim disappeared. The state felt that Jackson had threatened him and so he went into hiding. "What made this case interesting," says Chuck, "is that the state, in the absence of the victim, was going to use the transcript from the preliminary hearing to convict the defendant. The question was whether the judge would allow them to read the transcript of the victim's earlier testimony into the record even though he would not be present for cross-examination."

Even though Jackson was a very rough character, had been in jail before, and presented a version Chuck did not find very credible, Hogren took his case because he felt "the state has to prove him guilty." Hogren decided he would let the state try to convict Jackson on the preliminary hearing transcript and then challenge their right to do so.

The legal test never came off. While out on bail, Jackson was charged with another attempted robbery. In that case, he was represented by the public defender. His companion in the burglary attempt pleaded guilty and was sentenced from one to three years. Jackson escaped conviction due to a technicality.

The loophole was opened through an oversight by the state's attorney in which Jackson was not brought to trial on one of his offenses within the 120-day limit. That gave Jackson enormous bargaining power. The state's attorney, fearing he might lose his position if his oversight were to become known, offered a very attractive package. Jackson was to plead guilty to both crimes and in return he would be sentenced to but one year for each, with the sentences running concurrently. Because Jackson had already put in sufficient time in jail waiting for trial concerning this and other offenses, he would have met that sentence's length already and hence would be released immediately. Admitting that he did in fact commit both crimes, Jackson eagerly accepted the gracious offer and regained his freedom.

The last time Chuck heard of Joe Jackson he was back in jail for still another offense. "It's really discouraging," says Hogren, "because here is a 'career man' as far as crime is concerned, and he gets off amazingly easy through a loophole, while others who could use a break have the book thrown at them."

Nevertheless, to keep alert for legal technicalities is critical. Orville Williams was arrested in St. Clair County in Illinois and convicted of a crime. He served time in a penitentiary for the offense. Within five years of his release he was arrested in Cook County for unlawful use of weapons. Although that offense is usually a misdemeanor, because it occurred within five years of the offender's release, it was deemed a felony. In order to establish that, the prosecution stated in one count of an indictment that Williams had been convicted in Cook County of an earlier felony.

"Of course it hadn't occurred in Cook County, but rather in St. Clair County, so we brought that up at the trial," explains Chuck. "We held it back until the very end because we didn't want to give the state an opportunity to amend the indictment. I had spoken to a very famous defense lawyer, now a judge, about the strategy we should use and he suggested that course of action. The judge agreed that due to the error the indictment was defective, that the state therefore could not sustain the conviction, and so found Orville Williams not guilty."

It turned out to be a rather hollow victory, however. The state was also charging Williams with a misdemeanor—that of not registering a gun. The judge, obviously none too happy about having to let Williams off the felony hook on a technicality, found him guilty and sentenced Williams to the maximum: 364 days in jail.

In the case of a felony the defense has the option of a trial before a judge (called a bench trial) or before a full jury. In the past, Hogren has favored bench trials. More recently, however, he has leaned more in the direction of trial by jury. For Hogren, the rule of thumb is that a bench trial is preferable under the following conditions: when there is a technical legal point at issue—a point that a jury would have difficulty understanding; or when the concept of "reasonable doubt" necessitates that it be legally understood or may require a scholarly interpretation; or where there may be such sympathy for the victim because of his physical condition or the heinousness of the crime that a jury would be unduly influenced. In such a case, a judge is likely to be more objective and less easily appalled because "he's seen it all before." A jury is more desirable if the judge is reputed to be a "hanging judge," or if the defense wants to emphasize the human element and drum up empathy for the defendant.

A current case dramatizes the "human element" strategy. A police officer was in the subway posing as a helpless drunk. He

117 | THE RULES OF THE GAME

had three dollars in his pocket. Chuck's client went up to him, took out the three dollars, and started to walk away. "We would never want a judge to hear that case," states Hogren, "because there would be no hope for acquittal. Every judge knows it is very common for police officers to pose as drunks in order to trap would-be muggers. A jury, however, might look into the defendant's background: the fact that he has children, is a student, and is working. They may also feel, because there is some evidence to support it, that the defendant was actually trying to be a good Samaritan on that particular day and was attempting to help the person."

Incidentally, the jury strategy worked and the defendant was placed on a lengthy probation.

Nevertheless, a bench trial is highly preferable in some cases. It would have been better in the Bill Clemons case on which Chuck assisted. Clemons, tried by jury, was charged with attempted murder. It was alleged that he shot a cab driver in the neck, completely paralyzing him. The condition of the victim was brilliantly used by the state; they had the cab driver actually brought into court in a hospital bed. Medical apparatus was set up around him and two nurses attended the victim at all times. During any break in the judicial proceedings the nurses would rush up with medical equipment, insert a tube in an incision which had been made in his neck, and then connect him to a suction machine which made a great deal of noise. "It was extremely damaging for a jury to see that," says Hogren with typical understatement. Chuck had argued with his co-counsels that a bench trial was much to be preferred but had been outvoted. Clemons was convicted. "What is tragic," says Hogren, "is that I really don't believe Clemons was guilty."

When a jury is selected the defense and the state each may reject the ten jurors per defendant. They can be dropped for any reason at all: from a feeling that the prospective juror would not be fair or would be too influential among his peers, to a dislike for the length of his hair. Such jury rejections are called preemptory challenges. In addition, the state or the defense can drop anyone if they can "show cause," indicating the individual's obvious lack of fitness to serve due to overt prejudice or disability. Hogren obviously prefers black jurors, but unfortunately few blacks tend to get on jury panels, a matter that greatly distresses Chuck. If the defendant is black, the state will look for white ethnic types or suburbanites. Jury selection is an art and often is pivotal to the outcome of the case.

It is important who the judge is, even in a jury trial. Prior to the trial, usually many motions, including motions to suppress evidence, are made and the judge's rulings on those motions often determine what the jury will hear. Judges differ mightily.

Richard Elliott, twenty-five, is a drug addict. He has had severe emotional problems stemming from the fact that three family members, including a brother with whom he was particularly close, died within a very short period of time. The deaths triggered the drug dependency. He tried to deal with the problem by going to a methadone institute and although that was helpful, he still had the habit—supporting it by shoplifting.

Elliott went to court on a paternity matter. The mother of his child was receiving public aid and the state wanted Richard to support the child.

At court, Richard was ordered to contribute to the child's support. He said he was unable to because he was currently receiving methadone treatment and was making very little money. The judge was unswerving, saying, "You have to pay. If you can't, I want you to go out and look for a job. And I want you to keep a diary. Every time you go out I want you to account for every hour of the workday from nine to five. Write down what you did from 9:00 to 9:15, from 9:15 to 9:30, and so on throughout the day. I'm going to give you another court date and I want you to return with that diary accounting for exactly what you did, in order to show me you are making a good-faith effort in pursuing a job."

Richard complied. He kept the diary, and although it wasn't as complete as the judge had hoped, it did indicate that Elliott had gone to no less than thirty-five prospective employers. He was turned down by every single one. The experience was so psychologically debilitating that at the end of the thirty-fifth rejection he could endure no more and gave up.

The judge was not satisfied. He said thirty-five was not enough. He pointed to the diary saying, "Here, you didn't do anything on this day, and on that day you also didn't go out. . ." Hogren attempted to intercede for Elliott, saying that it was just emotionally impossible to meet with such a battery of

119 | THE RULES OF THE GAME

rejections day after day. The judge, having none of it, gave Richard another court date and told him to keep filling out the diary.

The next time there was a different judge on the bench. After hearing the case he announced, "If you are a drug addict you don't need to pay anything until you recover. You simply stay in that program until you are free of drugs. That's all I'm concerned about."

A completely different position. Chuck later learned that the earlier judge's wife had died a week before he heard the case and that trauma may have entered into his less than merciful determination. Fortunately, Richard is making progress in beating his drug habit and, according to Hogren, appears healthier every time he sees him.

The most common alternative to Hogren's services is the public defender system, an arrangement whereby the state provides a lawyer for people who cannot afford to hire one. For example, if a person is in jail and cannot make bail, the state will then appoint a public defender to represent him. Quite often, if he can make bail, a private attorney will take his case because the lawyer can take the bail money as his fee.

In misdemeanor cases two public defenders are usually assigned to a courtroom. They may have to deal with fifty or more cases in a single day. That means seeing people for the first time, interviewing them, and deciding what their defense should be. A client will not get more than a few minutes of time with the public defender in a misdemeanor case and goes directly from there to trial.

According to Hogren, with a few exceptions, public defenders are young and good. They are, however, "completely overworked; nobody can possibly deal effectively with so many cases in such a short period of time.

"There was an incident in a court to which two public defenders were assigned. They couldn't really cope with all the cases with which they were confronted. Because of that the defendants believed they weren't getting the attention they felt was necessary to present their defenses adequately. The defendants, who were locked up in the 'bullpen' behind the court, became very unruly, making for some rather nervous moments in the courtroom. Normally, however, the public defenders are very conscientious lawyers who are faced with an impossible task. They usually have some passion for justice on behalf of the poor or they probably would get on the prosecutor's side of the system. I think it is that passion for justice that motivates many of them."

In felony cases, more time is taken and there is an investigator for every two or three public defenders. There are also task forces of public defenders. These are small groups of people who are assigned specifically to deal with one type of crime. For example, there is a separate task force for murder. These task force members are specialists and can be very competent professionals.

Even though the felony public defenders are highly skilled—and some, having come up through the ranks starting in misdemeanor court, are very experienced—they also are vastly overburdened. Again there are but two or three per courtroom. They are expected to dispose of as many cases as possible and may deal with fifty people a day, going to trial with several. There may also be plea bargaining as well as a number of continuances. According to Hogren, about the only exception to the norm of overwork is the murder task force.

People independent of the public defender system first interview the defendant for the bail hearing. They turn the information over to a public defender who represents the person at the bail hearing. If the accused cannot make bail or cannot afford a private lawyer, he is assigned to a public defender for the preliminary hearing. He will be a different person from the one who handled the bail hearing. The lawyer for the preliminary hearing gets all the documents on the defendant on the very day of the hearing. If they decide to go to trial, the public defender and the investigator visit the client in jail to get more pertinent information. Such visits, however, are infrequent because there are just too many cases and too little time.

Defendants complain that the public defenders don't spend enough time with them: visiting them in jail, interviewing them prior to trial, and working on their defense. As a result, there is a lot of pressure to plea bargain (pleading guilty to a lesser criminal offense contained within the more serious one) in order to receive a lighter sentence. But, according to Hogren, the defenders are often excellent lawyers. "I wish I knew half as much as many of them know," he says. "I've learned a lot from working with them so often. Whenever we have two

121 | THE RULES OF THE GAME

defendants and I represent one, a public defender usually represents the other."

"Another problem for the public defenders," Chuck points out, "is that they aren't neighborhood-based; they don't have the confidence of the people they represent." One public defender told Hogren she wished that their system could be like the Cabrini-Green Legal Aid Clinic, where the office is a local institution. People could see the lawyer over a period of years, a degree of trust could be built up, and they would regard the attorney as "their neighborhood lawyer."

Another complaint about the public defender system is that it is under the jurisdiction of the chief judge and therefore is subject to his discretion concerning how many public defenders will be employed and other sensitive matters. It all hangs on his compassion for the rights of the accused, removing a great deal of independence from the public defenders.

Plea bargaining may occur either before or after a preliminary hearing. An assistant state's attorney is assigned to the preliminary hearing room strictly for the purpose of plea bargaining. In plea bargaining, the lawyers representing the client discuss with the assistant state's attorney a possible disposition of the case without going to trial.

Usually the state's attorney will make an offer. It can be accepted or further negotiated. If an agreement is reached it is presented to the judge and, if he consents, the plea bargain is entered into and the defendant changes his plea from not guilty to guilty to a lesser charge included in the more serious offense. The judge usually will review for the defendant his rights to a trial, to confront witnesses, not to testify, and not to make a statement of any kind. If the accused persists in his decision to plea bargain, waiving those rights and pleading guilty to the less serious charge, he is sentenced right there. In so doing, he also forfeits his right to a pre-sentence investigation in which a probation officer actually goes into his neighborhood and home, interviews him, and meets with members of the community in order to provide the judge with guidance in sentencing. Moreover, at the point that the defendant waives all these rights, the judge can look at his previous record and assess it in deciding on the sentence. From the standpoint of the court, plea bargaining helps to reduce the long backlog of cases by disposing of a number of them quickly.

122 | THE RELUCTANT DEFENDER

"Plea bargaining is a tough business and you have to be careful what you do," states Chuck. "The plea bargain is almost always a move downward with the aim of reducing the sentence. But it can be a very intricate process."

Hogren enters plea bargaining often. "I do it on the basis of going through the discovery material, looking at the client's background, discussing the case with him, and determining what the odds of presenting a successful defense are. The state will often make an offer, and I present it to my client with my advice as to what it is worth. Of course, the client makes the final decision, but generally, if the evidence against him is very strong there is little option but to bargain.

"We had one case in which the Church of the Ascension, across from LaSalle Street Church, was broken into by one of our clients, Johnnie Warner. Warner burglarized the Ascension school and the witness was none other than Father Norris himself. That, needless to say, was a case in which I recommended plea bargaining. Imagine the priest getting up in court, with his clerical collar and all, saying, 'I saw Johnnie Warner coming out of the window of my school!' There is almost no way that young man was going to be acquitted. Although he admitted to me privately that he did it, he still wanted to plead not guilty. I convinced him otherwise."

For Hogren, the primary reason to plea bargain is to get a sentence that will serve to rehabilitate rather than harden the client. "Lawyers, under our statutes, can outline an almost complete program of rehabilitation for a judge," says Chuck. "We can make suggestions indicating that we have contacted certain institutions and found an appropriate program that will take the defendant. For example, in a drug case, I would make arrangements with Gateway House.

"The prison system is so corrupt that the less time a client spends there, the less hardened he will become; so it is to be avoided at all costs," stated Hogren. Indeed, the major socializing agent of criminals is the prison system, which ironically, is designed to "correct" the behavior and attitudes of its inmates.

"I feel very strongly about getting proper programs for kids," says Hogren. "We had a young man here who was falsely accused of raping a four-year-old girl. He had never been in trouble before and was very timid and scared. I recommended him to Dave Mack and Steve Pedigo's Young Life program run

123 | THE RULES OF THE GAME

by our church. He will start with Young Life tonight and go again on Saturday. We want to get him directly involved in a constructive program. If he shows up at those meetings I will introduce that in court and it will stand in his favor."

Carl Jefferson was also preferred to Young Life. "Carl Jefferson was so violent that they had to kick him out of the YMCA here," recalls Chuck. "The authorities forbade him even to enter the place. He used to come into our office and harass the part-time secretary we had; he was just an obnoxious troublemaker. Jefferson has a great career of crime ahead of him unless Dave Mack and Steve Pedigo can head him off."

Yet Chuck defended Carl, obnoxious or not, when he got into a scrape with the law. "The case involved a purse snatching on Lincoln Avenue in which a woman named Mary Stock stated that she had been robbed by four white boys and one black youth, Carl Jefferson. He claimed he didn't do it.

"The identification procedure was outrageous. Carl was not arrested until twenty-three days after the incident. He was taken to the police station and, instead of putting him in a lineup, the police simply asked the woman, 'Is he the one?' 'Oh yes, he's the one!' she answered. It couldn't have been more suggestive."

Chuck then prepared a motion to suppress identification.* A date for the hearing on the motion was set. It was never held and the victim never came in to testify. The case was dismissed.

"That was a case in which a highly suggestive form of identification was employed," explains Hogren. "A motion to suppress was very much in order, and because it was filed the state realized it had a poor case and was not anxious to go ahead with it." Without the clinic, Jefferson probably would have been convicted and instead of heading for Young Life he would probably be getting a head start on a criminal career.

"Lynette and I talked about another case and decided to go the same route. In fact, the only reason that youth was not sent to an institution was that he was involved in a Young Life club. He received a two-year probation instead. Had it not been for Young Life, he would have been long gone. So I think relating people to other programs in the church is crucial and I feel

---

*A copy of a Motion to Suppress Identification is provided in Appendix 8.

more strongly about that now than ever before. But we have to follow through. We've applied to the Illinois Humane Society for $6,000 to do just that. Follow-through is basic to the success of any rehabilitation effort."

Hogren is diligent in his efforts to find a proper channel for his client. In the case of Keith Moran, Chuck went the extra mile. "We got a psychiatrist from the North Park Clinic to write a report on him. It was the first time that psychiatrist ever went to jail to visit a patient.

"Moran, now about twenty, had been charged with four crimes, all felonies: one was violation of probation, one was attempted armed robbery, another was robbery, and the other was burglary. He was guilty of all four. It was not a matter of mistaken identity or anything of that nature, because he admitted his guilt to me. All of those offenses were committed within a few months, so I requested a psychiatric examination to find out what had triggered it.

"The judge said the report was the best psychiatric report he had ever received, because he could read it without an interpreter. It was in plain English, easy to follow, and made a lot of sense. It told the judge why Keith had committed the felonies, what in his background caused him to behave in that manner and what he needed in the future to correct his behavior.*

"Keith had a very bad early life. His father abandoned the family when Keith was only five. I don't think Keith had ever been able to come to grips with that. As a result of his father's actions, his mother became an alcoholic and Keith, in turn, also became an alcoholic. So a part of his program consisted of alcoholic treatment.

"The judge was so impressed with the report that for four felonies Keith Moran was sentenced to from one to six years, an amazingly mild sentence. Having already served seventeen months on bail and being in jail at the time, Keith was immediately eligible for parole. But when it was considered, it was denied and we were rather disappointed.

"Lynette called the parole board in Springfield to determine why Keith's parole was denied. They provided three reasons. First, Keith had already violated probation which cast doubt on his trustworthiness; second, he lacked skills and so they intend

---

*A copy of the psychiatric report is provided in Appendix 9.

125 | THE RULES OF THE GAME

to teach him a skill or trade so that he can become employable; and third, he had not finished high school, and so, while in prison, he will be enrolled in a GED program."

Chuck had made arrangements that after Keith was paroled he and his entire family would become patients at the Near North Counseling Center. Hogren had informed the judge of those plans and the therapy became a condition for Keith's receiving an attenuated sentence.

After the parole request fell through, Hogren didn't give up. He drove down to the penitentiary in Pontiac to visit Keith and explain to him the reasons for the denial of his parole petition, hoping that his spirits would be buoyed and that he would take a positive view toward the future.

When proper facilities are not available, rehabilitation attempts can backfire. One such instance began with enrollment of the always mischievous Richard Thacker in that rigidly designed drug rehabilitation program which Mack Andrews had found too formidable.

Thacker had been found guilty of theft and sentenced to ninety days in the House of Correction. After the sentencing, Chuck went to the director of the rehabilitation program and asked if he would take Thacker—a hard-core heroin addict— into his program. He told Chuck he would, but warned him that the program was strict. Chuck then went over the rules with Thacker who said he could live with them because "anything is better than jail."

Richard entered the program. The regimen of an hour and a half Bible study in the morning, followed by an hour and a half prayer time on one's knees, a lengthy worship service after lunch, and then, following a recreation period, being dispatched to a rescue mission for the evening as a living example of a rehabilitated drug addict was more than Richard could endure. He left after two days.

To Richard the program was intolerable. He said they wouldn't let him smoke and he couldn't stand all that religion. The day after leaving the program Richard returned to pick up his clothes. He went inside the building and explained his intention to get his clothes. The person in charge said, "Oh, we gave those clothes away. God gave us those clothes to distribute to the other people here who are in need." Richard then went back to his neighborhood and told everyone who would listen that he was in a drug program in which "God had stolen his clothes."

"That's the full story. That's all he got out of a Christian drug program," says Hogren sadly. "It left him very bitter. To attempt to witness to him now would be very difficult since his experience was so unpleasant.

"Therefore we feel we have to get our own facility. We're pushing hard for a farm where the church itself operates the program on a bit more reasonable basis. A person won't have to come out of jail and spend an hour and a half on his knees the first day in addition to other biblical pursuits. We feel we can construct a slightly more humane process."

Thacker is not the only unhappy result of a poorly operated program. Doris Billings was sent to a similar drug rehabilitation program for women in Wisconsin. "She stayed awhile and then escaped," says Chuck with an unhappy look. "She claimed to have had a sincere religious experience while up there. But shortly thereafter Doris was back on the street as a prostitute and had completely rejected Christianity. She was actually a product of our church, having attended from a very early age.

"It's a very sad case. Her family life was terrible. Her father left when she was very young. Another man moved in but didn't marry her mother right away. After a year or so they did marry, but then began to get into bitter arguments. He left. It was a terrible experience for everybody, including me, who handled the divorce. All that was just too much for Doris, I suspect. She now has a baby but is so neglectful of it that she really can't keep the child. Despite the fact that she has spent her life in the church, Doris is a very wild person today," says Chuck, who has known her for years.

LaSalle Street Church towers over a needy neighborhood.

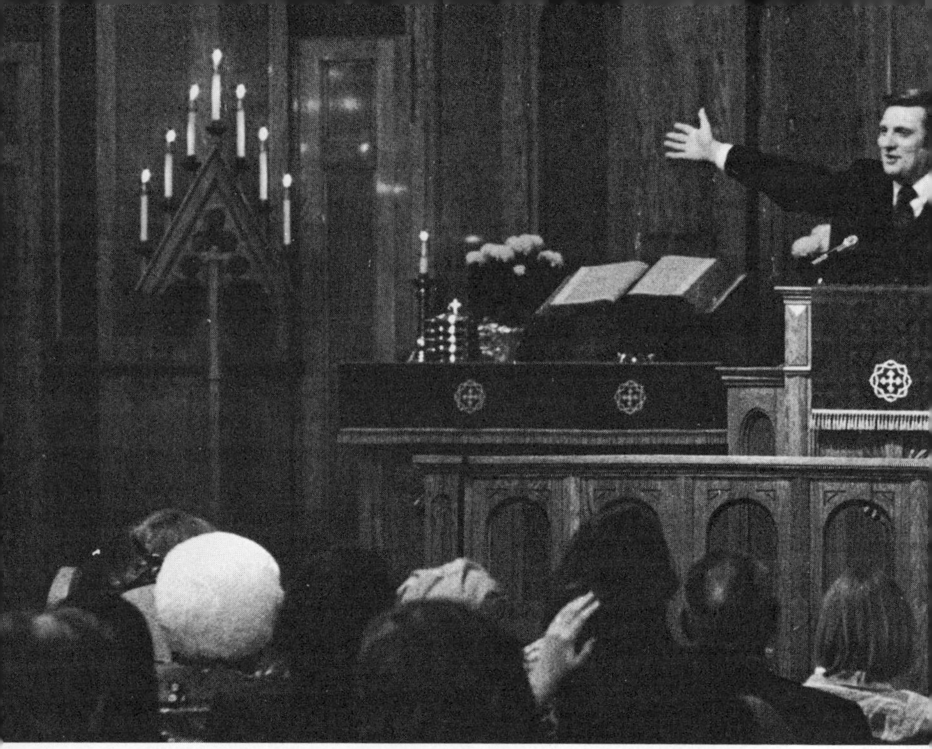

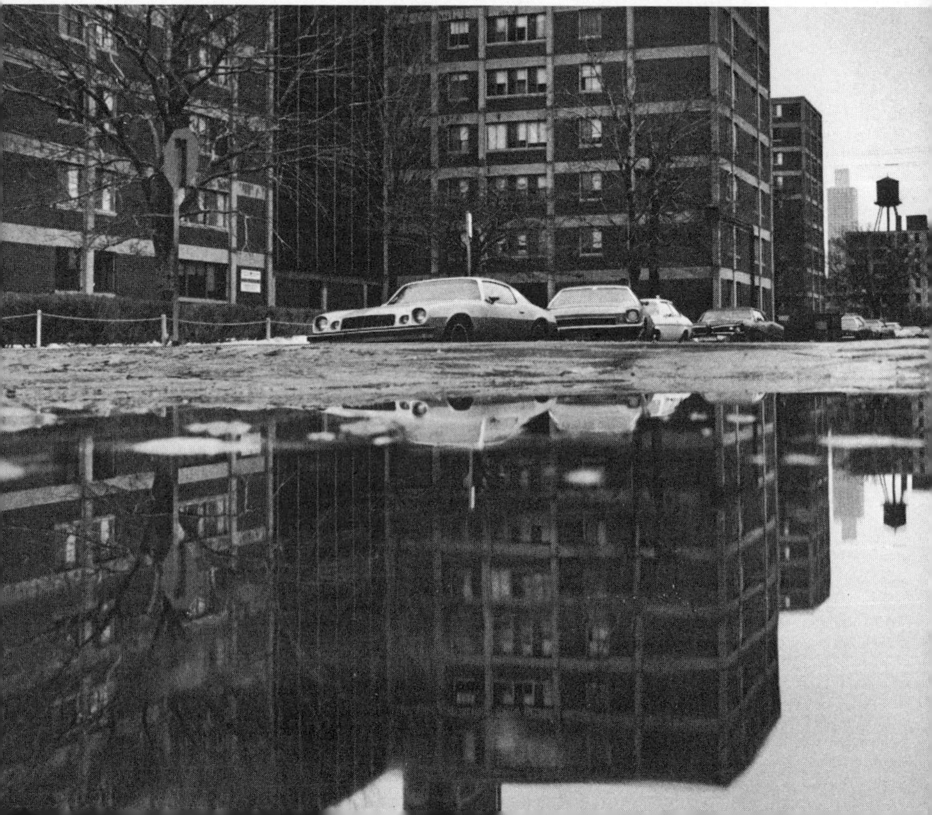

Pastor Bill Leslie of LaSalle Street Church, with his inner-city congregation.

A view of the Cabrini buildings.

Chuck counsels a client in his Isham YMCA office.

Gina Berg first assisted Chuck in the early days of the clinic.

Dan Van Ness, former associate of the Cabrini Green Clinic, consulting with a client.

Lynette Surbaugh assisted Chuck Hogren with telephone work and handled difficult callers.

Young Life leader Steve Pedigo.

Dave Mack of LaSalle Street Church.

Julie Malloy-Good is Chuck's current assistant/secretary.

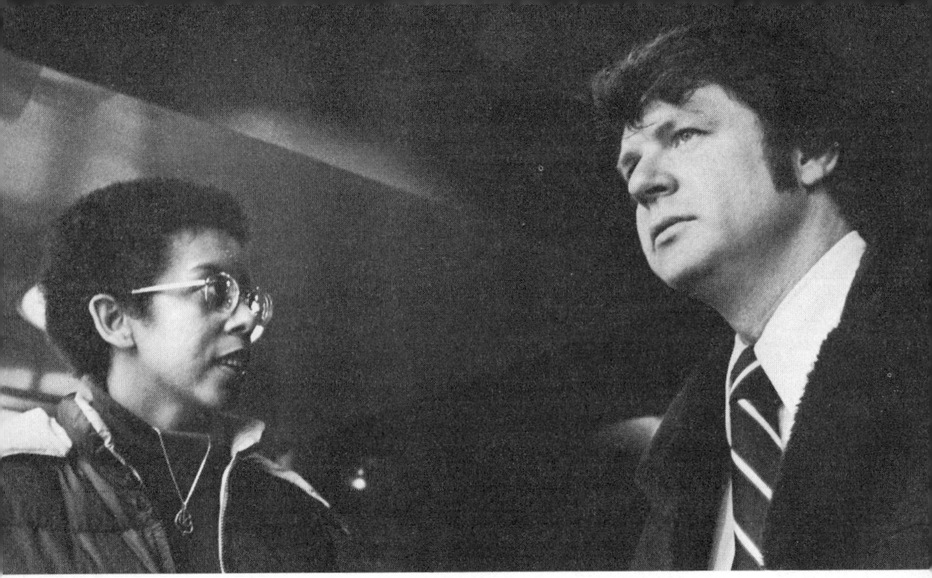

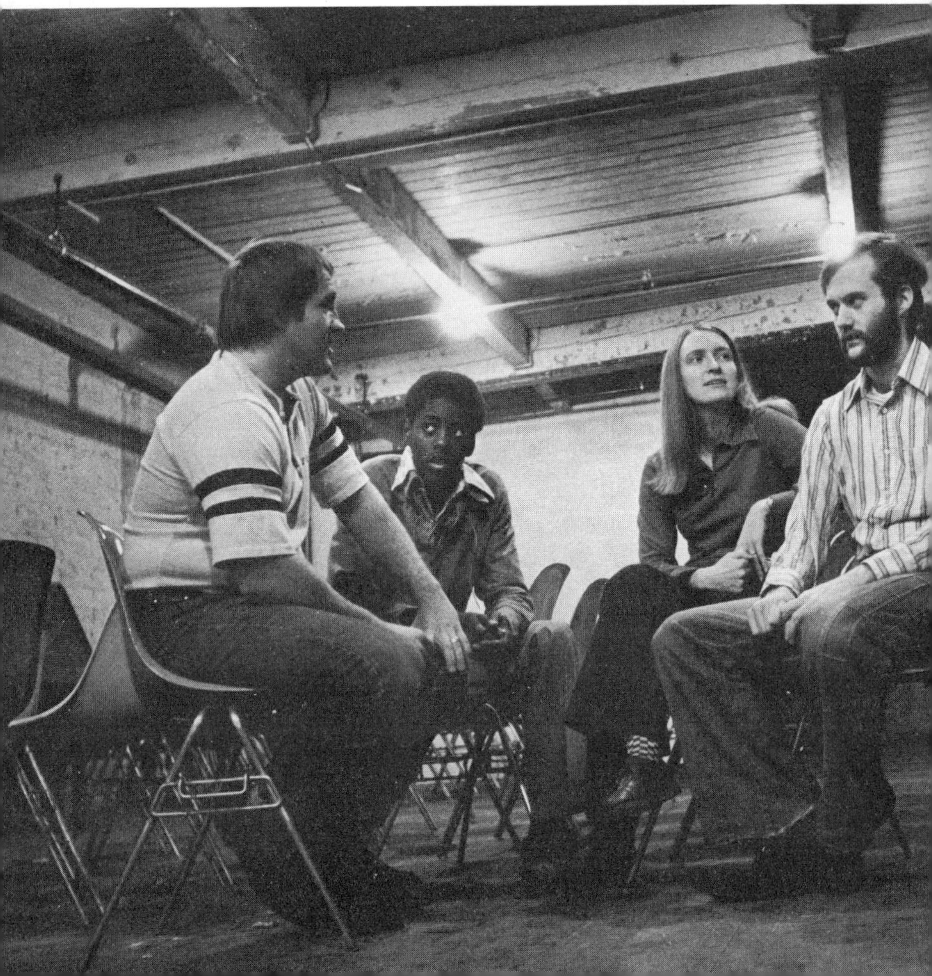

Author David Claerbaut and Gina at the Isham office.

The Isham YMCA.

Directors of the Young Life program, Dave Mack and Steve and Marlene Pedigo, meet with kids.

David Claerbaut, Dave Mack, and local youths outside the Cabrini-Green alternative high school.

THE YOUNG LIFE LINK

8

Wilbur Carter, now sixteen, has committed some rather serious crimes. He was on the verge of being sent to the Juvenile Correction Home in St. Charles, Illinois, to do time.

Hogren explained to the judge that Wilbur had been attending the Young Life club on Wednesday night, the evening on which Young Life stresses the evangelistic aspect of the program. Chuck explained that there was a possibility of further participation.

On the basis of Wilbur's participation the judge consented to probation. Wilbur, greatly relieved that he would not have to do time, returned to the neighborhood and attended the club.

Hogren described Wilbur's situation to the Young Life leaders, Dave and Brenda Mack and Steve and Marlene Pedigo. Steve Pedigo took Wilbur aside and talked with him about what his commitment to himself should be to change his behavior. Such a commitment often includes participating regularly in activities like the club meetings or basketball.

According to Dave Mack, although Wilbur was anxious to do everything right, in two weeks they didn't see him anymore.

128 | THE RELUCTANT DEFENDER

He wasn't interested in basketball, and club activities didn't stimulate much interest either.

"His next appearance," Dave explains, "was under rather tense circumstances. It was a club night and one of our Cabrini-Green staff people, Ken Rivers, had to eject a couple of kids who were in a gang of which Wilbur was a member. They headed for the door but then went upstairs in the church building. Ken went up the back way and caught them upstairs, going through the pockets of the kids' coats up there. Ken again asked them to leave, but they refused. Ken then proceeded to throw one of the guys out bodily. That resulted in a fight.

"The kids eventually left but returned later that evening. Wilbur and his cronies wanted back into the meeting. We said No, because we knew they were coming back to get Ken. In fact, we found out later that they had planned to turn off the lights on some prearranged signal and then stab Rivers. Anyway, there was a confrontation right there. So we invited the gang leader to come in and made an arrangement with him, and the group left."

Next morning the Young Life staff convened and decided that Dave Mack would go to deal with the gang. Wilbur and the fellows causing trouble the previous night were really a small part of that gang. Dave felt that if he could get to the leaders and offer Young Life as a recreational aid to them, it might clear the air immediately.

Mack talked to several of the lower-status gang members and asked if he could go to their next meeting. They told him they were having a meeting in their headquarters at five that night. They were reluctant to invite Dave to their meeting but then consented with the stipulation that the meeting not take place in their headquarters. As it turned out, Mack met them at a previously agreed upon place at five and they said he could come to their headquarters. Quite surprisingly, those headquarters turned out to be Wilbur Carter's bedroom.

"I went into the house," says Mack, "and there were several small children there. Wilbur's mother was ill and in bed watching television. In her late thirties, she was the only adult supervision in the household. The younger children were probably grandchildren from older daughters. Wilbur is most likely the baby of her own family.

"Wilbur's room was attractively arranged. I suspect the rea-

129 | THE YOUNG LIFE LINK

son they initially refused to let me come there was that I might find drugs or weapons stored in the room. One of the slogans written on the wall was something like 'My woman couldn't satisfy me sexually so I found myself someone who could.' There were all sorts of things in the room: fishnets, posters, colored lights, and a stereo set.

"The whole gang came in one at a time and weren't too surprised to see me. They were actually quite open and introduced themselves, as well as asking me why I was there. I was the only white person in that Cabrini-Green row house, but I wasn't particularly fearful because I already knew about half of the fellows from Young Life. Nevertheless, the guys I knew weren't the leaders and I was a little uptight about how I was going to be received by the leaders.

"They asked me 'What's happening' and I said that Young Life exists for young people in the community and that their involvement could take a variety of forms. Some of the fellows like to play basketball and the girls volleyball. We have a club and a camp which appeal to the kids, but as far as what else they were interested in, I told them I didn't really know. It was obvious that they weren't interested in any of the programs we had going currently. I said that part of my job was to organize the program and to find the money to carry it out, and that I was making myself available to their gang, called PHP, to help them to do anything they wanted to do. I told them there were only two restrictions: One, an activity had to be legal, and two, it had to be something which would result in some kind of personal growth. They said that it sounded 'hip' but that they'd have to discuss it. They talked about having a center where they could sponsor sets—dancing—just a place to have music and a place to come in and take it easy.

"Some of the lesser members, however, said they had some complaints about Young Life; that it played favorites, referring to the basketball group. I agreed with their concern and said I could understand how they felt, but that we really didn't know what else to do and that we needed their help in devising new activities. I told them we were open to other possibilities and that one of the purposes of this get-together was for me to be of help in formulating them.

"They asked me about Ken Rivers and what his position was. I said Ken is just like they are, but that he's seeking personal growth in a different way. I explained that he's in college and earning a living by working on the Young Life staff; he's a part of us, and when they show us a project in which we can aid them in seeking personal growth, they'll be eligible for the same kinds of things Ken is doing. They understood, although they weren't entirely satisfied.

"There was disagreement in the group and that's always a peculiar problem because a gang conflict can last for a long time, sometimes until one of the leaders of the conflict bows out of the scene either by dying or by simply moving on. Realizing that, I tried to gain as total an agreement as possible." By the end of the meeting Dave felt he had been able to communicate that Young Life was "for real": that the organization existed as a positive force in the community and would have to be reckoned with by the gangs. Since then, nine or ten of the members have attended at least one Young Life meeting.

But progress has been slow with Wilbur Carter. "We have a Honda program planned for the summer," Mack says, "where we'll get to see him on a regular basis. The only time you can hope to make progress with a kid is if you're spending a lot of personal, high-quality time with him. You have to get into some constructive stuff so you can alter some of his life patterns. We really want to work at developing values. If you have only one hour a week, there's not much you can do. Right now we just don't have anything that appeals to Wilbur."*

The account of Wilbur leads Dave Mack into a discussion of pimping and prostitution. "The leader of Wilbur's gang was a fellow named Sherwood. He had rather interesting attire: a black top hat, a double-breasted burnt orange sport coat with gold buttons and black trim, high shoes, and a cane. I don't know where he gets his money but a number of the guys have been involved in robberies, rather small-time stuff. I don't think this guy is into dope, so I doubt that he does much in the

---

*Minibikes had been donated to various urban YMCAs, including the Isham YMCA, who in turn asked Young Life to develop a "Honda program." Such a program envisioned teaching youth like Wilbur about the maintenance and constructive operation of minibikes. Unfortunately, the bikes were stolen from the Y before that program got off the ground. Nonetheless, after a series of dramatic experiences in recent months, Wilbur Carter now seems to be showing some response.

way of big-money heists. Sherwood may also be a pimp, but I'm not sure. The only other two times I had seen him, though, he was talking with the women of the street."

According to Mack, prostitution isn't very heavy in the community itself because sex is in such big supply. "In Uptown or on Madison Street is where the white folks come, and you'll see a lot of Cabrini-Green prostitutes there," explains Mack. "Quite a number of women from Cabrini go into other areas—they used to stand in the schoolyard there on Clybourn and Division, flagrantly soliciting in front of the police. They're also on Wells just south of Old Town. A number go up on North Avenue in the industrial area west of Halsted, especially when the men are getting out of work. Others are in the gangways in the side streets."

Pimps are part of a tradition. The pimp is usually someone in his twenties or thirties who pimps women of approximately the same age and a bit younger. He takes care of the women.

"We lived across the street from a prostitute," relates Mack. "Her pimp drove one of those garish green and gold Cadillacs with the funny horn and the lights on each fender. He would come and stay with her for three or four weeks, leave for a while and probably stay with another of his stable of women. We'd often see his car parked in other places around the area.

"The pimp provides the apartment through the money she turns in to him. He makes arrangements with the landlord who might want the use of her services once a week in return for the living accommodations. Prostitutes also count on the pimp for protection, something badly needed in view of their being alone out on the streets. If a would-be thug knows there's a pimp nearby who will shoot or cut on anyone who messes with him or his women, he'll be reluctant about bullying a prostitute. In addition, the pimp probably has connections into heroin, so if the woman is a drug addict he can get the stuff for her. It's a rather convenient setup. She doesn't have to handle the money and has an apartment to stay in. She also has a man who picks her up, takes her to work, and handles the drugs, food, and clothes. In turn, she does what he says.

"When the woman gets older it can be tragic. The separation generally comes from an unspoken mutual understanding. Out in the cold, she may decide to look for another job, like working as a waitress or in a lunchroom cafeteria or something like that. She knows that her attractiveness is gone and the future is pretty bleak."

Working in Cabrini along with his wife and the Pedigos, Mack has had extensive experience with gangs. "Presently gang activity is pretty low-profile," he says. "They often organize for mutual protection, friendship, and peer relations. Protection is important. A youngster may be walking to school, have some gang members jump him and take his lunch money or bus fare, and without any kind of gang affiliation that incident could be repeated daily. However, if it's known that he belongs to a rival organization they'll be deterred out of respect for his gang."

Nonetheless, the gangs can be vicious. One rather aggressive gang, according to Dave, is called the "G Boys," many of whose members come to the Young Life club. The gangs are violent and will defend themselves or even kill if sufficiently provoked. They're usually not so aggressive that they go out looking for violent action to engage in, but one faction of the G Boys is rather hostile. One of the fellows attended a Fun Day held at Lake Geneva; two weeks later he shot and killed a man. He's now in St. Charles doing time.

That is depressing, but not particularly surprising. Many kids, if not under the influence of drugs, can be friendly and reasonable—but when faced with the need for a fix, life becomes cheap.

Mack alluded to the lessening of gang activity in Cabrini-Green. "I think the decline comes in part from loss of the leaders from the South Side and West Side who were part of the gang culture of the sixties. They've grown older and are now in different activities. They used to rip off the government, control businesses and schools, and just generally intimidate people. Now they're in the straight world. One former gang leader was killed just last week; he had been working in a labor union."

Although not so tightly organized as they used to be—when each gang had a war council, a minister of war, a president, and a vice-president—gangs still retain a formal structure. "Although a meeting isn't run by *Robert's Rules of Order*, it's still operated in a very well-organized way," says Mack. "It's con-

133 | THE YOUNG LIFE LINK

trolled by the leader and each person knows when he can or cannot speak. There's a secretary present who takes notes of the entire meeting and at some points there are even dues paid. The treasury is watched over very closely."

The gangs are all male. "My experience on the West Side," says Mack, "is that any women associated with a gang merely party with them, sleep with them, or maybe are pimped by the gang members. Girls mainly are on the outside of the structure and just supply ready sex for the members."

Dave Mack has also had extensive experience with Mack Andrews. "Mrs. Andrews is a fine woman," he explains. "She has a job working for the Chicago Housing Authority. In order to retain her job she has to live in the projects and that's why she has remained in Cabrini. Living at home with Mack Andrews is an older brother, about twenty-three, and two younger sisters, thirteen and sixteen years old. His brother is not very influential, but his mother is particularly concerned about the girls and hopes she can help them.

"I got to know Mack Andrews when he joined a basketball team I formed with some of the fellows Chuck had referred to us. Juveniles who had made use of the legal aid clinic and who expressed interest in playing basketball were placed on a list. I'd call them up and invite them to play. We'd supply the shirts, enter the team in a league, and compete for trophies. Mack was one of seven or eight of the kids who showed up on a regular basis.

"Andrews said he wanted to get off drugs. In fact, getting off heroin would pretty well solve his burglary tendencies. The only way he could do that was to go to a place called Central Intake, register as a dope addict, and be assigned to a program. He had gone down there before, but since he could neither read nor write he couldn't fill out the papers. No one cared at all about helping him.

"Knowing he needed someone to help, I made an appointment for him. That first time he blew it and was out playing ball when we were supposed to go. So I called him up and said, 'Hey, I really want to do this with you.' I think the fact that I was really interested in going with him got him down there."

Going to Central Intake with Mack Andrews was a memorable event for Dave. "When I, a white, showed up with him, the person in charge of registering people didn't even ask Mack to read or fill out the forms; instead he read the forms to Mack and had Mack respond, writing in the answers himself. It wasn't even necessary for me to be there.

"All the while the registrar was eyeing me warily, wondering who I was. I was aware of that so I just held back and said nothing. Finally about halfway through he asked me, 'Are you a police officer?' I said No. The conversation ended right there and he continued filling out the forms. Then, a little later he said, 'Well, are you his probation officer?' I said No. He kept filling out the forms.

"When everything was completed, he was going to put Andrews in a drug clinic which used methadone and group counseling. It was located way down on the South Side. I said, 'Well, that's hardly feasible. Mack lives in Cabrini, and he's certainly not going to get up and spend the money to get down and back to the clinic by train every day. What he needs is a clinic nearby. He knows the clinic at Northwestern University on Chicago Avenue. How about that one?' So he said, 'Well, I'll call and find out.'

"He called and they accepted Mack. Finally he asked me who I was. I said, 'Just a friend.'"

The program started optimistically for Mack Andrews. He went every day for the methadone and group counseling, which encouraged Dave to take it a step further. He arranged with Glen McDonald of LaSalle Street Church for Andrews to enter the GED program at Kennedy-King Junior College on the South Side in quest of his high-school diploma equivalent.

Dave took Andrews and his mother down to Kennedy-King and Glen provided a special instructor for Mack. On several occasions Dave even provided bus fare for Andrews to make the trip.

Mack had a long journey ahead. He was tested at the outset and at age eighteen he was not even reading on the second-grade level. The GED program was such a huge uphill climb for Mack that he didn't have the necessary motivation to go anywhere with it. Dave then searched around for alternative programs but was unable to find any. There were just no programs for an eighteen-year-old person reading at such an elementary level.

Concurrently, Andrews became discouraged with metha-

135 | THE YOUNG LIFE LINK

done. He was required to go to a group counseling session and found it too far from his street experience to get into. Still, he did go regularly to the clinic for a month, providing a urine specimen daily to indicate that he was clean as far as heroin was concerned.

Right in the middle of that, Andrews was picked up for six counts of robbing a taxi. He made a partial confession, but stopped when the eyewitness was unable to identify him. He was released.

All this puzzled and disturbed Dave, so he talked it over with Andrews. "Evidently he stopped going to school at about age thirteen and then had nothing to do," says Dave. "He looked into something to do and found that one way to pass the time quite profitably was stealing. He would go into stores on North Michigan Avenue and case them out. He might spend hours and hours, day after day, and week after week, walking around looking at places—photography shops and offices. He'd walk in and use the ploy that he was looking for work and case the joint. By the way, that happens even in our church office; people come up and say 'Do you have a job?' and you know they're casing the place.

"Mack might feign interest in photography. That might make the unsuspecting photographer say to himself, 'Wow! This is really great! Here is my chance to relate to this black kid. I'll show him how to use the camera and everything!'" says Dave, chuckling with amusement. "So he would show Mack the camera, then lay it down, and go into the back room to pick something up. Upon his return, Mack and the camera would be gone.

"The biggest ripoff Mack pulled was for about $1,500. He was only fifteen at the time. As I understand it, it was in a business office on North Michigan. He got on an elevator and went up to an office. He walked in and told them he was looking for a job. He had been in that office a number of times before and had observed where they stored the cash. So one day he just came in with a gun, told the secretaries to hold it, walked right over, picked up the cash, and walked out. It was that simple."

That was one crime for which Mack Andrews was not apprehended. Such experiences embitter the police toward the community. In the taxi heist the people knew Andrews was guilty, but he got off. They told him he was lucky. Incidents of that nature cannot help but motivate the police to find other raps to stick Cabrini-Green residents with.

According to Dave Mack, Andrews was part of a whole system. He would steal cameras, go over to another street, and sell them for half their price to the owner of another shop. The owner would then turn around and unload them for their full retail price, raking in a monstrous profit—knowing all along that the camera was hot and that he was supporting a young person's drug habit.

Still, all that money would go only so far. It wouldn't be nearly enough to buy a car or anything so expensive. Certainly, if a kid were to try that, he would be questioned as to where he got the money. So Mack would give part of the take to his mother. She would ask him where he got it and he would tell her. His mother, needing the money and not wanting her son to be in any kind of trouble, would scold him but take the money—and life would go on from there.

For Andrews, the dope started with marijuana and moved along to heroin. Once on heroin, Mack teamed up with Terry Hart. They would "hook up," meaning pool their money for enough to get high on. The two would hook up for about $70 two or three times a week.

"I don't know where the heroin comes from," says Dave, "but it's on the street. I once had a counterculture person, a white girl named Sherry, about eighteen, coming to my office. Currently she's in a Young Life project in Colorado Springs. She had run away from home when she was eleven and had been on her own for seven years. She had been hitchhiking back and forth across the country, living with whomever she could and making money however she could.

"When she came to me she was living in the Rush Street area with street dealers who were taking in $1,000 a day pushing the stuff. Evidently it came from the syndicate, who sold it to blacks. They, for a small profit, would act as deliverymen, coming into the Rush Street area and carrying it into Cabrini, selling it to the dealers. The blacks get it from drop men who come from the Mafia or syndicate or wherever the heroin originated.

"Sherry told me that at that time the pushers were the only people she really admired, because they had the most expensive stereo equipment money could buy, all the dope they wanted, and all they had to do was sit around all day and get high. They were always high and always tuned in to the stereo stuff.

"With Mack Andrews I'd say we struck out completely. I tried to take him to camp. I made arrangements and everything, but he just wouldn't follow through on it. I tried not to give him any sense that I thought he blew it, but rather that I was trying to understand what was going on with him. I still try to reach out to some of that openness which made him tell me all about his past, but he doesn't respond. Whenever I see him on the street I try to think of something I can get him into and ask 'Can I pick you up for this?' 'How would you like to do that?' 'Come on over at a certain time, we got this basketball team . . .' He's always friendly to me but I think he's afraid and feels that he let me down."

Despite all the problems, it's safe to say that over 75 percent of the Cabrini-Green youth are not involved in crime. Why? "Strong mothers" is the most common response. "Their mothers hold and inculcate strong values," says Dave Mack. "The church is another strong institution in reinforcing the mother. She passes the church's values along and may raise a child very strictly."

According to Mack, gangs are primarily responsible for pulling the youth away from positive influences. The mothers battle against the force of the gang. "The night we met at Wilbur Carter's house there was a gang member, Tommy Smith, who was sort of a borderline type," recalls Dave. "He'd been to camp with us but was leaning toward the gang because he didn't really fit anywhere else. He had been involved in that fracas the night before, so we called his mom and said we wanted to meet Tommy and her at their home at five—the same time I was meeting with the gang. The mother kept him there until Ken and Steve came, and when she heard what had happened the previous night, she said, 'If you have trouble like that again, you go up alongside of his head!' Even though Tommy was sixteen, he knew he still had to show respect for his mother and would be accountable to her.

"After high school, many of these kids have great difficulty finding jobs. The jobs they do get are sporadic, insecure, and poor paying. They are almost as well off financially if they stay on welfare.

"The women generally become biologically productive—in many cases by sixteen or seventeen they will have had a child—and that creates some responsibility for them. The males often lack any responsibility to tie them down. So, if a guy doesn't go to school or get a solid job he may move from woman to woman, something which happens in our group quite a bit. The man may become a parasite of sorts, living off the women who have had his children. Some do that nearly full time, although they do get a job from time to time and hold it for awhile.

"In the Young Life club, though, an increasing number are breaking out of that pattern. We believe that if we can tie them in with the tutoring and other programs, and provide some solid direction for them, they'll be able to hold down a sound job.

"Chuck regularly sends us names of kids we might be able to help. What we need now are models, preferably adult models who will get involved and come to know the kids personally. If we could have people, especially Christians, come down and work in the community full time, getting to know what goes on every day in these youngsters' lives, we could really get things done. A special relationship with these young people is the foundation. On top of that we can build a lot of social and Christian programs which can be really effective. But unless we can have people who really understand the youth and establish rapport with them, it's nearly impossible. Just talking doesn't help. The only thing that currently prevents us from getting the type of people we need is money."

Despite the limitations, there have been successes. Dave Mack picked Ken Rivers up off the street. Ken had heard about the Young Life basketball team through one of his friends. He came and played and really couldn't quite figure out what was going on with Dave Mack. Here was this white guy who was really a coach (Dave had been a highly successful Chicago high-school coach), coming into Cabrini-Green. Dave was picking kids up and molding them into a team. He would enter them into tournaments so they could win trophies, and then tell them about Young Life and its camps.

Dave recalls that Steve Pedigo had taken over the team Ken

139 | THE YOUNG LIFE LINK

was playing on and, after discussing it with Dave, felt Ken should definitely go to the Young Life summer camp. At that time, Ken was entering his second year at Loop Junior College and his life appeared to be on the upswing. They talked it over with Ken and finally he agreed to go. "He went and heard the gospel," says Dave. "He wasn't really convinced there. Having doubts and questions, he studied the Bible with Steve and another group regularly on Sunday nights throughout the autumn and early winter. They talked about Christ and how you can really believe all that stuff that happened 2,000 years ago, as well as what Christ is doing today. Ken made a Christian commitment and became part of our staff. He was ideal because: one, he was a fellow who lived his entire life in the community; two, despite all he had gone through he had held together well; three, he was in college and working toward bettering his life; and four, he was bringing his Christian commitment and a genuine belief in what Young Life is all about with him. Right now he's running the same program that he was playing in a year ago."

Evangelism is definitely part of the Young Life program. Christianity isn't slamdunked down anyone's throat or manipulatingly presented, but fits into the whole Young Life concept of personal growth.

What Ken Rivers presents is a sound model. "As it is, the kids tend to respect pimps, any kind of pro athlete making good money, and musicians. Those are the only people they see. They don't see black lawyers or doctors who have the kind of stuff that spells success."

"What they do is watch television," Mack continues, "and see Dr. J or some other superstar like that. They look for the music on the radio stations and hear black superstars. In the community itself, the people who come in with the nice cars are the pimps who pick up the women and take them wherever they're going. That can be a hard model to beat.

"A few of the kids may hold on to a good black teacher or some other person who cares. But there just aren't enough. That's what makes Rivers so important. He's together, has a nice car, and is making a living. He's happy and living a solid life. That's the kind of thing we really strive for. There's just nothing else like that in Cabrini."

Ken Rivers is not the only happy story. "One of my favorites," says Dave fondly, "is Anthony White, who is fifteen. I've been at Young Life camps with him. I've played basketball, skied in the mountains, and sat down on a cliff above a lake in Minnesota talking with Tony. We talked about what it meant to be a Christian and what commitment means. He committed himself to Christ there in Minnesota. He has become a regular church attender, a part of the Sunday school, and is even one of our best tutors in the church tutoring program.

"We have four guys in the same category as Tony White, friends of his, who are really solid, committed kids. They are there every Sunday morning and every Wednesday night and they will be a part of the basketball programs, the camps, and other extra activities. All in all, from the camp last summer we had about twenty-two Cabrini kids, with about fourteen making commitments to Christ."

UNHAPPY ENDINGS

9

One day while working on this book I drove hurriedly down to the Cabrini-Green Legal Aid Clinic to tape an interview with Chuck Hogren. We had several late afternoon hours available for the taping before Chuck was scheduled to go to the home of good friends for dinner. On my arrival, Lynette informed me that the interview might be off. Chuck had just been notified that one of his clients, Joel Stevens, had been wrongfully jailed.

Stevens was on probation for a theft charge. During the probationary period, however, he had to appear in court for a civil action. He was late for the court appearance so a warrant was issued for his arrest. Joel's mother called Hogren and told him about the problem. Chuck went to court, requested and was granted an order to recall and quash the arrest warrant.* Although all that had been completed two weeks before, Joel Stevens had still been arrested and spent a night in jail on what should have been a dead warrant. Stevens, who luckily was

---

*A copy of an Order to Recall and Quash Warrant and to Reinstate Bond is provided in Appendix 10.

employed and seemed to be moving forward in life, was now in peril of losing his job, all because of a clerical error—failing to record the recall order quickly enough to prevent his being unjustly arrested.

What to do? Because the court was open until four-thirty, the first decision Hogren made was to hustle over to the court, located in the police station of the 13th District. He hoped to see the district judge in whose court the order was filed and have him order Joel released from custody.

Chuck and I left immediately, drove through Cabrini-Green and on into the depressed *latino* neighborhood in which the building containing the police station and court is located. We were up in the courtroom at about four o'clock, hoping to see the judge on duty. Much to our chagrin, there was no judge, no clerk of court, no one. Court personnel are supposed to be on duty until at least four-thirty but no one had answered the phone when Chuck had called twenty minutes earlier and no one was there now. The simple, well-worn courtroom was vacant.

It was also completely devoid of security. We walked through the courtroom and on to the back. We passed through doors and entered the clerk's quarters, off limits to other than court officials. The lights were on, the coffee machine was running, and several partially filled cups stood on top of the clerk's files.

Because the following day, Friday, was a court holiday we had to get in contact with court personnel or Joel Stevens would have to cool his heels in jail until Monday. It didn't look good. With the lights on, and all systems operating, the court officials had evidently left for an early holiday weekend.

We had no right to be in the clerk's quarters, but then there was no one on duty to help Joel Stevens out of his unjust plight, either. Chuck looked through one of the giant record books and found the entry order for Joel, dated some two weeks previous. At least that indicated that the order had been recorded at the court proceeding. Unfortunately, the writing was so light that there would be no way to photocopy it and take it to jail to spring Joel.

After finding the record, we walked across the hall and asked a secretary about the whereabouts of the court officials. She confirmed our fears, saying they apparently had gone home for the weekend.

We returned to the deserted courtroom. We stood there needing the actual order to release Joel and knowing it was probably in the cabinet files facing us. They were standing right next to the judge's bench in the courtroom proper, which posed a bit of a moral dilemma. It would be illegal to go through those files and remove Joel's order without permission. But then "it was unjust that Joel Stevens was in jail, too," said the ever-conscientious Chuck as we debated aloud whether or not we should take our chances and search the files. I asked Chuck if I should stand guard in a strategic spot to warn him if someone was coming. He suggested I step outside so if he were caught I wouldn't be involved. I had no interest in that.

We stood behind the bar, eyeing the filing cabinets. Then, just as we were poised to go into them, the secretary with whom we had talked came through the door. There was no doubt but that she was checking on us. She had no other reason to be there. We were caught redhanded and I felt my mouth rapidly filling with teeth as I pictured the police only a floor below being summoned to take us in. "Can I help you?" she said, exclaiming rather than asking.

Chuck recovered instantly and said, "Yes, you can. You see, we have this problem. I have a client..." and then proceeded to tell the sad tale of Joel Stevens. A bit uncertain, the secretary allowed us to go back into the clerk's quarters and look through those files. Having been there before without success, we returned to the courtroom files after the secretary left.

There in a file dated three months earlier we found the order to quash. It had been backfiled by three months, most likely by mistake. Chuck pulled it out and courageously marched back to the secretary. "This is what we need. Look, I'll be glad to sign a receipt for this document if I can take this over to the jail," he said.

Not being a court employee with any clout, the young woman seemed uncertain about how to respond. "You'll have to go downstairs and speak to the commanding officer of the police station to see what you can do. I have no authority to let you take this file out," she announced.

Without the file we headed downstairs. No luck. The

lieutenant on duty claimed to have no jurisdiction over the court files. Though affable, none of the five officers milling around the desk could help us. A phone call to a superior indicated that the court was closed until Monday and we would just have to come back then. I pulled Chuck aside and suggested that he request to be taken in a patrol car over to a place where he could find a photocopying machine, copy the file, and return. Chuck liked the idea but was once again sung the "no authority" tune.

"But the court should have put this order through at least a week ago, and if it had, my client wouldn't be in jail unjustly," Hogren pleaded. The officer responded rather dispassionately, "I know how you feel, counselor, but this happens a lot and there's always that one case where a kid should be in jail and he gets out. We can't take those chances."

It was clear that as far as the police were concerned, it was better that a kid spend a weekend in jail for no good reason than that a file leave the building even under the vigilance of a police escort. Moreover, that this "happens a lot" meant that plenty of people spend time in jail without justification. It didn't matter. To avoid that one possible negative exception, the police cordially declined to cooperate at all in our enterprise.

There was nothing we could do at the moment. All that was left was for Chuck to go over to the court in the jail that evening and attempt to get an "I" bond for Joel Stevens. If he couldn't pull that off, Stevens would be in jail for three more days.

Driving back, Chuck was fuming. "This is really first-class justice," he muttered. "This is what turns a young man like Joel Stevens against the system. He follows the system and goes to jail. He becomes bitter and loses faith in the law." What Chuck didn't say was that such bitterness augurs badly for the futures of the Joel Stevenses of the world, because such experiences with American "justice" are often foundation stones to a criminal career.

What seemed particularly remarkable to me was that Chuck never seemed the slightest bit upset over the inconvenience all this caused him. He was concerned only about the welfare of Joel Stevens. "Imagine the stress a family goes through in a situation like this," he lamented. "Everyone's upset, every-

145 | UNHAPPY ENDINGS

one's day is ruined, and Joel will probably lose a much-needed job. All because the system didn't function adequately." I had never seen Chuck angry before.

In any case, the Joel Stevens frustration was typical. Lynette remarked that "there never seems to be smooth progress from arrest to bail to hearing to trial in a case. There are always unexpected bumps and snags in the road, all of which exacerbate the problem." Sometimes those detours result from a client's oversights or deficiencies, sometimes from a backup in the court schedule, and still other times from some bizarre occurrence like this. In any case, the wheels of justice rattle rather than grind methodically.

"It almost seems surrealistic," Lynette mused. "Here we sit, discharging our daily tasks and thinking about what's on the schedule for the next day, all quite ordered and under our control. Yet there's a family nearby with plenty of problems already that now must undergo the additional chaos of the unexplained jailing of one of their members." The contrast between life in the middle class and life in the lower class is starkly summarized in Lynette's observation. Rather than living an ordered life, the poor live (or, more accurately, exist) from crisis to crisis with not even the American institutionalized system in support of them. In a law-centered, capitalist society, often such people can neither find jobs nor legal protection.

"Joel was really in a panic when he called this morning," said Lynette. "He called and asked if Chuck was here. As soon as Chuck answered he said, 'I'm at 26th and California; they arrested me last night and put me in jail.' The breathless nature of his speech indicated that he was not only distraught, but under pressure to complete the phone call. Chuck told him we'd get on it right away. All Joel said was 'They're putting me in jail . . . goodbye.' That was the way the call ended."

I wondered how Chuck puts up with it. The phone ringing endlessly—and with every case that closes, two more come in. And then just as things seem under control, either a mistake in the system or an indiscretion by a client wreaks havoc with the entire process.

So, instead of enjoying a leisurely evening with his friends, Hogren ate, visited briefly, and then dashed off to the jail in hopes of bringing a rather frightened young man back home to his anxious relatives.

At nine p.m. Hogren went to Bond Court at 11th and State. Upon his arrival, the judge wasn't there, but the clerk assured him the judge would return shortly. He did, and Hogren explained the situation to him. The judge agreed that a bond should be issued, so Chuck prepared a draft order for Joel's release. The clerk called the House of Correction to verify that Joel was there and then obtained the information from the mittimus papers (warrant for incarceration) necessary to prepare the bail bond. The bond turned out to be $500 (there would have been no bond at all if the clerk who handled Joel's order several weeks ago had done his job), so an identification or personal recognizance bond was prepared. The judge signed the "I" bond order and Chuck took it to the House of Correction.

When Chuck got to the jail itself, still another wrinkle awaited him. He was informed that the process for bailing people out closed at nine p.m.; it was now after ten. Chuck told the sheriff's deputy that the officer from the court had just called over and made the arrangements. The deputy checked it out and let Hogren in.

Once through that tangle Chuck was assured that in about forty-five minutes Joel Stevens would, indeed, be released. Forty minutes later, Joel came out.

"He was extremely happy to get out," says Chuck. "He said at seven p.m. he had given up hope of being released and had gone to bed for the night. They had to wake him up to tell him he was released."

Hogren couldn't get over how grateful Stevens was. "He was extremely appreciative, he really was," says Chuck with obvious delight. "He said he really appreciated that I had come down to jail and bailed him out because he knew that otherwise he would have to stay there until Monday. Since it was after eleven I gave Joel a ride home. He didn't want to call his family; he wanted to surprise them."

Although the Joel Stevens episode had a happy ending, not all of the clients' stories do.

Florence Jane Hawkins was charged with the strong-arm robbery of two girls. At the trial the judge held that she was not guilty of armed robbery, but rather of theft. That moved the offense out of the felony class down to a misdemeanor. The judge then allowed her to remain free on bond while an investigation by the probation department was conducted to determine what her sentence should be.

Just as things were looking up, Florence got herself in real trouble. At the investigation, Florence stated that she was employed by the Weston Grocery Store, when in fact she was not. She lied because she thought her sentence would be lighter if the court thought she was employed. It worked, for when it came time for sentencing, the judge placed her on work release. She would be free every day to go to her job, only at night she would have to come back to jail.

The judge then released her again for a week, under a stay of mittimus, to give her an opportunity to get her affairs in order in preparation for her stay in custody. Since she didn't have a job and since as an inmate supposedly on work release she had to pay five dollars a day for room and board at the jail, Florence knew she was in trouble. The proprietor of the grocery store evidently had been willing to cooperate with Miss Hawkins to the extent of vouching for her claim of employment, but he wasn't willing to wax philanthropic at the rate of five dollars a day.

Florence Jane Hawkins panicked. She didn't appear at the appointed time to begin serving time. She jumped bail on August 31, 1973, and hasn't been seen since.

Ed Walton, about thirty, became a client of the clinic through the Young Life program on Chicago's West Side. He was charged with murder. Chuck interviewed him and readied his case for the preliminary hearing. There were a number of complications. Finally, after a series of continuances the case was dismissed for lack of evidence because the witness who was to testify against Walton never did appear.

About two years later Hogren heard from Ed's mother. She told him Ed had been involved in the robbery of a tavern-supply store on North Avenue, just a block from the clinic office. The driver of the getaway car, Walton, had gone into the tavern with the two other robbers. The storekeeper pulled a gun and shot and killed him. Ed was the only one killed. The other robbers were apprehended.

"He was very fortunate to have had the charges against him dropped on the murder case," says Chuck sadly. "He was even employed, but yet felt compelled to go with some companions to rob that tavern-supply store. Ed had been a mental patient, an inmate of a mental institution. He was very unstable and that, I'm certain, contributed to his getting involved in the robbery. His mother told me he was tricked into driving the getaway car. I don't know how true her claim is, but in any case, I do know he was killed—a sad occasion.

"His mother came over to get his bonds refunded from some traffic cases we'd handled. She seemed broken up but philosophical about it. The whole situation illustrates what happens when there is nothing you can really do after a case is completed. I had noticed Ed was unstable on his earlier case, but there was little that could be done. The tragedy is that such an unstable young man is simply turned right back into the community, an environment that is at worst destructive, and at best no improvement over the environment out of which the person came. So, people like that wind up going right back into some other trouble. In this case, it cost him his life."

Mental illness is no stranger to low-income communities. Titus Parker was an assistant minister for youth at one of the neighborhood churches. In his early thirties, Titus was married with two children. Hogren recalls him to be a rather slight person, always dressed in very mod African clothing, his hair braided, and frequently wearing a turban.

Chuck worked with Titus on several community projects, including one aimed at organizing a not-for-profit community corporation. Parker was also rumored to spend most of his time training young men in judo, karate, and the martial arts. Parker believed that if there was ever another riot, he could raise an army on a moment's notice. Hogren had noticed, when he was over at the church for community meetings, that there would always be a group of young men drilling in another room.

Despite his martial avocation, Titus treated Chuck rather cordially. Chuck found him "cooperative, but aloof. He was very hard to talk to. He would talk in a rapid-fire fashion making it difficult to communicate with him." At meetings Parker would rarely sit down. He would usually stand along the wall as if he were a detached observer. Yet at many of those sessions, he would make long, meandering speeches outlining his position in a rather confusing manner.

149 | UNHAPPY ENDINGS

"Titus and his wife, Joan, owned a store which she operated," Chuck says. "The couple ran into marital difficulty and Parker seemed to be losing his grip on reality. In fact, for awhile he was released from his work at the church to try to get himself together.

"Among his symptoms was an inability to make decisions. I remember one time at the church when he couldn't control a group of kids. They were just running wild. The situation became so chaotic that Barbara Charles, a member of the church who owned a nearby clothing store, had to come over and reestablish order. Things got to a point where Titus was absolutely unable to cope with situations requiring discipline, so he was relieved of his ministerial duties for a period of time.

"Then I got the tragic news. Titus Parker had gone home and killed his wife. He then drove around for several hours, returned home, and shot himself.

"Titus had been highly regarded in the community, so a memorial organization was founded in his name which helps welfare recipients and other persons in need of social services.

"It was an extremely sad case," laments Hogren. "Here was a person who had a lot of ability, who was highly thought of—in fact, nearly worshiped by some of the teen-agers in Cabrini. I remember one, named James Sutton, whose parents had died when he was a youngster. Titus functioned as a sort of substitute father for him. James was terribly upset at the tragedy. And a tragedy is what it was—Titus had been very productive and then he completely deteriorated."

Situations like that one have a wearing effect on people like Chuck. Community workers long for a sense of unity with colleagues as they wage a mutual battle against the forces of poverty, crime, drugs, family discord, and other urban ravages. They need fellow workers with whom to have fellowship who also function as models of dedication and persistence. To have it all end in a burnout and double killing numbs the sensibilities.

Norman Gibson was another example of a person with great but unrealized potential. In 1974 Gibson, in his late teens, came to the clinic for help. He had been charged with armed robbery. Hogren handled the case and it was dismissed.

Then Norman got a break. He starred as one of the main

characters in the movie *Cooley High*. After the movie was completed, Gibson tried to get other motion-picture work but couldn't. It was either Hollywood or Cabrini-Green, and there was no vacancy in Hollywood.

Later, Norman and one of his friends, a client of the clinic named Jerry Hathaway, were accused of striking a woman. They were taken to jail. Gibson was bailed out shortly thereafter. As soon as he hit the street, Gibson, well known in the community, was shot and killed by two or three of the woman's friends. For Norman Gibson, stardom constituted a taste of honey, but only a taste.

Untimely death is common in Cabrini-Green. Tom Becker, a young man in his twenties, married, with a family, was an employee of the Isham YMCA. He worked in one of the recreation programs. He came in to the clinic office because some vehicles he had purchased had been repossessed, and as a result he had some wage assignments out against his checks. He wanted to know what Chuck could do to help him. Lynette made a series of phone calls and determined that Becker had actually purchased two cars.

"We were still working on those credit problems, when all of a sudden we heard that Tom Becker had been murdered," remembers Chuck. "He had been shot in an execution-type slaying. All we know is that he probably was involved in some drug traffic and rubbed someone the wrong way, so he was killed."

Circumstances in the community seem always ripe for trouble. Harry Robinson, a fourteen-year-old sophomore at Cooley High School, was charged with battery in an incident on West Division Street.

Four young men were in front of a building in the early morning hours when a woman walked out of the Farmer Brown Rib Shack carrying some takeout food. Two of the fellows jokingly called her some names because she wouldn't give them any of her food. The youths thought that was the end of the incident since they were just kidding with her.

The woman didn't think so. She went up to her apartment and later emerged with four other women, two men, and a little boy. It developed into a first-class rumble. Harry was

151 | UNHAPPY ENDINGS

stabbed with a two-edged dagger and taken to Cook County Hospital. His four stab wounds required a five-day hospitalization. One of the people who came out with the woman, Michael Templeton, was also seriously injured. He was beaten so savagely that his mind was affected for months and for awhile it was believed that he would be a vegetable. He gradually did recover.

Although Harry was charged with the crime of battery, the case was dismissed because the victim was in no condition to come to court. Moreover, the court felt that since Harry was himself seriously injured he probably was not the one who did the damage. According to Hogren, Robinson was not directly involved in the violence nor had he been the one who made the remarks to the woman. He had been charged with the others according to the theory of accountability.

"The incident illustrates," says Chuck with a sigh, "how you can be minding your own business but still get in serious trouble because two of your companions rather innocently make some remarks to a passerby—I don't believe they said anything malicious—bringing out a whole household; and that leads to an incident in which one person almost loses his life and my client gets four stab wounds such that he spends five days in the hospital." Meaningless violence.

Some clients either cannot or will not help themselves. Walter Rascher, a white man in his forties, is a prime example. He came to the Young Life clinic on Cicero Avenue when Hogren was working there as a volunteer. (Chuck wound up serving as that clinic's director for three years, all while he was also working at the Cabrini-Green Legal Aid Clinic.)

Chuck won't soon forget Rascher. "He used to call all the time and drive Lynette crazy. Finally I asked her not to talk to him but to refer all his calls to me. He would just cover the same ground over and over again. The issue was visitation with his children, something he had been denied on the basis of a psychiatric recommendation. The psychiatrist said his daughter was afraid of him and that it wouldn't be in her best interests for him to visit her at that time.

"He just could not accept that. When he called, he would talk in a very loud voice—you'd have to hold the telephone about two feet away from your ear. He would just bellow out the same material. 'Why can't I see my daughter? She's eleven years old and she loves me. Why am I divorced? Why can't I see my wife? What did I do, where did I go wrong?' He was absolutely impossible to talk to. It was obvious that he was mentally ill.

"I read the psychiatrist's report and told Walter that if he was ever to get visitation rights again, he would have to get another psychiatrist to examine him and write a contrary report. We sent him to various places but he wouldn't cooperate. He would say, 'I don't need this, I don't want to talk to them.'

"Months went by, and finally I got the court itself to appoint a psychiatrist for him through the court commission. He went and received a favorable report. He then got another lawyer because we told him we would just have to withdraw from his case. Anyway, he probably does have his visitation rights now."

Despite the necessity of having to withdraw from his case because of lack of cooperation, Hogren still keeps the door open for Walter. "I've kept a case in which he was being sued by his former lawyer for not paying his fees but that case is still pending. Fortunately, however, we don't hear from him much anymore."

Visitation rights weren't Rascher's only problem. He was an air-conditioning sheet-metal worker by trade, but during the time Hogren worked with him he didn't have a job because the union wasn't placing anyone. Rascher also had varicose vein problems in his leg, causing him to be hospitalized from time to time.

Hogren just shakes his head whenever he speaks of Rascher. "He is a loser because he can't accept the fact that he has to do something to deal with his own problems. The steps were so simple. All he had to do was cooperate with the psychiatrist. The judge actually wanted to give him the visitation rights because it's in the public interest that a father keep contact with his children. But Walter just couldn't see that. He blamed everyone but himself. He believed that his wife was turning the children against him—that was one of his favorite lines. He said she wouldn't even let him deliver presents on birthdays or at Christmas, that he had to leave them in the hall. Although that may have been true, he wasn't willing to follow advice.

UNHAPPY ENDINGS

"I did talk to his wife in the presence of her lawyer, and although she may not have been telling the truth, she seemed to be a fairly stable person. Her four daughters didn't get along with her so there may have been something to Walter's charges. But the fact remains that we couldn't deal with him because he would never follow through on suggestions. When he finally did consent to having the court-appointed psychiatrist examine him—since he had no other alternative after so many months—it worked. But he had really stalled his own case.

Ralph Roland, another white man about forty from the west side clinic, rivaled Rascher as a source of frustration. Also somewhat paranoid, Ralph had a drinking problem and a morass of traffic violations. Roland claimed that the suburb in which he lived was against him because he had tried to organize his neighbors in opposition to their suburb's being annexed by another municipality.

Although Hogren allows that that may have been true, Roland's legal problems stemmed from all the traffic cases pending against him. His driving misdeeds were so well known that he was notorious. All the local police and sheriff's officers in the southwest suburban area knew him.

"The judge seemed to have genuine compassion for him," says Chuck, "and stated that he wanted to get Ralph into an alcoholic treatment program. But Roland was unwilling to cooperate even after my efforts to convince him. In one of his cases the charge was striking a police officer. The judge didn't believe the officer's testimony and neither did I. So we won that one.

"After that, the cases came in torrents. Before one traffic case could be disposed of, he would get a number of new ones. It became obvious that to represent Ralph Roland on his traffic cases was a full-time job. He got one after another, and instead of getting one at a time he might get three at once. They would be serious moving violations, including driving under the influence of alcohol or driving without a license—offenses of that nature.

"That went on for over a year. Finally the judge (and for the most part we had the same judge) got tired of hearing the string of cases and said, 'We're going to continue your case. I don't want to hear it today. And when you come back I want you to go to the Central State Alcoholic Institute.' The reason Roland wasn't locked up long before was that the judge felt he was a victim of alcoholism and that, in some cases, he might have been picked on by the police. Sometimes the officers wouldn't come to court and testify against Ralph, and other times he could prove that he did have a license and that the police had charged him unfairly.

"It ended up with all but one of his cases being dropped, and for that one Ralph received a one-year conditional discharge with the understanding that he maintain membership in a local Alcoholics Anonymous chapter.

"We are now through with Ralph, but for awhile I thought it would never end. We'd win one case and then come to court and find there were five or six new ones waiting. He would call constantly with new cases, although I must say he was always appreciative of any help we gave him.

"It became so outrageous that at one point the judge wouldn't allow him to leave the courtroom once he came in in the morning—because he would go out, get drunk, and come back to court loaded. Toward the end, whenever he came to court at nine-thirty they would have the sheriff keep him there so he couldn't return at eleven or eleven-thirty in an inebriated state."

Chuck appreciated the understanding of the judge. He saw the judge later and found he had been elected to full judge and would serve as a circuit judge at the Maywood Court. "He asked me about Ralph," says Chuck. "He remembered him after all that time. He said, 'How is our friend doing?' I said, 'Fine, his cases are all over.'"

Gary Victory Patton, a white twenty-year-old who has been in trouble since he was nine or ten, is another of Chuck's nightmares. Gary is the product of a broken home from Chicago's South Side, Hogren's old neighborhood. "He's a classic case for a psychiatrist to use in pinpointing what can happen when a home breaks up after a relatively short period of time," remarks Chuck.

Patton was charged with stabbing a person at the Florence Hotel. (In telling the story, Hogren pointed out that the hotel had been named by George Pullman for his daughter, Florence. Including such detail is typical of Chuck's meticulous style.)

Patton was working at the hotel when four teen-agers entered and threatened him, saying he had made some remarks about a girlfriend of one of them. Gary denied it. The owner of the hotel, smelling possible trouble, told Patton to leave the area. Patton went up to his room and the four youths left. A half hour later Gary came out the back of the hotel carrying a straight razor. He came around to the front and there were the four, waiting. Patton told them to get out of his way. He then slashed one of them with the razor. After being charged, he was examined by a psychiatrist and found to be incompetent. He was incapable of cooperating with a lawyer, so Hogren tried unsuccessfully to have him committed.

"Patton was a glue sniffer," says Chuck, "and it had apparently affected his mind. After awhile, however, he seemed to improve. He met an older woman and moved in with her. They lived together in a hotel on the North Side. A later psychiatric examination was held and he was found to be competent to cooperate with a lawyer.

"Several years lapsed between the crime and the trial. When we did prepare for trial the state offered him probation, despite the fact that it was a felony. He had been charged with attempted murder. Patton didn't want to go to trial, so he took the probation offer: five years. The probation included a provision that he go to the Near North Counseling Center weekly for treatment.

"He didn't go very often although he's still out on probation. It's been over a year now. I really doubt that he'll be able to do five successful probation years. Gary is the kind of person who just gets into trouble. He has no self-discipline and always wants someone to work with him. He came to church regularly for awhile and even got into a Wednesday night Bible study sponsored by Mike and Chris Spethenson, who sort of took him under their wing. But he's drifted away.

"Gary is a likable young man. But he never finished high school, has been involved in stealing cars, and has a record the likes of which I've never seen for a person of twenty. At nine or ten he had already been charged with sexual assaults—unheard of! He's the type of person for whom you just wish there could be some follow-through. In his case, however, there was an attempt. But he's not able to keep up his end of the agreement and technically he's violating his probation at this time."

Perhaps the most disheartening case of all for Chuck is that of Warren Wiley, a twenty-six-year-old Cabrini-Green resident who was charged with attempted burglary. Someone had broken the plate glass window of a television repair shop and Warren and his partner were leaning into the window when he was arrested.

Warren was fortunate. He was placed on two years' probation. "I admonished him to be particularly careful," recalls Chuck, "since he had a severe problem with alcoholism and he had difficulty holding a job because of it. He used to make a near violation out of hanging out on the corner."

Chuck didn't hear from Warren again until about a year later when he was charged with another offense. This time he was arrested for having a concealed weapon on his person, a revolver. It was a felony because Wiley was already on probation for the burglary charge.

Warren did admit to having the gun but said he was carrying it because someone had threatened him. That turned out to be true. He felt that the risk of being arrested was less than the risk of being killed by the person who threatened him. His reasoning shows the terror in which many Cabrini-Green residents live. In his case it was terror sufficient to put Warren Wiley back in trouble with the law. At any rate, Warren was standing outside a building on a street corner with his cronies as a police car went by. When he saw the car he dropped the gun and tried to kick it down a stairwell. Unfortunately for Warren, he missed, and the revolver remained lying next to him. He was easily apprehended.

"So we went to court with him," says Hogren. "It's very difficult to defend someone in that type of case. A motion to suppress evidence would not have been productive, so we started negotiating. I knew Warren had a severe drinking problem. He even came to court drunk one time when he was out on bail, and the judge locked him up for his own protection.

"The decision was that the best thing for Warren was to get him into an alcohol treatment center," explains Hogren. "I convinced the judge of that and he gave Warren three years'

157 | UNHAPPY ENDINGS

probation. I also talked to the judge who placed him on probation earlier for two years and received permission to take this course. He assured us he wouldn't revoke Wiley's probation. He could have re-sentenced Warren on the burglary due to his violation of probation by carrying a gun. So I had to deal with two judges and both agreed to a most generous disposition.

"I also went to the alcohol treatment center which the city of Chicago operates and about which I had heard very good reports. I was favorably impressed with the center after visiting it and talking to the personnel there. I made arrangements with them for Warren to enter right from jail; he was to leave jail with me and walk right over there and be treated for six months.

"It was very difficult to get Warren to consent to enter the center. He was not at all cooperative. The center wasn't excited about taking him because he claimed he didn't need the treatment. Ordinarily, one has to feel he needs treatment before the center will admit him; otherwise they feel they may be wasting their time. But he did finally agree that it would be better to be at the center than in jail. When the day came, I went over to the jail, picked up Warren's belongings, and walked him over to the center." Chuck was relieved, feeling the Wiley dilemma was finally under control.

One day, however, as Hogren was driving down Larrabee Street whom should he see on the corner but Warren Wiley. In utter shock he brought his car to a screeching halt, got out, and shouted, "What in the world are you doing here on the corner?" Wiley had lasted at the center less than one week. He told Chuck he had just walked off, never receiving the treatment for which the judge had placed him on probation. At present, Warren goes to his probation officer once a month, but is not getting any treatment for his problem. He spends his days on the street corner.

"It's a great disappointment!" says Chuck. "With all that going for him he didn't follow through on it. The judge had to lean over backward because his case included not only the concealed weapon charge but the violation of probation as well. A condition of the second probation was that he remain an in-patient of the alcoholic treatment center until they discharged him—and he blew that too! He didn't live up to the agreement.

"The center must have let him go. It's a secure place with guards on duty. It would be very difficult if not impossible just to walk off. I suspect that he didn't respond or cooperate, so the center, not wanting to keep him, officially discharged him even though he didn't merit it. So, although he is technically not violating his probation, he's certainly violating the spirit of it because the understanding was that he was to stay six months."

Chuck was devastated by the experience. "Those are the kinds of things that make me feel like quitting," he says with his shoulders sagging. "It's very discouraging after having worked that hard. It was a lot of work to negotiate that kind of sentence, then to go to another judge and get him to agree to it, in addition to going over to the treatment center and talking them into taking Warren when they really didn't want to because of his attitude.

"I felt betrayed and very angry at him. Warren was sorry for my sake that he had skipped out, but he claimed he just didn't need it. He's only fooling himself. I talked to his mother earlier and she said Warren was drunk constantly, twenty-four hours a day. He was almost never sober, sometimes not even on court days. The whole family was really behind this arrangement and that's important in situations like Warren's. But for him, it just wasn't enough."

Where did Wiley get the money to keep his John Barleycorn proclivities satisfied? "Warren is unique in that he was injured in two auto accidents and is getting disability money. He uses it for booze. Because he lives at home with his mother and two sisters, his expenses are minimal," Chuck explains.

Other less affluent "corner boys" seem to work in teams in which shoplifting is developed into a near-science. In addition, money is extracted from petty crime, purse snatchings, muggings, possibly pimping and dope pushing, and any kind of sporadic or short-term jobs which can be converted to liquor.

It is also very common to take over a woman's public aid checks. "Tom Flack, a lawyer and private investigator, told me of one woman he represented who lived on Franklin Street," says Chuck. "She had about five children and there wasn't a stick of furniture in the apartment. It was just bare. People were sleeping on the floor.

159 | UNHAPPY ENDINGS

"Tom asked her what she did with her rather substantial check and she said she gave all of it to her men, because if she didn't, they would have nothing to do with her. That's how she kept her men, by giving them her public aid check."

Hers was the sad plight of a vulnerable woman. Through a series of involvements with men she had a number of children. The children in turn chained her to her apartment, making her a social prisoner, painfully in need of companionship. In order to obtain that companionship she has to remain sexually and financially available to her parasitic suitors. The results of that vicious cycle are suffering children—left without food, furniture, or a healthy home life.

All the problems don't emanate from clients. Chuck spoke of a judge named Kenton, whom he finds unnecessarily severe in his judgments and expectations of Cabrini-Green defendants. Kenton is new and Hogren expects him to mellow. But in the meantime he often presents obstacles for Hogren.

While we were sitting and talking of frustrations, the phone rang. It was Roger Henderson. He had been calling Chuck at least twice a day, sometimes as early as seven-fifteen in the morning. After considerable exasperation with Roger's calls, Chuck had vowed to Lynette that he would get tough with him. But as I sat there listening, it was obvious that Chuck isn't able to play that role. He saves all his toughness for the courtroom. There was hardly any sternness in his voice, and it was clear that Henderson would come away from the call without feeling he had bugged Hogren in the least. So Roger Henderson talked on in a paranoiac vein, sapping Hogren of the little energy he had left for the evening. And five court appearances were scheduled for the next day.

THE TRIUMPHS

10

"I get very nervous about murder cases because the penalty is so severe: a minimum of fourteen years," says Chuck, who rarely reveals his anxieties. "I feel I'm responsible for the person's life and if I don't come through it could be destroyed in a penitentiary. I have trouble sleeping and I get depressed over pressure like that.

"A lot of times I can't seem to get rid of cases. They drag on for what feels like an eternity. Delays have been a terrible problem for us—seldom being able to get cases quickly to trial for one reason or another. And that just compounds the frustrations. Recently a new procedure was instituted in which cases will go to trial much more rapidly than in the past. That was much needed. Now we'll be able to dispose of cases and move on to other ones.

"Also, when you don't get the cases to trial you don't get the experience you need to deal with the next case. Legal ability is based in large part on experience, and without that experience you deteriorate as a lawyer. In the earlier days we had a trial once a week, all kinds of trials. Now there are very few. The courts are just too crowded—and we get more felonies than ever. A lot of times the people are guilty, so going to trial is futile. That leaves us with no option but to move the case along through the plea bargaining process."

"I do get very depressed at times," Hogren admitted. "One day I received a call at home before I even got to the office. A person told me that one of my clients had been arrested again on the same type of charge I had dealt with before. I then came to the office and got a call from another client saying he, also, was back in jail.

"It was devastating. To have two clients whom we felt were successfully dealt with, whose problems we believed had been solved, go right back to where they had started years before. It was just too much! We were starting all over again. That's happened frequently, and it's extremely hard to cope with—knowing we weren't successful in helping a person beyond what his legal problems were. We weren't able to deal with his life.

"Lately we've been trying harder or praying more or something, and we're finding that the Young Life program is of great value. Lynette has made calls to people trying to get their assistance and that has also been helpful. But it is still very hard to deal with that repeater situation."

When the horizon seems gloomiest, Chuck gets "the feeling that I'm just wasting my time here, that this is completely useless—not worth spending another minute on. But then something will happen and I come back and start all over again."

Fortunately, there are victories as well as defeats. One was the case of Ulysses Edwards, twenty-three. He was charged with the armed robbery of a news vendor, a man who had a newspaper agency. The vendor operated out of a little house where the papers were delivered. He would get up very early, around four a.m., and wait for the trucks to come from the *Sun Times* and *Tribune*. He hired delivery boys who would come after the trucks had dropped off the morning papers. The youths would sort the papers and go out on their routes.

One morning when the vendor was up early, at 4:55 a.m. two people wearing masks came into the little house. They

163 | THE TRIUMPHS

held him up and robbed him. The vendor didn't know who the assailants were immediately, but about a half an hour later he said he believed that one of them was Ulysses Edwards. "It wasn't the world's greatest identification, since he had to mull it over," grumbles Chuck. Nonetheless, Ulysses Edwards was arrested.

Edwards had an interesting defense. He claimed that at the time of the robbery he was in the emergency room of Henrotin Hospital. He was there from four-thirty a.m. on. He stated that he had been on a playground riding a bicycle and had fallen off and injured himself. He said he was with a friend, Robert Dobbins, twenty-seven. Because Dobbins had a welfare department green card, entitling him to free medical care, Ulysses borrowed the card and used Dobbins's name at the hospital. Unbelievable as it seemed, that four-thirty a.m. injury constituted Edwards' defense.

Dan Van Ness, who handled the case, listened to the story and was skeptical. Nevertheless, he followed through on what Hogren calls "the most thorough investigation we have ever had in this office." First, Dan subpoenaed the records from Henrotin Hospital. The records showed that a Robert Dobbins had indeed arrived at four-thirty a.m. and they had his signature to prove it. With the signature in hand, Van Ness set out to find Dobbins in order to get a sample of his handwriting.

Robert Dobbins was nowhere to be found. Dan looked for him for months. He traveled to possible addresses all over but couldn't locate him.

Then one day Van Ness came up with still another address for Dobbins. He asked Hogren to accompany him and Chuck quickly agreed to go along. "We drove up north to a hotel in Uptown, far away from Cabrini-Green," recalls Chuck. "When we got there, there was no Robert Dobbins on the names posted in the lobby. So we pounded on the door and the woman clerk came out. We asked her, 'Is there a Robert Dobbins who is a resident of this hotel?' She said, 'Yes, he's in the office with me right now.' We went around the corner into her office and there was a young man. We asked 'Are you Robert Dobbins?' He said, 'Yes, I am, but I was just checking out, getting ready to leave. Five minutes later, and I'd have been gone.'

"Dan lives in the Austin area of Chicago as a part of the

164 | THE RELUCTANT DEFENDER

Austin Community Fellowship of Circle Church. He now runs a law office there. His group has regular prayer meetings, and for months they had been praying he would find Robert Dobbins. Now we had found him with but five minutes to spare. He was actually leaving the state, and had he left we would never have been able to locate him. In fact, had he even been in his room we probably wouldn't have found him since his name wasn't on the directory. We felt it was a miracle of sorts."

Dan told Dobbins why they were there, and that he was a very necessary witness in the Ulysses Edwards case. Dobbins said he would cooperate in any way he could. In further discussion, Dobbins corroborated Ulysses Edwards's entire story and agreed to supply a specimen of his handwriting to assist in the matter.

Dan then hired an examiner of questioned documents, Donald Doud, who is one of the best-known such experts in the country. Doud, who has offices both in Chicago and Milwaukee and divides his time between the two cities, has written books and lectured extensively at Northwestern and other universities concerning questioned documents.

Since Ulysses Edwards was indigent, Van Ness and Hogren asked the court for an order to pay Doud the $200 fee to examine the documents. The request was granted and the specimens were turned over to Doud.

After careful examination, Doud wrote:

> In my opinion Robert Dobbins did not execute the signature on the Henrotin Hospital report No. A 11884. There are a number of differences between the signature on that document and his known specimens. The enclosed comparison exhibit illustrates by means of arrows some of the more fundamental of these differences.
> It is my opinion that Ulysses Edwards, the individual who purportedly executed a page of exemplar specimens in the presence of Daniel Van Ness, also signed the name "Robert Dobbins" to the Henrotin Hospital Report No. A 11884.
> The questioned signature agrees in identifying characteristics with the known specimens of Ulysses Edwards. These include skill, letter forms, proportions, and spacing. The only significant variation noted was in the introductory stroke to the "D" which appears in the questioned signature, but not in the known specimens. While this characteristic cannot be explained in the evidence, it seems reasonable to believe that it was either incor-

165 | THE TRIUMPHS

porated into the "Robert Dobbins" signature used as a model, or was due to some accidental circumstances.

The signature comparisons on the right side of the chart illustrate the close agreement between Ulysses Edwards' writings and the questioned signature on Henrotin Hospital Report No. A 11884.

166 | THE RELUCTANT DEFENDER

Van Ness and Hogren gave a copy of Doud's report to the state's attorney who was prosecuting Edwards. He read the report, discussed it with his supervisor, and dismissed the case. The state felt that if someone of Doud's stature were to come to court and testify that the person who was charged with the crime was actually in the hospital at the time it was committed, the defendant's alibi would hold up.

Ironically, at about the same time, the vendor waffled, saying, "Yes, I may have been mistaken in my identification." According to Chuck, "He wouldn't admit it earlier, but now he acknowledged that he might have been mistaken, that it might not have been Ulysses Edwards who did it."

But even that victory was tarnished. "The sad part of the Ulysses Edwards story deals with File 'B,' " says Hogren. "As soon as Ulysses was discharged he was back on the street again. Not too many months later he was arrested and charged with burglary. Ulysses and three others were going into a building on Fremont to burglarize it. While they were there the police were called, there was a shootout, and one of Ulysses' companions was killed. Ulysses was found hiding under a tarpaulin in the basement of the building. He was using the name James Crenshaw.

"Dan was crestfallen. He had exerted all that energy in enlisting Donald Doud to prove Edwards's innocence, all to have Edwards get caught under a tarpaulin in the basement of a building he was burglarizing. There were negotiations and it ended up with Ulysses pleading guilty and receiving a sentence of one to three years in the penitentiary."

The case of Kevin and Morris Harper, both in their early twenties, constituted a more clear-cut victory. The two were driving south on Orleans Street when they came to a fire station next to Seward Park. As they were approaching the fire station, a fire truck was backing into the station garage, having just returned from responding to an alarm.

According to the Harpers, they stopped and let the truck proceed into the station. They then eased the car forward so that it would pass the truck as soon as the truck cleared the street. As they did so, a fireman came up and kicked the car, putting a dent in it. When the two got out and looked at the dent they were attacked by more firemen: they were hit, knocked down, and kicked.

The police came and, instead of investigating the case to see who provoked the incident, charged the Harpers with battery. Morris was charged with striking a fireman on the left side of the face with his fist while Kevin was alleged to have kicked and spit at another fireman. The firemen, who were white, were not charged at all.

"We went to court with the case and were ready for trial," says Chuck. "One fireman appeared but the state said they couldn't go to trial that day because the other fireman was not available. So the case was continued.

"We went back again and the same thing happened: another continuance. We returned for a third time and this time no firemen appeared at all. The judge then dismissed the case.

"Evidently the state saw there was going to be some opposition, that we were going to question the firemen. We had photographs of the car showing the dent and were well prepared to defend the Harpers."

Had the clinic not been there, the Harpers would probably have been convicted unjustly. That is not to say that they had nothing to do with provoking the incident, despite their claims to the contrary; what is important is that they were the only ones charged and when the state discovered that the Harpers were going to contest it, they apparently didn't feel they had a case strong enough to present.

Albert Stewart's case required perseverance. He was charged with the armed robbery of Joshua Jones. Jones claimed that he had been robbed in the room of a boarding house. He was tied up and many things were taken out of the room. The robbery occurred in March 1974, but Stewart was not arrested until July. Stewart denied any involvement in the crime. During the period between March and July, Jones admitted to having seen Stewart on several occasions but did not at that time report to the police that Stewart was his assailant. Jones had no explanation for that.

"The state's attorney didn't feel they had a very strong case," states Hogren, "because of the time lag in the identification as well as the fact that the victim had seen Albert Stewart during the intervening period and had not reported him. So, in an effort to get a plea of guilty, they offered Stewart probation. That required that they reduce the charge from armed robbery to robbery. They were willing to do it because they didn't have a really good shot at getting a conviction if the case went to trial."

Jailed in July, Albert was still incarcerated in November when Chuck entered the case. Stewart said he definitely wanted to get out for his mother's birthday. He said he didn't care what it took—he would plead guilty even though he maintained he was not involved—but he wanted to get out for his mother's birthday.

Probation or not, Chuck didn't want him to enter a guilty plea, so he requested a conference with the judge. Hogren told the judge that he did not concur with the guilty plea, but since he had only been on the case for about a week and Stewart was adamant about getting out for his mother's birthday, he had no choice but to relay Albert's wishes to him, the judge.

"I will not accept a plea of guilty unless you recommend it," the judge responded. Chuck said he would not. The judge then said, "Under the circumstances, if Albert Stewart wants to get out for his mother's birthday and the state admits it does not have a strong case against him, I am going to issue an 'I' bond." That was a most unusual ruling, for armed robbery customarily calls for bail in the neighborhood of $10,000.

Once out on bail, Albert came back to court for every scheduled appearance. Although Joshua Jones, the victim, was present at the preliminary hearing, he could not be located for the trial. The state tried to subpoena him but he was never located. "Maybe Jones realized his mistake and didn't want to come to the trial," says Hogren. "In any event, the state, knowing it had a thin case, didn't look that hard for him either."

The whole ordeal ended in a dramatic and highly unusual fashion at the trial. The court called out Joshua Jones's name and the judge said that if no one answered, the case would be closed. Albert Stewart was never convicted. "I believe he was innocent," asserts Hogren. "He must be doing well because I have never heard from him since."

Resolution of family strife brings Hogren particular satisfaction. One such case involved a youthful mother of four and an

169 | THE TRIUMPHS

illegitimate father who helped support the children. Tragically, the mother could not cope with life's miseries and committed suicide.

The father, Chuck's client, subsequently gained temporary custody of the children and they were cared for by his mother, Martha Carson. Shortly later, the maternal grandmother went to court and filed a petition seeking custody of her deceased daughter's children. Her grounds included a charge of negligence on the part of Mrs. Carson.

Several hearings were held, with a social caseworker making reports. The caseworker refused to take sides, finding both homes suitable for the children. That still left the problem of the children being in the care of the father's side of the family when, in fact, his acknowledged paternity had not been legally established.

Hogren worked out a temporary arrangement in which the maternal grandmother could visit the children on Saturdays. "That visitation was important," stresses Chuck, "because the young mother had had other children who were half-brothers and sisters of these four and it was important that a relationship be maintained among all the siblings."

The arrangement worked out so well that it eventually became permanent. "Everyone was happy and the children are now well taken care of."

Despite these successes and others involving Arthur Scott, Allen Pendleton and the Oak brothers, Roy Harris, Carl Winters, etc., Chuck takes the defeats hard. His gentle exterior belies his competitive spirit and intense desire to do an effective job.

One evening, after enduring an hour of a ponderous church board meeting I got up and went into the adjoining office to get some coffee. There, with a rather glazed, aimless look on his face was Charles Hogren. Usually a faithful attender of the board meetings, Chuck showed no inclination to join the meeting. "What's the problem?" I asked.

In a courteous but flat tone Chuck replied, "We got an adverse jury verdict on a murder trial today."

After working two years on a murder case involving Roger Henderson's brother, it had finally been completed. Hogren was no longer the chief attorney for the case, but was assisting two others. He may as well have been the principal attorney, considering how hard he took the decision.

It wasn't until much later in the two and a half hour board meeting that Chuck came in. Afterward, I asked him if the case was eating him up as much as it appeared. "Man, is it ever! Won't sleep well for awhile" was his reply.

Chuck said that the jury had decided the case less on whether the prosecution had proven the defendant guilty than on whether the defense had established his innocence. "The rationale for the verdict clearly indicated that," he said with fatigue and disappointment.

I inquired whether the judge might step in and order a new trial. "It's possible, but it's very, very unlikely. It almost never happens," he said wanly. "Our best hope is to appeal it."

Despite the bleak outlook, Chuck obviously was not about to give up. He was regularly making brief phone calls whenever he was out of the board room. In the meantime, an anxious and upset defendant would simply have to hope for a break in the judicial process.

One of Hogren's toughest losses occurred in the case of two teen-agers, Dan and Paul Baxter. They were charged with armed robbery and attempted rape.

A young woman had gone out to a store late at night. She claimed that when she came out of the store two men were by the door. They followed her about a block to her building. As she was about to enter, they grabbed her, put a gun to her, and took her to another building. There they robbed her and tried to rape her, though unsuccessfully. The assailants then fled and she called the police.

About two months later Dan and Paul were at Rainbow Beach on Chicago's South Side. They saw a couple of young women, one of whom was the victim, who looked attractive. They went up to them and started a conversation. During the course of the conversation, the victim thought she recognized the two as her attackers. She told her friend to keep them engaged in conversation while she slipped off and found an officer. The officer came over and arrested them.

"It was a classic case of faulty identification. It should never have been considered adequate!" exclaims Hogren. "Anyway, they made bail and we got ready for trial. We were doing all right until it came time for the defendants to testify. They were asked, of course, as to their whereabouts on the night in question. Since the incident was now many months old, it was difficult for them to remember. One client, however, actually said that his mother had told him to say he was baby-sitting. That didn't go over very well. The other client admitted that he was unemployed but claimed he'd been working on his car which had broken down that day. It was impossible to corroborate that, however, so his testimony didn't help the situation any either.

"It was very painful to watch that process of them being torn apart in the cross-examination. That was my fault, since I probably should not have allowed them to testify in the first place."

The judge found them guilty and sentenced them to the minimum: four to five years in prison.

To Hogren it seemed a terribly unjust verdict. "It was a classic case of reasonable doubt!" says Chuck in lingering disbelief. "She gave a description of the assailants after the robbery and then not until several months later did she identify them.

"Although I could be wrong, I really feel the Baxters are innocent. At the trial, I emphasized the confrontation on the beach, that had they seen her and had they been guilty, they would have run the other way as fast as they could, for fear of being recognized. I also stressed another factor, that her brother who lived in the apartment where she was going had seen one of the assailants and couldn't identify him. There was just no corroboration of her testimony," says Hogren.

"But the judge based his ruling primarily on the defendant's testimony: that his mother told him to say he was baby-sitting. That just illustrates the fact that you have to rehearse and rehearse and rehearse the testimony of witnesses even when they are telling the truth, or they may be easily dismantled under the onslaught of cross-examination. It also goes to show that more cases are lost on the defense than on the state's side."

The Baxters are now in prison. "I've contacted them by phone a number of times, and I'm hoping they'll be paroled soon. They've been in prison for several years now and should be eligible for a parole hearing shortly," explains Hogren anxiously. At the time Chuck talked about them, the youths had served about two and a half years of their four-year minimum. The rule of thumb for parole goes pretty much like this: For a one-year sentence, parole may occur after about ten and a half months; two years—twenty-one months; four years—thirty-six months.

"It was a very bitter case," Hogren recalls. "The father, of course, was very disappointed. The whole family, especially the older brother, was overtly discourteous. They gave me very brusque treatment. They felt I hadn't prepared enough, that I could have done a lot more research, especially on the girl's background.

"I got quite a few phone calls from them for weeks afterward. I told them that I had done the best I could under the circumstances, but that the one defendant's testimony concerning the baby-sitting alibi did not help their cause.

"I understood what the kid meant—that he and his mother had sat down and tried to figure out where he'd been. I tried to get that across in court. To the best of her knowledge, the mother had gone to the track that night and so one of the fellows was given the chore of baby-sitting for the younger children."

Not unexpectedly, Chuck internalized much of the Baxters' criticism, blaming himself. "I've been very unhappy, very upset about it," says Chuck, showing obvious signs that the three-year-old adverse verdict still preys on his mind. "I feel guilty about it and sort of blame myself because I think I could have done better if I had to do it all over again. The case came up faster than I expected it to, so I wasn't as prepared as I would have liked. I lost sleep over that one."

It never seems to occur to Hogren that he may be demanding the impossible from himself. Deluged with cases, he is his own interviewer, researcher, and attorney; one wonders how he is able to present an effective defense at all.

Asked about how he deals with defeat, Hogren replies, "If I have a bad case, I may wake up at three or four in the morning because I just can't sleep. I get up for awhile and then go back to bed. Sometimes I have difficulty eating and I become very reclusive. It's just very tough to take the losses."

173 | THE TRIUMPHS

Fortunately, not all judges operate as capriciously as the one in the Baxters' case. Chuck had an extremely pleasant experience while trying to bail the beleaguered cat lover, Lisa Thompson, out of jail.

Knowing that she had put up $500 for bail on her traffic cases, Hogren couldn't understand how she could have been sent to the House of Correction, from where she called Lynette.

By the time Chuck got to the court late in the afternoon, it was closed and the judge had gone for the day.

"There were three clerks still there, finishing up some paper work," recalls Hogren. "None of them really wanted to get involved in Lisa's dilemma because it was the end of the day. They were tired and about to go home. But one of the clerks did say, 'I remember her being in here and I'll see what I can do. Follow me.'

"We ran out of the courtroom into another one where the judge ordinarily would be. Court was over and he wasn't there, so we scurried around looking for him. Finally the clerk went back into some offices and found him.

"The judge was a young man. He came up to me and said, 'What can I do for you?' I explained that I represented Lisa Thompson, that she had serious problems—fifty-two traffic tickets—and that we had raised the bond money for her.

"The judge said that when she had been in court on one of the charges she had hurled some papers at him and verbally abused him. She did not mention anything about being on bail. He said he dismissed some of the moving violations, but neither she nor anything in her folder indicated that she had made bail. So, he set bail at $1,000, requiring her to pay $100. She didn't have it and was sent to the House of Correction.

"The judge, upon seeing the bond in the amount of $500 and realizing it covered the same charges for which he had set bail, acknowledged it was a mistake and took steps to correct it. He decided to issue an 'I' bond in the amount of $1,000. We couldn't find any clerk to write the bond because it was now after hours, so we went to the chief clerk's office and found a person there who could write bonds. There's only one place in the building where 'I' bonds are kept and fortunately the desk drawer was open. So the clerk took one, prepared it, and the judge signed it.

174 | THE RELUCTANT DEFENDER

"The judge then called the jail himself, told the person who answered what had happened and that I was coming over to get Lisa. He determined over the phone exactly what documents I needed, so we wouldn't have to waste any time. He prepared them and sent me over to the House of Correction. A little later that evening I bailed Lisa out and drove her home. She was reunited with her eight or ten cats." It was a humanitarian act on the part of the judge, to rectify the mistake after being so shabbily treated by Lisa, and Chuck appreciated it. "It certainly demonstrates that all is not evil and vicious in the system, by any means," he says with a smile.

Chuck counts few successes sweeter than the case of Rodney Tolan, who was charged with armed robbery.

Rodney, who owned a car, was on the north side of Cabrini at a party. Three of his friends, John Fulton, Joe Darwin, and Eddie Freeman, asked him to drive them to the south side. Tolan agreed to do so. On the way he had a flat tire. Seeing an open gas station, he pulled up in front and motioned to the attendant to ask him if he could use the air hose. The attendant said he could and Rodney proceeded to fill the tire.

While he was doing that, his three companions got out of the car and went into the service station. After filling the tire, Tolan went in to the station to get change for some cigarettes in addition to the washroom key. Upon returning from the washroom, Tolan found, much to his surprise, that his companions had tied up the attendant and his associates in the back room and robbed them of all the money. Rodney and his companions got back into the car and drove away. They traveled only about four blocks before they were apprehended.

Rodney's defense was that he had no knowledge of the others' intention to rob the service station. The state's position was that, even though he didn't, he was accountable because he drove the getaway car. After all, he could have driven off alone and left them there. But he didn't.

Chuck believed it might be better not to go to trial, because of the theory of accountability. Rodney did drive the getaway car and, besides, the court might not believe his claim of ignorance anyway. Morally Tolan was innocent, but legally he might not be. To risk a trial, possibly losing the whole thing

THE TRIUMPHS

and having Rodney sentenced to a minimum of four years in prison, might be less prudent than to plea bargain for a lighter sentence. "I was very worried about it," says Hogren, recalling his uncertainty.

Chuck talked with the state's attorney at the preliminary hearing and the prosecutor said, "If Rodney pleads guilty to a lesser charge of robbery, we'll give him a year's probation." Hogren leaped at the offer. However, when the state found out that the others intended to plead "not guilty" because they wouldn't get anything less than a prison sentence by pleading guilty, the state's attorney changed his mind, claiming that he had to keep the case together and try all four as one.

Chuck succeeded in gaining a severance—separating Rodney Tolan's case from the others because his defense was different. Initially, Fulton, Darwin, and Freeman said, "No, we were never at the station; it's a matter of mistaken identity." Rodney said, "Yes, we were all there, but I had nothing to do with it." So, the defenses were in conflict and Tolan couldn't be tried with the others.

After Hogren obtained the severance, but prior to the trial of Rodney's companions, Chuck again tried to bargain for a one-year probation. He had to deal with a different state's attorney, but one from the same office as the first. The prosecutor would hear none of it. "One year's probation for that? Never! That offense requires several years in a penitentiary," he said.

The state's attorney was, however, willing to strike a deal. "If Tolan will take the stand and testify against the other three, then we'll give him one year's probation on the lesser charge of robbery."

Chuck presented the offer to Tolan. He refused, saying, "No, my life would be in jeopardy if I did that. I've already been threatened by Eddie Freeman. My life wouldn't be worth a nickel if I went on for the state. I'd much rather do time in the pen alive than go on the stand against them."

When the state's attorney heard that Tolan wouldn't testify he said Tolan would have to do time in the penitentiary. The other three then went to trial, and although they initially denied involvement, when the jury was chosen and was seated in the box they knew things didn't look very favorable because the victims were present in the courtroom and ready to testify.

They decided right then and there to change their tune. Pleading guilty just prior to the beginning of testimony, they were given prison sentences.

Then came a break. Rodney's case was transferred from the criminal court to the Civic Center and a new state's attorney was appointed to handle it. Hogren talked with him about probation. The prosecutor reviewed the file and noticed that the other three had pleaded guilty. After further negotiation, he agreed to five years' probation. Tolan snapped up the offer.

"We dealt with three different state's attorneys from the same office, all making different offers," says Chuck. "Fortunately the final one agreed to probation. The judge was very upset about it. He didn't think the case merited probation, but he went along reluctantly with the agreement.

"I am happy to say that Rodney Tolan is very ambitious, almost a hustler type. He made the most of his opportunity and went into business for himself immediately. He developed a company which makes and sells sheets. He has a garage on the South Side, receives the material from a mill in the South, and has some people from Cabrini with sewing machines help him make the sheets. He then sells them door-to-door.

"He is very industrious. He has done other door-to-door type selling as well. I've never heard of his getting into any trouble again.

"In fact I still hear from him from time to time. When he started his business he asked me to help him set it up. I referred him to a corporation lawyer supplied by Fourth Presbyterian Church who could certainly help him. Because of that referral, Rodney got first-class advice about how to go into business."

With about half of his probation served, Rodney, twenty-six, is married and has several children.

"He was very appreciative," recalls Hogren warmly. "I represented his brother later on another matter. I've met the whole family and they all appreciate the help they have received. It's tremendously gratifying."

Some clients have rather unusual ways of showing their gratitude to Hogren for his help. Richard Elliott, the shoplifter, regularly came bearing gifts. "Every time I saw him he gave me something from his store of goods," says Chuck. "I have a collection of items—neckties, sunglasses, a very nice shirt—in a filing cabinet. Once he asked me if I wouldn't like a nice tie.

177 | THE TRIUMPHS

He asked me what my favorite color was. I told him brown. Lo and behold, shortly thereafter Richard appeared with a very expensive brown silk tie. At first I did wear it, but I've set it aside since. I think it was lifted from Marshall Field's and I'm going to take it back there."

Such methods of expressing gratitude make the scrupulously honest Hogren uncomfortable. They do, however, provide an insight into the kind of moral code by which some of his clients operate. Good people are those who will help them and bad people are those who hurt them, regardless of what side of the law the people are on.

Appreciation and changed lives energize Hogren's spirit. Mark Mayberry, age twenty, was arrested on a variety of charges, the most serious being the armed robbery of a store on East Delaware. Mark and two accomplices went into the establishment with a handgun, ordered the victim to the rear of the store, tied him up with a vacuum cleaner cord, and stole a jacket and the money from the cash register. The police arrived and arrested the intruders while they were still in the store.

Mark was unemployed and a heavy user of alcohol at the time. Since then he has changed his ways and, from the penitentiary, writes Chuck appreciative letters like those below:

> Dear Mr. Hogren,
> I am in another penitentiary now. I was shipped out Friday. Things are a lot better here. Mostly we have had a lot of tests. I don't know whether I am going to stay here or not. However I will try to. I heard the only thing they have over here is they're school. Well, that's all I want anyway.
> Mr. Hogren, I want to thank you for coming to court, trying to help me each time you did. I know you knew I was likely guilty. I have never been arrested for something that I didn't do. I know your caseload was and still is full but you seemed to take out time. I know you couldn't do much for me on this case but I am grateful and maybe when I am out I will have some way to show it.
> I have to ask you one last favor. You see, my bond slip is in my name and my mother really needs the money. The check will be in my name and she won't be able to cash it. Can you get the slip transfered to her name or some way get the check cashed for her? If you can help please call her and let her know because she is going to send me some of it and I need it too. I know you probably won't take it but she will probably try to give you some of it too. I've written her and asked her to call you

but I don't know if she has yet. I hope I'm not asking to much. But if you can help, I will be much obliged. Well, I am going now. I wish you all the good luck, a Merry Christmas, and a Happy New Year!

Take care. Mark.

Dear Mr. Hogren,

Please give my best wishes to your staff and especially your secretary and tell her that I hope that she doesn't think bad of me for coming to your office high. I was in a kind of depressed state and I couldn't wait for it to wear off because I had to get there before you closed down. Tell that young attorney that I am grateful for his appearing as your sub and trying to keep them from snatching me but Frank Wilson was set on locking me up. It's funny that I don't hold any grudges against the court or the state's attorney. I guess it's because of all the things I have done. I have been throwing bricks at the pen for a good while.

All of that is behind me now though, I have been looking ahead, far ahead. I only want to better myself. My birthday is on the ninth and I will be 19 and soon to be 21. I've got to have something, to be somebody. I have lived fast without gaining and now I believe I truly see the light. I only wish I could have noticed myself ten years ago.

Sometimes when I am just lying in my bed thinking of people I have known I think of you and your warmness and your straight forward answers. I didn't know much about lawyers and I am glad you didn't kid me about the case. I want you to know that I think of you as one of my best personal friends and I will always wish the best for you at home and at your office. I am closing my letter now. If you have time write me back. I will write you again.

Take care. Mark.

THE MEN IN BLUE

11

Ira Ronald Clark, age nineteen, had recently come up from the South and was living with his brother who owns an antique store on LaSalle and Division. Clark was shot once in the head by a white police officer, Wallace Polk, while he and two companions were being arrested for burglary at the rear of a row house on North Cambridge.

The police claimed that Polk and his partner separated while chasing the three suspects for about a block and a half. When Polk rejoined his partner the three youths were on the ground. Ron Clark ran to a tree as Polk called to him to stop and when Clark made a sudden move, Polk fired.

Residents of Cabrini-Green who witnessed the shooting had a different version. They contended that it occurred without provocation while Ron was kneeling on the ground. Beatrice Parker, who said she saw the shooting from her bedroom window only ten feet away, claimed Clark was virtually prone on the ground when Polk abruptly put his gun to Clark's head and fired. Abraham Norton was with his family on their back porch when he saw the killing. Norton stated that the three youths were stretched out on the ground with Polk and his partner standing over them. Norton claimed Polk shouted racial epithets and other abusive things at Clark, repeating, "Don't move! Do you want to die?" and then shot him, after which Polk yelled, "Die, you nigger! Die!" Others who came over after the shooting said that Ron, who died in nearby Henrotin Hospital, was lying face down with his hands clasped behind his head.

No guns or other weapons were found on any of the three.

Who is to say exactly what happened? The fact remains, however, that that type of incident—the killing of a suspect who has no weapon—almost never occurs in white, middle-class neighborhoods. It is common, however, in Cabrini-Green and other poor areas. And incidents like that polarize the police and the community.

Dr. Paul Mundy of Loyola University has said, "Among the police are the most noble and most savage of society." Policemen are often not regarded as humans, but merely automatons in blue uniforms. Yet the entire span of human quality is there. Just as there are honest and honorable politicians, lawyers, physicians, and teachers, there are also honest and honorable policemen. But just as there are corrupt and uncaring politicians, lawyers, physicians, and teachers, there are also corrupt and uncaring policemen.

The police brutality cases and other excesses dealt with by the legal aid clinic include both the actions of the less honorable among the police and the actions of those who make instant and sometimes incorrect decisions under pressure. They also involve policemen who may feel so much tension and frustration with a given day's activity that the breaking point is reached and cutting loose serves as a way of venting rage and frustration.

Nonetheless, the instances of misconduct are not rare. Charles Fisher came into the clinic. He said the police had come to his home when he wasn't there. They left a note for him to come down to the 18th District station for questioning about a burglary he had witnessed. He went voluntarily the next afternoon.

While he was there he signed a statement indicating that although he had seen the burglary in progress he did not know the names of any of the participants. He claimed he would be able to recognize some of their faces if he were to see them again.

Evidently the police weren't happy about that limited form of identification. Charles said that while the questioning was going on an officer pounded on his leg four times with his fist. Fisher was then released to his mother's custody.

According to Hogren, "It is fairly common for clients to say that they were in some way beaten or intimidated by the police following their arrest, and not always at the station. On some occasions victims have been driven to other locations and beaten in an alley or en route to the station."

Barry Carlton also had a scrape with the police. Carlton was charged in a misdemeanor complaint with the offense of battery. He was alleged to have intentionally and without provocation caused bodily harm and an abrasion to the left side of the neck of a patrolman, Ernest Harrelson.

According to a statement sworn to by Darlene Gray, age sixteen, Barry was drinking with some friends in the hallway of a Cabrini-Green high-rise building. Three sixteen-year-old girls were with him. The arresting officers came up to see where the beer drinking was taking place. They asked Barry to come to the station. He gave his drink to Darlene and said he was coming. One officer then threw him against the wall, while the other tried to put handcuffs on him. When Barry said it wasn't necessary to put handcuffs on him an officer told him not to get smart and threw him to the floor. Carlton required treatment at a hospital for the injuries he sustained in the scuffle. While this was going on, Darlene ran down to the Carlton apartment to call Barry's mother.

An interesting aspect of the case is that the arresting officers filled out a report which indicated that the defendant did not resist arrest. That was in direct contradiction to their verbal statement in court. "How that happened, I don't know," says Hogren, "but it came out at the trial that on the report, written on the very day of the incident, it was clearly stated that the defendant had not resisted arrest."

Further, there was quite a bit of suspicion on the part of Barry, his mother, and others that officer Harrelson had himself been drinking. In fact, when they got to the station—a substation in the Cabrini building—the officer had become violent and said he was going to kill Barry. Mrs. Carlton, having accompanied her son to the station, was fearful that Harrelson would kill her son right there. At the substation Mrs. Carlton complained to the commanding officer that patrolman Harrelson was drunk, so he ordered Harrelson to take a breathalyzer test. According to Mrs. Carlton, however, Harrelson was not required to take the test cold. He was given an opportunity to influence the machine by smoking a number of cigarettes prior to having the test administered.

At the trial, the judge acquitted Barry Carlton. The reason for the acquittal was that although the officers got up in court and claimed that Barry had struck Harrelson and had to be restrained in order to get him to the substation, the arrest report indicated no such problem. That constituted contrary evidence. Moreover, the judge felt that no battery had occurred. The injury to the officer which he alleged to be a neck injury turned out to be, at most, a fingernail scratch.

Because of the conduct of the police, Barry Carlton filed a brutality complaint with the Director of Internal Affairs. The following reply was received:

> Pursuant to the registration of the complaint an investigation was initiated concerning the allegations of misconduct on the part of the accused officer. After exhausting all investigative resources, no evidence was obtained which would justify sustaining the allegation and taking disciplinary action against the accused officer.

This is a standard, preprinted form. The officer's name does not even appear on it, and it is addressed "Dear Sir/Madam" in order to make it applicable to all situations. It indicates that this is a very common response to brutality charges. Chuck found that, in complaints of that type, 91 percent end with such a letter being sent to the plaintiff.

Jerry Hampton, who had applied to take the Civil Service examination to join the police force, probably had second thoughts after his experience with the men in blue. Hampton had been invited to the home of Mary and Amy Johnson for the evening. The three were in the living room listening to the radio while a twelve-year-old sister of the Johnsons, Yvonne Barker, was running through the house.

Suddenly about twenty uniformed officers came bursting into

the house. They had no search warrant but came because they suspected that some material, stolen earlier from a freight car, was probably stored in the house. As it turned out, nothing was found and their suspect, Jerry Hampton, was not charged with burglary. Based on the ensuing row, however, he was charged with battery and disorderly conduct.

After breaking in, the police ordered all the occupants into the kitchen and questioned them. The officers, obviously dissatisfied with the results of their "investigation," then set off a genuine confrontation. They stood around the kitchen table and in a mocking tone sang "We Shall Overcome" and "The Battle Hymn of the Republic."

When little Yvonne took down a knife an officer pulled out his gun and shouted, "Stop, bitch, or I'll shoot!"

With that Jerry exclaimed, "Don't shoot her!"

Another officer turned and snarled, "Who are you to tell him what to do? You aren't his boss!"

"I'm not his boss, but she only took the knife down to open the back door," Jerry replied sarcastically.

"Take him out," one of the officers ordered. Two officers grabbed Hampton.

Mary Johnson, later a witness in court, then said, "If he's going, I am too."

With that, Amy Johnson started kicking one of the officers. He responded by throwing her onto the kitchen table. "Can't you see she's pregnant!" one of the residents screamed. The officer, obviously enraged, continued to jostle her around.

The officers then turned out the lights and put a flashlight in Hampton's face. They handcuffed him and took him downstairs. When they got outside, the cuffs were removed and several officers began hitting him. "Run get your mother!" Jerry shouted to Theresa Johnson who was also at the scene.

An officer then jumped out of the car and hit Hampton in the face ordering him to "shut his mouth." In the gangway, the donnybrook continued with Hampton being choked and hit in the face.

At the trial, the judge did not find Jerry Hampton guilty. However, because Hampton was known for having a hair-trigger temper and turning hostile whenever provoked, he was placed on six months' supervision. The judge said he realized what had probably happened in the melee and said he would continue the case for six months. If after that period no further trouble occurred it would be dropped. It was dropped.

Pastor Bill Leslie talked about the police. "The police admit that only about 200 of the then approximately 13 or 14,000 kids in Cabrini were involved in the Martin Luther King riots. They remarked to me that many of the mothers kept their kids in when that 200 were on the rampage. I can tell you that the mothers deserve a lot of credit for keeping their kids straight. Many place a heavy moral emphasis on life and the kids respect them."

Leslie has had his own experiences with the police. "One night I was working with the kids in our youth program," he says. "I was wearing a hooded sweatshirt and placing in my car a chair I had taken to the church from home. I was parked in front of the church. As I brought the chair out, two unmarked squad cars suddenly pulled up alongside my car, jackknifing it in. The officers jumped out and slammed me spread-eagle over the hood of my car. They wanted to know where I was going with the chair. I told them, "That's my name up there on that sign; I'm the minister of this church." They were embarrassed and apologized immediately. Now if I had come out with a suit and tie on, I could have carried that chair anywhere I wanted.

"The harassment so many of the Cabrini-Green people go through produces a lot of bitterness. But in talking with the police, I find they really believe that harassment will keep down crime. They admit to doing it. They say that if the kids know that if the police get close enough to them to see what they look like and are able to identify them, it will have a deterring effect.

"Harassment takes many forms. For example, the police may stop a black youngster driving through the community with four kids in the car. They'll tell the occupants to get out of the car and search it for drugs. In some cases reported to me, the police have had some marijuana up their sleeve and then claimed they found it in the glove compartment of the vehicle."

Policemen interviewed for this book also acknowledged that harassment goes on. Two, Bill Martin and Sid Levin, officers at the substation in the Cabrini-Green high-rise building, talked about it. "If a policeman just stops a car with four teen-agers in it, he has no reason to do that," said Martin, a fifty-five-ish, gray-haired black lieutenant. "Simply seeing them is not enough reason. The kid is driving, sees the blue car light go on, and says 'Doggone!' Scaring him like that is just not necessary.

"Getting tough is not always defensible. If you get your tail kicked by the police without justification, you're going to be resentful," Martin continued.

"Or if you as a citizen are doing something wrong but everyone else is doing it too and you're the only one to get your butt kicked, you'll also resent it," Levin, a bright-eyed, forty-five-year-old sergeant chimed in. "A policeman always has to make judgment calls. Interpretation is the name of the game, and what a policeman may call justifiable, a citizen may feel is harassment. Besides, a policeman in a bad mood can find a way to harass justifiably."

Levin harked back to his own youth with a mischievous grin. "Just to give you an illustration of how effective butt-kicking is, my first experience with the police happened when I was about ten years old. I was climbing up the side of a billboard and a policeman came up and whacked me across the rear with his nightstick. He didn't really hurt me, but I was sore for about four or five days. I decided I'd lay low for awhile and get even. Finally one day I got up on that billboard and as the policeman walked underneath it I dropped a brick on his head. So you see, just being real tough isn't always so smart."

Fear of the police is paramount in Cabrini-Green. The case in which Leon Grand and Elbert Hayes were charged with armed robbery and aggravated battery provides some examples.

A thirty-five-year-old white woman was walking down Larrabee from Montgomery Ward's with her eight-year-old son. As she reached the building where her husband worked she was accosted by two men who robbed her and viciously beat her with a gun butt, almost breaking her nose.

One of the defendants was picked up on the following day and taken to the police station. The other simply walked into the station to inquire why his friend had been arrested. That circumstance definitely augurs well for the two defendants' innocence. That's not all. The police officer reportedly now states that he knows those two did not commit the offense. The woman's son was unable to identify the defendants in a lineup, although when he came to the preliminary hearing, he lied, claiming he had identified them.

However, because the woman identified Grant and Hayes, they have to stand trial. The identification procedure itself was rather bizarre. While the victim was in the hospital, photographs were taken to her and, on that basis, she made a tentative identification of one and a positive identification of the other. The two were then brought over to the hospital the following day for the woman to make an in-person identification.

The case has another interesting twist. Just thirty days earlier, Grant had had a run-in with the police officer who arrested him. Grant saw the patrolman drive recklessly through the community, killing a six-year-old boy. A hostile crowd quickly gathered at the scene. The police officer asked Grant to hold back the incensed throng. Grant, having seen the officer's negligence, refused to honor the request. Fearful for his own safety, the officer radioed for help, bringing an ambulance and a spate of other officers to the scene. A month later the same officer, who now admits he may have been wrong, arrested Grant on armed robbery and aggravated battery a full day after the woman was accosted.

The attack on the woman occurred at about eleven on a Saturday morning. At least fifteen people were sitting on a nearby stairway and witnessed the event. Only one of them will testify in defense of Grant and Hayes. Others have been contacted but say they don't want to get involved. They're afraid they'll be charged with something if they contradict the police version of the incident. They are so fearful that they won't testify even though it may mean a minimum of four years in prison for two of their neighbors.*

Locating witnesses and getting them to testify is one of the real frustrations for Hogren. In one case, a woman claimed she had been beaten and robbed by two of Chuck's clients. She was in the hospital as a result of her injuries and made her identification of the defendants there. According to the defendants, the woman was heavily sedated at the time and was really in

---

*As this book goes to press, Grant and Hayes have indeed been declared guilty. Hogren intends to appeal the verdict.

no condition to make an accurate identification, but the police told her what to say.

Chuck went to the hospital and questioned the victim. "Did the police bring the alleged assailants to the room?" he inquired.

"Yes, they did," she replied.

"Is that how the identification was made?" Chuck asked.

"Yes."

According to Hogren, it was a very suggestive identification, but legal under the circumstances. Fortunately, the woman had a roommate and she, of course, would be the best person to corroborate the defendants' claim that the victim was not in a proper state to make the identification when the youths were brought in. Chuck subpoenaed the hospital records, found who the roommate was, and got her records. Regrettably, the records indicated she was also in poor condition on the day in question.

Chuck located the woman, nonetheless, and talked to her. The woman claimed she couldn't remember the event and would have to think about it. Hogren called her back and again she repeated she had to think about the matter. Finally she told Chuck that her doctor had instructed her not to get involved, leaving Chuck and his clients in a perilous position for a defense. The case is now being tried.

In another incident, Chuck located an ideal witness in a murder case. It wasn't easy to find her, but after knocking on door after door Hogren reached the key witness.

Murder being the charge, self-defense was the defendant's plea. At issue was the character of the victim. Hogren needed to demonstrate that the victim, a teen-ager, was a violent person, one who would be the aggressor in almost any situation.

Chuck wanted the woman to testify to an event she had experienced which was illustrative of the victim's violent character. She had seen the victim in his front yard as an elderly couple came up the street pushing a grocery cart. Seeing them approaching, the youth went into the yard and piled up some rocks behind a bush. As the elderly couple passed in front of the yard, the kid leaped out from behind the bush and began hurling rocks at them.

The witness opened a window and yelled at him to stop. He did, but when she came out of her home, he started throwing rocks at her. He then crossed the street and threw more rocks at the woman's house, breaking a window. After she screamed, he moved on and threw stones at the house next door.

In the actual murder incident, Hogren's client claimed he shot the victim as the youth and three others were about to break into his house. The state contended that the youngster was shot while still in the street from the defendant's porch. At any rate, the testimony of the woman concerning the rock-throwing episode would be helpful to the defense in indicating the youth's aggressive propensities.

Again, the witness wanted to think it over. She said she didn't want to get involved. Her neighbor prevailed upon her to testify, claiming that injustice might result if she did not. Her response was that she had gotten involved in a similar situation before and it had backfired. Hogren stressed that a person's freedom might be on the line. He begged her to come, offering transportation to court and other courtesies. Finally, she simply stated that her son told her not to go. She was intractable. She said she lived alone and was afraid of possible retaliation by the victim's family—hardly an imagined fear, given their reputation.

Hogren says, "That was one of the most frustrating experiences I've ever had. The man was convicted."

On the same day Chuck was describing that discouraging experience, he had to talk to the proprietor of a store who claimed that one of Hogren's clients had robbed him. "That presumes he will even talk to me," says Chuck. "Then we have an appointment with another witness at five-thirty in her home. I'm taking Lynette along because you always have to have two people interview witnesses, and she's very good at easing people's fears, especially women's."

Policemen in Cabrini-Green have been known to take oppressive advantage of the people's powerlessness. One well-respected white pastor long in the neighborhood is privy to a practice illustrating this. "I know that many times when a crime was committed the police would come around and arrest a whole pile of kids they knew had been in trouble before or who they were suspicious of. Then they'd come around and have sex with a kid's mother as a necessary condition for dropping the charges against the youngster and allowing him to go free. I've known that to happen nine or ten times.

"White policemen and black mothers! Many of the families lived in two-room dwellings, so the kids could see what was going on—that their mother was going to have sex with the officer. The kids I have talked with were very, very bitter about that."

Doris Billings, a twenty-three-year-old heroin addict already mentioned, had a distantly related experience with the men in blue. Chuck, having known Doris since she was eight, has been in the Billings home often for dinner. "From a broken home, Doris somehow drifted into prostitution," says Chuck, speaking in euphemisms. "She would be in and out of it sporadically."

Late one evening Doris was sitting with several other people on the stairway of her building in Uptown. She had a gun under her coat, a .22-caliber sawed-off rifle. A police officer drove by and questioned her. He picked up her coat and noticed the gun. Doris was charged with unlawfully carrying a concealed weapon on or about her person.

Although Doris admitted being guilty of having the gun, she felt she was unjustifiably searched. The policeman, she felt, really had no reason to stop her and conduct the search; the situation did not constitute "probable cause." Chuck agreed. "It has been my experience," says Hogren, "that in such cases policemen will occasionally fabricate a story in order to justify their search. Many times the story will hold up in court. Nonetheless, I told Doris we would prepare a motion to have the matter determined by a judge."

At a hearing on the motion to suppress, Chuck went through an elaborate recitation of the facts, stressing that the police officer simply had no valid reason to conduct the search. He even had Doris testify.

Fully expecting a vigorous denunciation along with a wholly different version of the event by the state's attorney, Hogren was shocked when the prosecutor simply rested his case. He didn't refute Hogren's presentation. He said nothing.

Chuck couldn't believe it. Neither could the judge. "What do you mean? You haven't even cross-examined the witness," the judge asked incredulously.

"We have nothing to present. We do not contest the version given by the defense," rejoined the state's attorney.

"I have no choice then but to find that this was an illegal search and seizure," stated the judge. "Therefore the use of the gun as evidence will be suppressed."

The state's attorney pressed on. "Without the gun we have no evidence—we have no way of proving our case," said the prosecutor. "Therefore I move the case be dismissed."

"Case dismissed!" ruled the judge.

As they were leaving the court Chuck's head was spinning. Cases just aren't won that easily. He turned to Doris and asked, "What in the world happened here? Why didn't they fight the case? Do you have any idea?"

Doris knew. "In the past few weeks since I was arrested I've gotten to know that police officer pretty well," she said with a grin.

Getting cut in on some action is often tempting for the police. "In one case two youngsters were charged with possession of narcotics," remembers Chuck. "During a recess in the trial I noticed the detective who had uncovered the drugs out in the hall talking to the defendants. I asked them what the discussion was all about. 'Oh, he wanted to make a deal and be dealt in on the drug money in exchange for going easy on us,' said the youth."

"One problem the police have is that a lot of the crime that goes on in this neighborhood is committed by people from other parts of the city," says Bill Leslie. "They can come in on the subway or by car, commit a crime, and then leave—knowing that no one, not even the blacks living here, will be able to recognize them."

Leslie has talked to a number of policemen about respect for the residents as persons. "They say that things happen so fast around here that part of disarming a person involves catching him by surprise. They also contend that it's always the nice guys among the police who get shot and killed. You can go down the list of all the Chicago policemen who've been killed, they say, and invariably it will be the nice guys who tried to treat everybody with respect. They say, 'We're out there putting our lives on the line and we're not going to take any

191 | THE MEN IN BLUE

chances.' From their point of view it's a tough job for what they're getting paid. I'm not sure I'd want it either. When you add the lack of cooperation they get from the community to the other difficulties of the job, it's tough."

To form my own impressions for this book, I decided to talk to the police myself. That is no easy task, since Chicago policemen aren't given to generous ventures of self-expression to those who write about the urban scene. Nonetheless, after spending a day with them I found them generally cooperative and responsive, albeit often in contradiction. They were, for the most part, nondefensive and even self-critical at points. Moreover, they seemed to evince genuine concern for the community they were to "serve and protect." Even the most authoritarian among them seemed to have at least a well-intentioned paternalism toward the Cabrini-Green residents, feeling it was their job to protect the "law-abiding" citizenry. There were no "niggers," "black bastards," or any other such epithets hurled by any. The strongest term used was "punks," and then only to refer to several youths who attacked an officer on duty.

Chuck had arranged an appointment for me with Sergeant Hutton, officer in charge of neighborhood relations. Hogren warned me that Hutton was very reluctant to see me but had consented to a ten a.m. appointment in his office.

When I arrived, I found Sgt. Hutton in a telephone-boothlike office surrounded with people. I peeked in and he told me he'd be at least a half hour late for our appointment. I went into an adjoining courtroom to wait. There, child support and public aid cases were being heard by a rather free-wheeling female black judge. At one point when a defendant either didn't seem to understand or was reluctant about responding to a question regarding his "livelihood," she asked him what his "hustle" was.

I sat in the back row sporadically reading a paperback but tuning in to the more interesting and amusing aspects of the goings-on. Chuckling with the rest of the audience at one point, I was surprised when a bailiff marched up to me and warned me that if the judge were to see me reading rather than paying rapt attention I would be held in contempt of court. I soon left for Hutton's office.

Hutton motioned me in. "I don't remember what you're here for, but this isn't confidential, is it?" he asked me brusquely, in the company of four or five others, not police officers.

It seemed a *fait accompli,* so I said, "No, it doesn't have to be."

"I remember this has something to do about writing a book about Cabrini-Green and the police, doesn't it?"

I explained my mission to him, emphasizing my desire to get the police side of the Cabrini-Green/police relationship.

Expecting Hutton to launch into a dissertation on the trials and tribulations of working in Cabrini, I was surprised at his response. "Go ahead, fire away," he said, leaning back in his chair.

I did. "What is the number-one problem the police have in Cabrini-Green?"

"Lack of cooperation on the part of victims. They sign a complaint and then don't show up in court."

"What about police-community relations?" I asked.

Hutton jumped that one. "I guarantee you I could go over there day or night, walk a block and fifty people would call me by my first name. Ninety-nine percent of them are wonderful people; I got lots of friends over there. If I were to go over there now a hundred kids would run up and say, 'Hey Bilko!' That's my nickname.

"Here, look at this. You can't see it from there, come over here," Hutton impatiently ordered, motioning me over to his desk to look at a picture under the glass. "This is my godchild," he said proudly as he pointed at the picture of a black infant. "See? Blacker than the ace of spades!" I was embarrassed for the blacks sitting in the office. "I got lots of friends over there," Hutton repeated with bravado.

"What about hostility toward the police?" I queried, hoping to elicit some comment about community problems. Up to that point one would have gotten the impression that the crime rate in the community was zero, the residents being too busy seeking to recruit godparents from among the police.

"We don't put up with vandalism," Hutton said firmly. "You can see vandalism in some of these buildings. When we notice a kid doing that, we grab him! And of course when you crack down on some kid destroying property he ain't going to like you. It produces hostility.

"Look, if you get in a fight with someone, what happens?" Hutton asked, remaining on the offensive. "You get hostility, that's what happens. Right?

"We don't have trouble in the community," he added. "I got fifty-seven officers detailed in Cabrini and 80 percent of them are volunteers. I've been here since 1962 and my car has never been touched. It says 'neighborhood relations' right on it. They all know my car.

"And another thing, we run basketball tournaments, baseball leagues, and summer camps with the kids. I've never had any difficulty with anyone in Cabrini. Yet all we get is bad publicity. Who ever writes about Elax Taylor (the local resident who opened his basement to youth as an informal recreation center)? You should talk to him. He's right over at 911 Hudson. You never hear about him." (Hutton did get his wish. Shortly after the interview, Taylor was publicly honored for his generosity.)

"What are the main causes of crime in Cabrini?" I asked, pressing to break through Hutton's *macho* shield.

"No comment. I've got my own ideas about that, but I don't want to talk about them."

We then went back to the subject of community relations. Hutton was eager to tell me about Christmas baskets for needy families, the distribution of free tickets to Cubs and White Sox games for the youth, as well as other initiatives on the part of the police to show care for the Cabrini residents.

It was informative and encouraging to hear of Hutton's efforts to relate to the community. There was little doubt that he did care about the people and considered them his friends. Nevertheless, he remained foursquare in asserting that the relationship between the police and the community was nothing short of idyllic. It all seemed quite defensive. I found it interesting that he demanded that I leave my name and address with his secretary as I left.

I pushed on, hoping to talk with others. I ambled over to the patrolman in charge of the tactical unit. He courteously but firmly informed me he couldn't talk to me at all. It would have to be cleared with the director of press relations "downtown." He said I might want to go down a floor and talk with the district commander.

Downstairs I went, in search of the commander. I spoke to a

pleasant forty-five-year-old officer with wire-rimmed glasses named Gene Keller. Keller tried to reach the mysterious director by telephone. While he did, I sought to worm some information out of him. "We had some trouble over in Cabrini just yesterday," he volunteered. "We got a call about an abandoned automobile. We dispatched two officers to the scene. They looked at the car, and as they were examining it two young punks came up. One had a lead pipe and started swinging at the officers, knocking one of the men's glasses off. The police were just doing their job, but the kids wouldn't even let them explain that they were just following up a complaint. They just don't understand authority over there," said Keller matter-of-factly.

After reaching the director of press relations Keller informed me that the official could give no clearances, but that any officer who wanted to talk could do so on his own. Keller then arranged for me to go over to the substation located in one of the high-rise buildings to talk to Lieutenant Martin and Sergeant Levin. In addition, the helpful officer arranged for a patrolman, Earl Rammer, to drive me over to the substation.

Rammer, about thirty, is a handsome, husky, *macho*-appearing white officer. He exudes guts and sensitivity.

The day was warm and sunny as we drove over to the substation. I sensed an openness in Rammer and so invited his reflections. "I feel the Chicago Police Department is doing an injustice to the blacks, Puerto Ricans, chicanos, and for that matter, to the whites as well. They're not being adequately protected," he announced.

"Look, 80 percent of the people in Cabrini-Green want more, not less police protection. Only about 20 percent want the police out. In that building 160 people want the police here," he continued, pointing at the project building containing the substation, "and 40 don't. I've got four little girls. I don't want me killed by some gunner. These people are no different.

"You read about police raids and gun pinches, but no one will ever know how many crimes have been prevented by those activities. The police department is scared of bad publicity. I've worked this area for seven years. I remember when the tactical unit was sent in here to break up the gangs. A sixteen-year-old kid started shooting at them, and they returned fire. I'm not here to get killed and neither are the people. The community group rose up, we got bad publicity, and the tactical unit was pulled out.

"Back around '70 five girls were hit on Cleveland Street by gang gunfire. One lost an eye from a bullet. So the police, in order to demonstrate to the community they wanted to help and be friends, took on the 'walk and talk' assignment. The police were there to show they wanted to help. Although we were never told directly, it was clear that the department didn't want us to arrest anybody. Anyway, the police take off their gunbelts, put 'em in the car, and then go out and play baseball with the kids. So what happens? You get two dead coppers."

Parked next to the project building in the lot, Rammer went on. "While 'walk and talk' was going on, other people in the community wanted you to get tough, stop playing baseball, and break up the gangs. 'Walk and talk' is fine, but not till you've gotten the gangs out. One gang member can terrorize 5,000 people.

"See that woman out there?" said Rammer in a protective voice as he pointed in the direction of a young black mother walking in the sunshine in front of the car with several cutely dressed, pigtailed little girls. "She doesn't want those little girls killed. So you go in and try to protect the people against the gangs. Sure Mrs. Williams maybe doesn't like it, but I say the hell with Mrs. Williams because her kid is a gang fighter anyway.

"Yet the publicity is all bad. I'm not for controlling the papers but any time a former officer gets in trouble they write 'an ex-policeman'; they never write about 'ex-barbers.' If an off-duty policeman is caught selling drugs they make it clear he's a cop. Policemen, ministers, and teachers all get the negative treatment. And it makes the public hate policemen," he said poignantly.

I asked Rammer what makes police work so frustrating that some men on the beat can take it no longer.

"For one, going in front of judges and state's attorneys who don't care," he quickly retorted. "The papers and the politicians scream for gun control, but when you make pinches they get off. How often can an officer make gun pinches and see 'em get off? I made thirty-seven pinches in three months and every time you make a gun pinch you're risking your life.

"Another problem is that the department doesn't back up

the cop. We occasionally make bad judgment calls and the department doesn't support us. You don't always have time to think it over, you have to act. About 1970, we got a fire call. It was a school north of here that the kids were trying to torch. Me and my partner and several firemen are out there fighting the blaze with maybe $25- and $50,000 worth of equipment. Between 800 and 1,000 people start gathering. I'm not exaggerating either. Now some bricks, bottles, and cans start coming. They start falling closer and closer. Now they're flying over our heads. Two cops and a few firemen and about a thousand people. So I go to the car and take out the shotgun. I fire a warning shot straight up in the air. Then I level the gun on the crowd. And did they scatter! The result is that the fire is put out, the equipment is preserved, the police and firemen are safe, and no one got hurt.

"So what happens? When I get to the station I get criticized for using the gun. They say you're not supposed to fire a warning shot. I say, 'What do you want me to do, shoot at them?' 'No, of course not.' But still the department can't give me any better ideas.

"We need a policeman's bill of rights. All I want to know is clearly what I can and cannot do. Right now it's all discretionary. One time you do something and you get a departmental honorable mention. You do the same thing later and you get criticized.

"Another problem is widespread lack of respect. One of the reasons for that is that the family doesn't teach respect. Another is that the teachers in the schools aren't tough enough. When the schools let the kids do anything they want, allow them to pass to the next grade even though they haven't learned a thing or hardly attended at all, there's not going to be much respect for authority.

"Although the kids have no respect for the police they will give with you if you give with them. I work in a *latino* area now which is loaded with gangs. I get along pretty well with the kids. But they know I'm occasionally going to check 'em out for guns and knives. Now if I happen to see a wine or whisky bottle I may look the other way, but still, even though I'm friendly with them and they know me, they know I'll check 'em out once in a while.

197 | THE MEN IN BLUE

"Lots of kids are following in the steps of their older brothers who go out, rob and steal, and get away with it. When they see their brother burglarize successfully, what are they going to think?"

Rammers talked of the frustration of getting a conviction. "I sometimes have to go to court even on my day off. One time recently we caught a bunch of kids breaking into an apartment. I looked through the window and actually saw the burglary in progress. We arrested the kids and took them to the station. While I and my partner were still making out the burglary report, one of the kids walks right out of the station. The youth officer had decided to release him in the custody of his parents. The guy whose place was turned upside down can't believe his eyes. He says, 'Hey, isn't he one of the kids who you caught?' I said, 'Yes, sir.'

"Look, you can take any major felony involving a twenty-year-old, and I'll guarantee you it's not the first time he's been in trouble. He's a repeater of the same or lesser crimes."

Rammer, despite his authoritarianism, seemed genuinely concerned about protecting the people. There was no evidence of malice toward the community in general; his way of solving crime was simply to get tough. According to Sgt. Levin, Rammer is a better than average policeman. The *macho* image coupled with articularity is, in Levin's judgment, typical of the Chicago cop.

I thanked Rammer for the ride and readied myself for the walk through the project area over to the substation. I have had a good dose of inner-city experience in Milwaukee, Detroit, Grand Rapids, and Chicago—experiences that included intervening in school knife fights and encountering the usual verbal threats to my physical safety. Although I'm not easily intimidated, somehow the prospect of walking unattended through the project area of infamous Cabrini-Green didn't appeal to me. But Officer Rammer remained in his car observing me until I was safely in the substation ready to meet with Martin and Levin.

I asked the two officers why such an anti-police attitude pervaded the community. "Many families are up from the South where, with some justification, the policeman is viewed as the oppressor," said Levin, sounding like a sociologist. "Also you have two different mores operating: the blue-collar, white mores of the police and the black mores of the community. That leads to abrasive circumstances."

"Sometimes there's a lack of respect for the police," chimed in Martin, "due to lack of respect for citizens. For example, on a traffic stop if the citizen talks back to the police, he's often told to shut up. The police don't have ultimate authority over the citizen. Yet the police sometimes feel a citizen doesn't have the right to contradict them and so they talk down to the citizens. You don't need too many officers doing that to influence a community.

"Also, in many instances the white policeman—although sometimes a black policeman too—doesn't respect the black welfare person. He feels that person is inferior and treats him accordingly. So the policeman is resented. Soon the community responds to him negatively simply because he's wearing a blue uniform.

"But some good police work goes on here too," Martin was quick to add. "When the tactical units make valid raids on narcotics, they're doing good and necessary work."

"Anytime anyone is arrested in the community there's resentment," said Levin. "We get calls from people in the building telling us about drug traffic to a certain apartment. But still people respond negatively to the police *per se*, even if they're in valid pursuit.

"You have one poor person being chased by four cops and you have the classic American underdog situation," Martin added philosophically.

Both officers seemed to agree when I added that the poor person probably has little going for him in other areas of his life so there's also the tendency for his peers not to want to see him "picked on."

"Still I have yet to run into anybody in my two and a half years here who told me that he wanted the police out of here," said Martin. "The so-called law-abiding citizens have no animosity toward the police being here. There's really no clear-cut line between the pro-police and anti-police groups in the project. Most of the people are passive, just like the rest of the national population. They just don't give a damn."

"But what about the frustrations?" I asked. I told them about

Harvey Reines who had to get out of the community because he felt it was making an animal out of him.

Levin and Martin challenged this, claiming it was infrequent. Each could think of only one or two policemen who couldn't tolerate working in the neighborhood.

Levin did offer an interesting insight into the difficulty of asserting authority. "You go into a situation and say, 'I'm the authority.' But if you're the only one who sees you as the authority, it doesn't mean very much. You say, 'I'm going to lock you up.' But that's no big thing—the kid's probably been locked up several times before."

"It all depends on your goals," Martin interjected. "If you think you're going to solve all the crime problems in Cabrini-Green as a cop, you'll burn out fast."

"What about violence against the police?" I asked.

"In my two and a half years only one policeman was shot in Cabrini-Green and he was shot by a fellow officer. There was only one incident where the police were fired upon."

Levin was chuckling as Martin made the statement; Levin had been the victim of the errant bullet.

With regard to community problems, the officers felt that alcohol was the chief plague. Surprisingly, neither officer had any idea of how rampant heroin addiction was in Cabrini.

"Then why all the crime?" I asked, trying to look naive.

"Because the people don't feel it's morally wrong," Martin answered quickly. "They don't feel guilty about stealing and robbing."

"The people are aware that white-collar crime goes on and so there's less sensitivity to street crime, although that by no means justifies it," offered Levin. Both officers asserted that crime is indeed relative since so much white-collar crime is perpetrated in the city and is overlooked.

Neither Levin nor Martin believed that fear of punishment greatly deterred crime. What was needed were strong moral values.

"Where parental values are strong, stronger than those of the peer group, you get less crime," Levin stated.

"My kids argue in favor of their peers' values, but when they get older they'll raise their kids with the same values I taught them," Martin said confidently.

Martin and Levin felt they had an advantage working out of the substation. They were the "people's police," rather than anonymous officers riding around in beat cars.

Martin, with his community orientation, was unimpressed by Rammer's record of gun pinching. "As far as gun pinching goes, whenever a policeman's activity is low he knows he can always get a gun pinch around here. There are all kinds of businessmen who carry guns here; even doctors will carry them in their medicine bag. You punch 'em and they'll tell you that the next time you see them they'll have another gun for their own protection. Some policemen take advantage of that when they need arrests."

The interview ended and the genial Levin drove me back to the clinic. Commenting on overaggressive police he said, "I can't prove this, but I think many policemen are unduly influenced by those sensationalized police programs on television. They think that's the way it is and try to emulate what they see. The fabric of reality is just not thick enough for them to operate intelligently."

A MIXED BAG

12

Hogren never liked to involve himself in divorce litigation and rarely handles such cases anymore. "When I graduated from law school I remember one of my first assignments was to go out to Du Page County and handle a divorce matter. I remember sitting in the courtroom and before my case was called I had to listen to many other divorce wranglings. I got so depressed I don't think I ever really recovered," he says. "I drank coffee by the barrel afterward, trying to regain some energy; I was so completely depressed. It actually took me several days to get over the shock of sitting in that room and listening to divorce after divorce after divorce. I vowed I would never take another divorce and I never did until I came here."

When Hogren came to the clinic he quickly saw that he had to handle at least some divorce cases. "Marital breakdown was a real social problem in the community and something had to be done. People couldn't collect benefits they were due, children weren't supported, and we had to pursue delinquent husbands." Later, however, when Chuck and Lynette found themselves inundated with divorce cases, Lynette located other agencies in the area to which she referred potential divorce situations. Nevertheless, the experiences left a profound imprint on Hogren. "There's nothing more depressing than sitting in divorce court all day and listening to marital tragedies. How a person does it I don't know," he says shaking his head.

Some of the divorces the clinic handled were among the saddest cases in its five-year history. They illustrate the unhappy plight of women trapped in the web of poverty. Take the case of Edith Wellington, a woman of about thirty. She said her husband deserted her and their three children without supporting them. In addition, there was a large number of outstanding debts which the husband refused to pay despite his ability to do so. Edith's credit soon became affected and she was financially plagued for about two years.

According to Edith, her husband, who was both on drugs and pushing them, worked for an auto manufacturer and made in excess of $200 a week. He had two cars and was living with a girlfriend at a different address. Edith was receiving public aid despite the fact that her estranged husband had such high earnings. He threatened her with physical harm if she tried to get any money for the children. Hogren was finally able to obtain a divorce for Edith which provided that her former husband had to pay $20 a week per child to the Department of Public Aid for the children.

"That shows the problem many women have in the Cabrini-Green neighborhood of getting their husbands to support them and their children. It's a constant source of irritation," asserts Hogren. "The whole legal process in the Wellington case took over two years. What is most pathetic of all are the unnecessary threats and anxiety associated with this type of experience for the woman."

The case of Ellen Shore, thirty-one, is even more poignant. Ordered to pay alimony, the husband refused, claiming that he hadn't received the court summons to appear at the session in which the order was given. He was trying to vacate the decree. David Ott, a law student, handled the case and got the deputy sheriff into court who swore that he had, in fact, handed the summons to Mr. Shore. As a result, Shore's lawyer was unable to get the decree overturned. A default judgment against Shore was obtained and he was ordered to pay $45 a week alimony.

The problems had just begun. Shore claimed he was earning only $75 a week, working as a timekeeper in one of the federal programs and so wasn't able to meet his financial obligation to Ellen. He became very angry and threatened Ellen's life if she persisted in her legal efforts. Ellen became so fearful she was afraid to go to her job. "She became highly paranoid," recalls Hogren. "Her whole outlook on life seemed to deteriorate because of the situation. Her husband said he would rather kill her than pay her any money.

"In addition, he had another woman who was actually living with him in the next apartment. Evidently he had found someone else and didn't want any responsibility toward his former wife and children. He was openly engaged sexually with this woman in front of his own wife and children.

"Ellen was being dehumanized by the whole process. The judicial procedure lasted over a year and she emerged with very little for the three children. The trauma showed on her to the extent that she became visibly despondent about having to be put through that kind of treatment in order to get a little support for her children. It was very bitter, very unpleasant."

Recently Hogren handled the case of Ann Allen. The clinic had handled her divorce case in which she obtained custody of the children. Her husband, however, contrary to and in defiance of the decree, waited outside the school and abducted one of the children. Ann didn't know where he might be keeping the child.

Chuck then put on his private investigator's hat and went out with Ann to look for the child. They went to several addresses where they thought the child might be. At one location they called the police from a corner phone booth, telling the officer where they were and why. They waited in front of the building until the police, very cooperative in the matter, arrived. Anticipating possible violence, the officers accompanied them as they went to the door, attempting to find the child. It was a dead lead. They then went to two or three other addresses, looking without success for the missing child.

When they finally did locate the child they went back to court. The father, in turn, decided that he wanted custody of all the children and so filed a petition to gain custody legally. The court, in an effort to dispose of the matter justly, appointed a social worker to make an investigation of both parents' homes. The father balked at the prospect of a social worker coming into his house and never consented to the arrangement. Ann, however, also demurred, regularly making up excuses why she wouldn't be able to keep proposed appointments with the social worker.

Since that time the father has lost interest in gaining custody of the children so, by default, Ann has them. He has a second family which he also has to support and that adds to his burdens. Earlier, he actually took another, younger child but Hogren was able to get that child back also. At any rate, the torment Ann Allen was put through will never be able either to be legally assessed nor financially compensated.

Domestic injustices abound. A Japanese woman who had been a war bride came into the clinic. Evidently her husband, a Viet Nam war veteran, had met her in Japan, married her, and brought her to the States. Five years and two children later, the husband simply took off with the youngsters. It bothers Hogren to talk about it. "Here's a woman who speaks very little English, whose husband just disappeared with the children. Now she's all by herself. She did have a lawyer who was trying to track her husband down but it was a very frustrating thing, because tracking down a person is very difficult. She was in the country legally—a citizen. It was one of those situations we come across once in a while in which there is just nothing we can do."

Desertion is common. "A woman," says Hogren, "will be left with three or four children and the husband will be nowhere to be found. They'll send the sheriff out to his last known address to serve a summons regarding the divorce complaint. Usually the sheriff returns unable to find the defendant. We then have to publish a notice in the newspaper and serve the summons that way, but we're unable to get any child support through that method. Desertion is a way for a father and husband to evade supporting his family by just disappearing. Often the case remains open so that, if and when the husband is found, he can be required to pay alimony and child support."

Tracking is frustrating. "The first thing we do is to find out from the wife where the man might live, where his parents are, and any possible address she might have for him. Then we send

205 | A MIXED BAG

the sheriff of that particular county out to look for him. We often look in the South; some we have found in California. If he's not found that way, there's little else we can do but to publish a notice in the newspaper in order to obtain the divorce.

"Some of the men are never heard from again. Some wives have told me they have absolutely no idea where their husbands are and haven't heard anything from the man for five or even ten years. In fact, many don't know if their husband is still living. It makes me very angry—it's very frustrating to deal with, but it's very common."

Some of the civil skullduggery the clinic encounters is particularly sad. Bernard Green, now in his seventies, can neither read nor write. He claims he was an illegitimate child but has his father's name. Now that his father is dead, Ben wants a part of the inheritance. He alleges that his sisters cheated him out of the inheritance because he was unable to read. Hogren, however, has never been able to confirm that charge.

There are a number of snags in the case. Ben's father died fifteen years ago in Mississippi, so all the documents surrounding the estate are quite old. Chuck has sent numerous letters attempting to get some money for Green but so far none have been successful.

It bothers Hogren. "Ben is very difficult to communicate with and what makes it so unsatisfying is that we just couldn't get anywhere. Some people you just can't help. Like Ben, they come to you with a serious problem. You'd like to do something for them and yet it seems that nothing can be done."

"I believe the guy has a right to some money," says Hogren. "The father evidently had some land which was sold and I think his sister tricked him into signing a document agreeing to take a thousand dollars for his full share of what should have been a much larger estate. Unfortunately, years have gone by and we are unable to get any hard evidence to favor his case. We're still trying—we haven't given up yet—but it's a case of relatives not talking or not giving out as much information as we would like. In addition, the lawyers who handled this years ago in Mississippi are no longer available or are unwilling to answer letters."

That Ben is black may also be a factor, making the white southern lawyers less interested in reopening that family's can of worms. It's more convenient to let it drop and die its own death. For Ben, however, life is miserable. Unmarried and poor, he lives an isolated life. "He has some relatives around here," says Chuck, "but they think he's crazy. They humor him along saying, 'You'll get some money someday, you'll get some money someday.' He does act quite strangely and maybe he is crazy; but that's probably from having endured so much frustration and having had so many doors slammed in his face over the years."

Ben Green is one of life's pathetic figures, one who is poor and has been down and out for so long that he may be partly deranged from the battery of defeats. "You would like to help him—if only to break the string of defeats," says Hogren, "but it doesn't look good."

There is hardly a more pathetic figure than Rose Barker, a white woman in her middle seventies. Chuck remembers her as having heard about the clinic on the radio. "She said I was God's answer to her prayers, that she had been looking for someone like me all her life, and that God had finally answered her prayers by sending me into her life," recalls Chuck with a look of disbelief.

Rose first stated that she had worked in a hotel as a desk clerk. There was a tenant of the hotel who would "borrow" money from her from time to time. In all she gave him $3,000, with him promising her eventual repayment. He never made good on his promise.

Another time she was at home when a woman using the alias of Mrs. Blair came to her door and said she was from the Social Security office. She asked why Rose hadn't answered her letters. She told the bewildered Mrs. Barker that there was a thousand dollars waiting for her at the office, but in order to pick it up Rose was to pay Mrs. Blair $96 so she could take care of administrative details. When the dust cleared, Mrs. Blair, through some elaborate scheme, had made off with $500 of Rose's money, promising to return with the thousand dollars in the morning. It is unlikely that Rose will ever again see "Mrs. Blair" on this side of the eternal divide.

Rose Barker constantly fell for confidence schemes and, according to Hogren, was "the most unhappy person I have ever seen. It was pathetic to see how completely unhappy she was

207 | A MIXED BAG

over a long period of time, and how unable she was to cope with it.

"She was a woman who had severe mental problems. She told me once that her father had died when she was very young. Later she said that I was her father. She always looked on me as her father. She also told me she had been divorced some years back and that her husband was a part of the Mafia and that she had almost been killed on a number of occasions."

Rose wrote Chuck a number of letters. Those letters indicate more sharply than anything her impaired condition. An excerpt from one reads as follows:

> OFFICIAL BUSINESS*PERSONAL
> 'AMICUS CURIAE'
> Mr. Charles V. Hogren:* *Personal,*
> 'Cabrini Green Legal Aid,'
> (325 N. Hudson St.,) 1515 N. Ogden Ave.,
> Chicago, Illinois. 60610.
> Dear Mr. Charles V. Hogren:
> Honorable Sir, THANKS for your kindness, car, et al, and letter of *August 27, 1975,* relative to STATUS *of my situation with Mr.* EDWARD PLAIN lll, *also, his address, also, I am happy to report my situation is* IMPROVING *very well, Legalwise, etc.,* under existing, extenuating conditions, so often beyond my control, *being* INJURED SO CRITICALLY, ET AL, hence, please, EXTEND *the further* 'CONTINUANCE' *for ME, KEEPING MY 'FILE' OPEN;* due to the many undue delays et al, I've encountered, LOSS of My $500.00, as of JULY 2, 1975, by Mrs. J. BLAIR*ET AL, as I reported to YOU*ET AL, thusly, also, as YOUR LETTER *was mislaid among the MANY LETTERS I receive from 'MISSIONARIES' PLEADING for MONEY, AID, ETC., TO ASSIST THOSE IN NEED, which I endeavor to do,* also, *being* SO CRITICALLY INJURED, SUFFERING EXTREME PAIN, *being partially* DISABLED, HANDICAPPED, ET AL, *hence* URGENTLY NEED ASSISTANCE PHYSICALLY, FINANCIALLY, ET AL, *not just to be* 'self-serving,' *but for my attending Physicians, et al,* OFFICIALS*OTHERS, *as follows:*

"She's an example of the type of clients one of the articles about the clinic brought in," says Chuck. "She's a genuine mental case, and because there's no one around to help her she remains the prey of unscrupulous types who want to take advantage of her deteriorated state. We looked into her cases, but when it came right down to it, we were unable to help her. She had a house in Longview that needed work and she could have kept a full-time lawyer busy handling all the cases she had involving that. There was an almost endless supply of legal hassles. Despite her despondency, she thought God would pull her through. She has since left town. I hope she is happier."

Communication breakdowns impeded the civil case of Norma Hess. She had purchased a home on West Jackson Boulevard in 1963 for $15,000. After making her mortgage payments faithfully for eleven years she still owed a balance of $12,000. She came in to tell Hogren about the problem. Chuck contacted the mortgage holder and asked him to send her a copy of the passbook showing the accurate balance. Hogren then wrote Mrs. Hess asking her if she was satisfied with the new balance. She has not responded. In fact, she has never responded to any of Chuck's letters or phone calls.

"I wrote her concerning the status of her account, asking her to inform me if the mortgage holder had provided her with a new payment book and if she was satisfied," explains Hogren. "I had a great deal of difficulty communicating with her anyway, but the upshot of the matter is that I don't know whether she is satisfied or not. I simply can't reach her. I've written letters and they have come back. I'll just have to keep trying.

"It's disappointing, because she has a valid case. But communicating is extremely difficult. I can hardly read her handwriting. Talking with her is extraordinarily difficult. I don't know what actually happened. Like Ben Green, sometimes over a period of time papers are lost, records are misplaced, and receipts disappear. I doubt that we accomplished a thing, despite the blocks of time we spent on her case."

Communication between Hogren and many of his clients can be very problematic. He has all the problems that attend a middle-class person who is trying to communicate with a lower-class person. All of those impediments, about which books are written and lectures are given, come to a focus at the legal aid clinic. Indeed, before Hogren says a word, his whiteness and middle-class character make him a symbol of the oppressor—the white community—which, according to the Kerner Commission, creates and maintains ghettos and keeps poor people poor through shady business and political machinations. In addition, Hogren symbolizes the white middle-class court system, the schools which have flunked the clients, the employers who won't hire them, and the police who seem only too happy to arrest them.

Chuck takes all that in stride and is empathetic. "Often the client has no knowledge of the law and that in and of itself can be frightening and difficult. There are a lot of emotional barriers to surmount in getting them to understand the judicial process."

The case of Raoul Melendez, a tetnty-eight-year-old Puerto Rican, is a prime example of faulty communication. Melendez was arrested for driving under the influence of alcohol. Although Hogren is not certain whether or not Raoul was guilty, there was reasonable doubt; moreover, Chuck has not seen Melendez since the disposition of his case.

"The case was continued a couple of times," says Hogren. "I couldn't communicate with him so I asked for an interpreter. Finally we had a full trial and the judge found him not guilty. However, because Raoul had refused to submit to a breathalyzer test when he was arrested, his license was suspended for three months. That was a very minor matter compared to being convicted of driving under the influence of alcohol. Nonetheless, because of that three-month license revocation, I couldn't convince him he had won the case. He left the courtroom believing he had lost. It was frustrating, as it was a victory that I was very happy to have achieved for him. Being unable to tell him in a convincing fashion that he was legally not guilty was maddening."

The perils of Vanessa Wacker, a woman in her twenties who was a tenant of the Chicago Housing Authority, living in one of the low-income project buildings, evidence the need for legal protection.

Vanessa was served with a summons ordering that she be removed from the premises of her apartment because a fire had damaged the front door. She wasn't home when the fire, which began outside the building, had occurred. Nevertheless, the CHA wanted her to pay $800 for the repair of the door in addition to evicting her.

The origins of the fire were never determined, but Hogren suspects that it may have been set by an angry boyfriend. Probably the CHA felt that Vanessa had some undesirable friends and that by getting her out of the project they would also be rid of her unsavory associates. After a good bit of legal maneuvering on Chuck's part, the CHA, realizing they couldn't penalize Vanessa for a fire she didn't start, dropped the case.

A year later, however, Vanessa was served with a similar complaint, stating exactly the same grounds: those which had been dealt with in the earlier case. Again the CHA lost the case, based on the fact that an identical complaint had been disposed of a year previously. So Vanessa Wacker continues to live in her apartment but is well aware that if it weren't for the clinic's availability she could easily have found herself penniless and without shelter.

Consumer complaints also come in. In 1975 Mary Jones bought a used 1968 Ford from a dealer on Western Avenue in Chicago. Although the bluebook value (the car's value in a competitive market) of the vehicle was only $400, Mary paid $1,275 for the vehicle. She paid $100 down, signed a contract, and left.

Within two weeks four of the major systems of the car collapsed. The car was inoperable. Outraged, Mary refused to make any further payments and the car was repossessed. The dealer turned around and sold that same car to another gullible consumer for $900. According to Hogren, "They must have fixed the wreck up enough to drive off the lot."

Mary was given credit for the $900 but was held for the unpaid balance of the $1,275 purchase price. Charging that the car was worthless and that the dealer had refused to repair it upon her request, she still balked at making any further payments. Before the dealer had an opportunity to file suit against her, law students from Northwestern University who were working at the clinic prepared a twenty-page complaint against the dealer. The document dealt with five statutes concerning truth in lending. They sued the car dealer and the finance company for $5,000.

Chuck immediately received a call from the lawyer representing the car dealer. "Forget the Jones payment, we'll wash out the balance and call it even," he told Hogren excitedly. Mary Jones was not satisfied. She wanted the suit to stand. According to Chuck it is still pending and "she will never get anything near the $5,000 from it because the dealer does have a defense against certain of the allegations." However, he hopes that her challenge of that sleazy operation may have the preventive effect of making the dealer more reasonable in future business transactions.

Bonnie Morris, in her late twenties, went to a furniture store and saw in the showroom several items that appealed to her. She purchased them on the installment plan and had the furniture delivered to her home. The furniture that was delivered, however, was not like the furniture she'd seen in the showroom. For example, whereas the coffee table on display was made of fine wood, the delivered item was actually constructed of wood-grained paper glued over some very cheap wood. In addition, the bed fell apart almost instantly.

A very upset Bonnie Morris demanded that the store take back all of the furniture. They, having sold the contract at a discount to a finance company, refused. Bonnie then discontinued making payments. She was sued for $1,816.46.

Chuck negotiated back and forth for a long time and finally the suit was settled at $400. "This is a very common occurrence," says Hogren. "In fact, Bonnie brought three other people with her to the clinic office, all of them having purchased furniture from the same dealer and all having been ripped off. Although we couldn't take all their cases, I used that fact in settling the case. I told the lawyer that I could truncate him with similar cases if he didn't come up with a reasonable settlement.

"People living in Cabrini often see things put in front of them which look very attractive. They're offered a purchase opportunity requiring little or no down payment. It's all very enticing and the person signs his or her life away, almost literally. Then when the 'goods' are delivered and are inferior, the purchaser, knowing of no recourse, is stuck with the payment.

"It's a slick operation. The store sells the contract at a discount to a local finance company and washes its hands of the whole affair. The old legal theory was that putting such a contract in the hands of a finance company cut off all defenses on the part of the purchaser concerning inadequacies in the quality of the material. Since the contract was held by a finance company, an independent party who knows nothing of the quality of the goods except what is stated on the contract, the store was off the hook. That was part of the old commercial code and, before that, of the negotiable instruments law. They were designed to protect business people from capricious complaints. The law has since been changed in favor of the purchaser."

Such fraud is lucrative for the unscrupulous perpetrators. The furniture company sells junk at outrageous prices, knowing that over the long haul they will collect more than they lose; moreover, if repossession does occur, the store can simply touch up the merchandise and sell it again—while still holding the original purchaser to the contract. The finance company's strategy is based on holding the person to the contract. Although there are defaults along the way, those reversals don't exceed the bonanza of the interest killings they make on the victims who do pay either partially or fully.

That was not Bonnie Morris's only unhappy consumer experience. Her sister went to a different store to buy furniture, but because she was on welfare, she was refused credit. The store wanted cosigners. She asked Bonnie to cosign but the store balked at her because Bonnie wasn't employed full time. A brother was then called and, because he had a full-time job, his signature was accepted.

A few months later the brother lost his job and the payments weren't being made. A law suit was filed against none other than Bonnie Morris in the amount of $1,155. Although her sister had signed for the furniture, because that sister was on welfare and the brother was unemployed, they went after the then-fully-employed Bonnie for the money since they could garnish her wages. The store had earlier obtained Bonnie's signature on the retail installment contract by telling her it was a credit check. Bonnie had signed the paper and the store eagerly had filled in the blanks.

Chuck went to the lawyer representing the furniture company and informed him of the swindle. The lawyer agreed that Bonnie might not have known what she was signing, but he emphasized that there was no doubt that it was her signature on the contract. The result? The case was settled out of court with Bonnie having to pay a reduced sum.

"The case of Bernice Adamovich, a woman in her fifties, was one of the outrageously trite things we've gotten into," says

Hogren. "Such cases are often very important to the person involved, but in the long course of justice they really have no significance and should never be adjudicated."

Bernice came to the clinic stating that she had taken care of her elderly mother for a long time and that when her mother died she had not received the full amount of money due her from the Department of Health, Education and Welfare. She wanted legal help in collecting it.

It turned out to be an elaborate case with a series of appeals, one which Chuck entered late, filling in for another lawyer. Expecting that a substantial sum of money was involved, Hogren was alert for the upcoming hearing. There, for the first time, he discovered that the whole issue revolved around the whopping sum of $36.30.

When Chuck introduced himself to the hearing officer or judge and started laying out the case, the officer was aghast. "Do you mean to tell me that you are only talking about $36.30?" he bristled. "And you're taking up the time of this administrative hearing to talk about that. I'll tell you what I'm going to do. I'm going to *give* you $36.30 just to get you out of here. It's worth our time not to have to deal with this."

Bernice was delighted. She had won her case. A few days later she sent Hogren some items she had crocheted as a token of her appreciation.

Unfortunately her case was not closed. The judge who ultimately had to sign and advance the legal papers in the matter died before everything was finalized. His successor refused to go through with the decision and Bernice was, once again, bereft of her $36.30. She was convinced that she was the victim of a colossal miscarriage of justice.

Ever persistent, she appealed the disposition. The appeals council didn't budge. It ruled that the latter decision was correct and it would stand.

To Hogren, the whole issue shows not only some of the petty aspects of the clinic's work but also how "one judge could have compassion, seeing this older woman who felt she was entitled to $36.30—although she actually was not—while another would call the play from a strictly legal standpoint."

A number of other cases have had unusual if not unbelievable elements. Tyrone Smith, married and about thirty, was a church musician who had the reputation of drinking too much—in fact, he was a confirmed alcoholic. Nonetheless he somehow was able to get up every Sunday morning and retain his position as church organist.

"One day he and a companion were out in the suburb of Cicero," relates Hogren. "Now that, in itself, is interesting: two blacks in all-white, hostile Cicero. They claimed they were out there looking for work."

Unfortunately for Smith and his compatriot, the police felt otherwise. The two were arrested for armed robbery.

Smith had a remarkable version of the event. After being unable to find work the two decided to get something to eat. While in the restaurant, Tyrone recalled that he had left a rifle wrapped in newspaper in the car. Smith claimed he was taking the gun to a sculptor who wanted to copy it for a decoration to be hung over the sculptor's living room mantelpiece. He said it was not an operative weapon and didn't even have a firing pin.

In any event, remembering that the window of the car was broken and fearing that the gun would be stolen, Smith carried the gun into the eating place. The story becomes a bit foggy from that point but Smith steadfastly asserted that he did not, as the counter man charged, rob the restaurant.

Unfortunately, Tyrone Smith and his friend were apprehended not far from the scene, their pockets bulging with coins: rolls of coins disturbingly similar to those missing from the cash register of the restaurant. Ever ready with an explanation, Tyrone claimed that his associate had gone to a currency exchange and gotten the coins for his children.

To Smith's good fortune, however, the counter man— obviously afraid—left his place of employment shortly after he reported the robbery, and the state was unable to find him by the time of the trial. As a result there was room for some aggressive plea bargaining. It resulted in Smith's receiving three years' probation accompanied by treatment for his alcoholism. He seems to be doing well now.

Smith may have missed his calling; he should have become a novelist. Subsequent investigation turned up no currency exchange, no evidence of the faulty condition of the rifle, nor any concerning the existence of a willing wood sculptor. It did, however, reveal that Tyrone was drunk at the time of the robbery.

215 | A MIXED BAG

Probably the most bizarre case in the clinic's history was that of Barry Matson, twenty-four, a wounded Viet Nam veteran.

According to his mother, Barry was very religious although he had drifted a bit in recent years. His case involved a fortyish woman named Rosalind Thornton.

According to Mrs. Thornton, her husband was a contractor who had been working next door to a tavern. She asked him to drive her home but he refused, wanting to continue working. She then went to the Aquarius Lounge to call the jitney cab company. (A jitney is an unlicensed, illegal cab, a plain car which operates in low-income neighborhoods. It picks up a large number of people, running almost like a private bus service.) A car pulled up in front of the tavern with Barry driving and his girlfriend, Mary Castle, sitting in the front passenger seat.

Rosalind, thinking it was her cab, walked over and asked if she should get in. They said, "Yes, get in." So Mrs. Thornton got in the car. As soon as she was comfortably situated, Mary Castle put a large knife up against her neck.

Rosalind claimed they took her to Mary's apartment in a high-rise building. There they took her rings and some money. They then forced her to remove her clothing and Barry raped her.

After keeping Rosalind there for hours, they drove her back to her neighborhood and let her out of the car. Barry and Mary were arrested shortly later. Barry was charged with robbery and aggravated kidnapping.

Barry Matson came to Chuck through a chaplain at the county jail, the streetwise Cabrini-Green veteran, Father Mark Santo. Barry had asked to see the chaplain, and upon hearing Barry's version, Santo was so impressed by the apparent injustice that he personally put up the $500 necessary to bail him out.

Such an act by a chaplain is simply unheard of, but Santo felt the situation extraordinary enough to warrant such action. He called Chuck and asked if Hogren would come down and hear Barry out. Chuck did and agreed to take Matson's case. Mary Castle's defense was handled by someone else.

Matson presented this version: He and Rosalind Thornton, whom he did not know was married, had been seeing each other regularly, and upon occasion he had taken her to a hotel right behind Malcolm X College, the Alamac. He said the desk clerk there, Frank Waters, could verify that they had been there on at least three occasions, registering as husband and wife. Hogren talked with Waters, who confirmed Matson's claim, saying that Barry and Rosalind were regular customers of his.

Barry mentioned another witness, Leonard Darwin, as one with whom he and Rosalind had double-dated. Chuck also talked to Darwin, who said, "Yes, that's true, Rosalind Thornton was with Barry on at least two occasions." Then Matson gave Chuck the name of a Bernard Louis Shore who said he had seen Barry driving a brown Buick with Rosalind as the passenger in the front seat.

Barry said he had dated Rosalind for about four months and then dropped her for the younger Mary Castle. When Rosalind found out, she threatened to get even. The frame-up, according to Matson, was Mrs. Thornton's way of getting even.

Barry said that Rosalind had been at the Aquarius Lounge and saw him and Mary Castle in one of the booths. Rosalind came over, placed her rings down on their table, and told them to keep an eye on the jewelry while she danced. Rosalind had had a good bit to drink and became so unruly that she was later ejected from the bar. While she danced, seemingly interminably, Barry and Mary took the rings. Barry said he had initially taken them from the table for safekeeping, but later pawned them. He showed Hogren the pawn tickets and said that he got at least one of the rings back and returned it. In any case, he said the rings were taken only because Mrs. Thornton was drunk and most certainly would have lost them.

Barry thought the incident had ended, but three weeks after the night in the Aquarius Lounge he was arrested and charged with the two major felonies. He said he was in shock.

With Barry's story and his three corroborating witnesses, Chuck was loaded for bear. Rosalind's anger over being jilted provided a motive for the frame-up. At the preliminary hearing Hogren questioned Mrs. Thornton, asking her all the pertinent questions.

"Didn't you know the defendant at least four or five months prior to the date of the alleged incident?" Hogren inquired.

"No. That was the first night I saw him."

217 | A MIXED BAG

"Haven't you, in fact, spent evenings with Mr. Matson at the Alamac Hotel?"

"No, I did not."

And so the questioning went. Hogren had expected her to lie at the hearing and he wanted to get it squarely into the record. He did not, of course, tell her that he had Waters, Darwin, and Shore waiting in the wings to refute her version. His strategy was to go to trial, have her repeat the lies, and then bring on the three witnesses to demolish the veracity of her testimony. Hogren would then claim that "since Mrs. Thornton was lying about not knowing Matson, she was also lying about the felonious charges against him." Moreover, proving that she had lied about her relationship with Matson both at the trial and at the preliminary hearing would impeach Mrs. Thornton as a witness.

Almost two years elapsed between the preliminary hearing and the trial. There were a number of continuances but the main problem was that in the meantime Rosalind Thornton died of cancer.

Nevertheless, the trial strategy remained the same. The charges against Barry would be shot down by impeaching the earlier preliminary hearing testimony of the late Mrs. Thornton through the testimony of Waters, Darwin, and Shore. The stage was scrupulously set.

A week before the trial the phone rang. It was Barry. "I have met the Lord and I must tell you the truth," he said with a sense of urgency. "None of the story I gave you was true. It was completely made up. I had never met Mrs. Thornton. Everything she said was true."

Chuck was shattered. "My whole defense was a sham and the question was what to do," he says with a look of lingering disbelief. "I had spent so much time developing that elaborate defense. We were ready to go to trial, and it was the best defense I had ever developed. All false," says Hogren with an amused chuckle. "It sure looked good on paper though. Anyway, I told Barry that I couldn't allow him to testify to his false story. All of his witnesses were false. He had found three people who agreed to lie for him."

Hogren then talked with the state's attorney. Although he did not have Mrs. Thornton, there was a very thorough and lengthy transcript from the preliminary hearing. Since the victim was dead, but had been subject to cross-examination at the hearing, it was permissible for the state to introduce her testimony as evidence at the trial. The situation was utterly hopeless.

"So I talked to the state's attorney and worked out a plea bargain," says Hogren. "It amounted to five years' probation with the charges reduced to lesser felonies. The first two years of the probation were to be spent on work release. Barry was to work in the morning and go to school in the afternoon. That meant avoiding the penitentiary and being out working each day. Barry was delighted with the settlement."

Hogren was hardly prepared for the next jolt. Shortly after Barry began his work release, Chuck received a call from him. He said he needed more time off, out of jail. He wanted his weekends free. Hogren assured Barry that he was very fortunate to get work release in the first place and so he should be contented with that. Nevertheless, Chuck said if all went well for several months he would go to court and request a reduction.

Not long after Barry's request Hogren received a phone call from a local pastor. "Please don't represent Barry Matson! Don't let him out of jail; he needs to be in the penitentiary rather than getting time off!" the clergyman exclaimed. The pastor then informed Chuck that the allegedly spiritually reconstructed Barry had been spending his afternoons with one of the minister's female parishioners rather than going to school. What was worse, Matson had gotten the young woman pregnant.

The minister was distraught. "This young woman has been coming along so well and we've been working with her regularly," he said. "Now she is destroyed. She's away from the church now. Barry is nothing but a confidence man to beat all confidence men. Don't ever believe a word he tells you!"

For the earnest Hogren, it was the final episode in what had become a personal and professional nightmare. "I don't think I have ever been taken in so completely in my life," he says. "It was simply incredible. Right from the outset the chaplain and I were convinced of his story. I had interviewed all the witnesses; they had dates, places, and everything. Then when Barry told me he had lied I felt completely betrayed.

219 | A MIXED BAG

"Still, when he said he wanted to tell the truth I felt, 'Well, I guess it's better that he admits it. We'll try to deal with it that way.' Then to find out he was violating his work release..."

Hogren, for his own sanity, seems compelled to fill in the missing pieces. "As far as the conversion story goes, I think something may actually have happened to him because it was to his complete advantage to stick to his original story. With the plaintiff dead, he was almost a lead-pipe cinch to get off. The state would simply have read the preliminary hearing into the record with all her denials of Barry's claims to their relationship. Then all I would have had to do was bring the witnesses in and he would have been home free.

"Nonetheless, whatever his spiritual experience was, it must have been temporary. It may have been one of convenience, as he wanted to impress that girl from the church. He may have told her about the case and found her insisting that he tell the truth. Who knows? Anyway, Barry Matson is a con man and the most believable one you will ever meet."

Chuck hasn't heard from Barry Matson for over a year. By now he has finished his work release and is living out his probational sentence. How that is going is anyone's guess, and asking Matson about it certainly carries no guarantee of finding out.

DREAMS

13

The days are long and the cases keep coming. Some days exhaustion is written all over Hogren's face. On a number of occasions he has come dangerously close to "burning out."

The concept of urban worker burnout is of great interest to Bill Leslie. According to Leslie, burning out means running out of steam, reaching a point where you're unable to make decisions, unable to conjure up feelings for the people with whom you work. You have nothing left to give.

"I read an article recently," says Bill, "that discussed the condition of people who work with problem-riddled persons in the city and how the workers are called upon to give, give, give. When all you see are problems, pretty soon you find you've given all you have to give. There is simply nothing left. Often you don't see big changes either in the people or in the systems afflicting them, and you become bitter and tired. You figure you've done your job and want to get out.

"The instance of burnout is very high among social workers unless they move up or go downtown into a supervisory post. The statistics are high for inner-city educators and attorneys.

I've also observed a lot of burning out among ministers who work with the poor.

"Many times two to four years is all you can give before you're exhausted," says this youthful-appearing seventeen-year veteran of urban ministry. "When I first came to this community there were a lot of liberals in here believing they could usher in the kingdom of God in the city. Harvey Cox's book, *The Secular City*, had just come out and everybody was celebrating that. Now I don't know of any liberals left within miles of this community. I think they observed that things were getting worse rather than better. They just didn't have the mental toughness to stay at it—they burned out.

"Now it's not beyond evangelicals to burn out, but they do have resources the others don't have. One is the pietistic relationship with Christ and another is the belief in the filling of the Holy Spirit. In short, you have a theology that can keep you there. In addition, you develop a supportive community that really cares for you, loves you, and helps patch things together."

Leslie then turned his attention to Chuck's fatigue. "Chuck almost burned out in the spring of 1976. Lynette came over and told me he was postponing cases, becoming indecisive; he simply wasn't functioning. We had to get him out of the city for awhile to pull him together."

Hogren had mentioned his near burnout while being interviewed for this book. As might be expected, he felt rather guilty about it. He blamed himself for some of Lynette's discouragement, feeling he had spread his depression to her and left her carrying an excessive amount of the mental and emotional load. Chuck credits church staff meetings with preventing much of his potential burnout; there, the people working in several ministries convene to talk, pray, and even celebrate together.

Bill Leslie continued on the subject of urban burnout: "I almost went the burnout route myself last spring. Others in the church have totally burned out. They would come, make a commitment to the city, give all they could give, and move on because they were just plain tired.

"Some of us who have been on the urban scene for awhile have tried to find the secret to survival. Bud Ipema, Ray Bakke, and I came up with four things that have helped us hang on in the city. The first thing was that we have a theology of God and his kingdom. It was that theology that kept us here. It wasn't simply an awareness of pressing urban needs that kept us going. The idea of extending God's reign, asserting an institutional as well as an individual witness, making a "commitment to turf" such that you work in a community no matter who lives there—all those things along with the notion of the sovereignty of God and his concern for the city are included.

"Second, nearly all of us have had some diversion; we were all simultaneously participating in some kind of graduate study where we were growing as persons. That got us out of the community and enabled us to focus our minds on something else. It was significant that I almost burned out just after completing my graduate work. I started spending all my time wrestling with people's problems without any diversions. I felt locked in there, with nothing new going on.

"A third thing is that nearly all of us have been a part of a small group, one that supported us and picked us up when we were low. When Gilbert James (of Asbury Theological Seminary) had completed six years of directing the urban ministries program for seminarians in this city, I asked him, 'If you were talking to urban ministers, what is the one thing you would especially recommend to them for survival?' He said, 'Get a pal, someone you can be close with, and track with him, because you will really need that.'

"Fourth, it's important just to get out of the city once in awhile. You have to get away from the broken glass, violence, and hurt that pervades urban poverty. You need a little time for yourself. You need to see trees, fields, the sky, because that helps you feel you're back in control of your life. That control thing is really important, because to be an urban worker means you are a servant, and you won't always be in control of your life if you're really taking servanthood seriously."

Such talk of servanthood and ministering to society's victims brings thoughts of "blood and justice" to mind. Most of the Cabrini-Green Legal Aid Clinic's time is spent on justice. What are Hogren's feelings concerning the victims of community crime, especially violent crime?

"I have a lot of sympathy for the victims," says Hogren assertively. He should. Danger is everywhere. Chuck has been a victim at least four times himself, once of an attempted robbery.

"I was walking up Blackhawk Street to a meeting at the Olivet Center," he says. "It was a midafternoon on a nice day, and with my car being repaired and the center only three blocks away, I decided to walk. I had walked about two blocks when a couple of teen-agers came up to me and asked me what was in my briefcase. I said nothing to them and kept on walking. They followed me. When I got about 100 feet from the door of the center, they stopped me physically. They demanded my briefcase. I said No and kept going. One kid ran away when he saw I was resisting. The other continued to follow me. Neither had any weapons so I just kept walking up to the door.

"As I was opening the door with my one hand, the kid grabbed for my briefcase in the other. He then hit me in the face with his fist and, with both my hands occupied, I was unable to defend myself. The blow drew blood but wasn't hard enough to loosen any teeth or require any stitches. I managed to get through the first door and into the foyer, but the next door was locked so I had to ring a buzzer. I began to knock very loudly on the door. Fortunately, somebody came and the kid ran away.

"That incident was witnessed by at least ten people who were sitting on the stairs of the center, none of whom I knew. They did nothing either to encourage the youth or to help me. I suspect that was partly because I didn't ask for any help. Also, I was white and all of them were black."

Sometimes knowing the neighborhood people helps. Late one evening Chuck was leaving a meeting at St. Matthew's Church, and as he approached his car he noticed a teen-ager sitting on the hood of the vehicle parked in front of his. Hogren became, in his words, "rather apprehensive," but kept heading toward his car. When he drew even with the car on which the youth was perched the kid spoke to him. It turned out to be one of his clients. "We passed the time of day for awhile and I was on my way," says Hogren with a laugh of relief.

Chuck has made his commitment to the city, purchasing a home just north of Cabrini-Green in a mixed neighborhood. He lives there alone with his two large dogs. His clients are often shocked when they hear he lives nearby. They take for granted he would be living in the suburbs.

225 | DREAMS

The dogs are there for a reason. On three occasions Hogren's home has been burglarized. "I lost a camera, a coin collection, and money," he says. "The house was turned upside down. The third time the perpetrator was a teen-ager who was caught by the police and everything he got was returned."

After purchasing his home Chuck was also a victim of an unsavory but common institutional policy. He found he was unable to get insurance for it because of its urban location. The underwriter told him that it wasn't the company's practice to write policies in the city. The usually mild-mannered Hogren was incensed. Knowing that such a practice was illegal, and propelled by his passion for the city and for urban dwellers like himself, Chuck drove to the downtown home office of the company in question. There he pounded his fist on the table and demanded that they write him a policy. They did. When he told the underwriter later, she simply couldn't believe it.

Actually Chuck's problem was part of a much larger and more insidious practice called "redlining." According to Bill Leslie, who has made the fight against redlining a major avocation, "The banks look at areas and attempt to determine what communities won't hold up for the next twenty years because that's the usual length of a home mortgage. Then they refuse to lend any money in those communities with a poor prognosis. That all but guarantees that no property will be bought or sold in the area, so it simply dies.

"From the owners' standpoint, if you own a multiple family dwelling and you can't sell it, you're likely to try to get as good a return as possible on your investment. In order to get as much money as you can, you have to do what is called 'managing toward demolition.' The first thing is not to make any improvements on the building. That not only saves repair money but also keeps real estate taxes down. Then as your stable tenants move out to better quality buildings you replace each family with two or three to obtain more rent from the same property. You can see that this is going on just by looking at the overcrowdedness in many schools. When they build a school in a community they have single-family housing in mind as the standard community practice. But as the family size and the number of families increases, the schools bulge.

"In any event, as the apartment buildings begin overcrowding without any improvements, the number of building violations accumulates. Of course, the city building code inspector will come around but initially he's paid off with a couple of hundred bucks and nothing is done. Eventually someone will raise a serious objection—a community group, some ministers or somebody else. Or someone will be seriously injured due to the substandard conditions. Then the city comes around and gives the owner ninety days to make the necessary improvements.

"Often what follows is that the owner will 'torch' the building, burn it down—frequently with the families in it. Sometimes people die in the blaze. Others lose all their possessions. By torching, however, insurance can be collected and the owner is off the hook.

"In Ray Bakke's neighborhood just north of here they've had over 400 fires in four months. Many of them are torchings. In fact, much of the land you see that is vacant once had apartment buildings on it. They were torched, burning the people out. We had one white family that got burned out two times in a year and a half, although some of it may have been their own doing. Fires are very, very common in Cabrini-Green, far more so than ever before. It's a big part of the deterioration and decline of the community."

In discussing his attitude toward victims, Hogren told of the experience of a nearby McDonald's franchise. "Lynette and I used to eat lunch there regularly; then suddenly it was closed. There were metal grates over the door and everything. Wondering what had happened, I asked John Stevens about it. He said the place had been shot up. Robbers had gone in, disarmed the guard, and shot the place up, injuring one of the employees. It was the third time in a month the place had been held up. It makes me sad to hear of that sort of thing, because for one thing, it destroys jobs in the community. A lot of younger people worked there and depended on that McDonald's for their livelihood."

"I believe, however," says Hogren, "that you must have more than sympathy for the victim, because sympathy does not aid the victim at all. Real aid comes in dealing with the person who commits the crime and in trying to prevent more crime by changing conditions that foster it. That is accomplished through the church, education, drug and alcohol rehabilitation, and by developing a genuine community. We need an open community center like this YMCA, only much more comprehensive, which serves people like that woman who just came in here. (A young black woman accompanied by an infectiously friendly four-year-old boy had come in requesting help in notarizing some papers. Hogren had notarized her documents without charge.) When you have services available in the community, people don't have to go to the Loop or a currency exchange and be taken for a lot of money in executing simple transactions such as notarizing papers.

"We have to see the importance of urban concern. I think Bill's sermon about how God loves the city should be printed and distributed; it's a classic. He deals directly with what the problem is here. People have to become concerned because God's people live here, too.

Returning specifically to concern for the victims of crime, Hogren says, "I think one of the reasons I'm here is to try to effect some lessening of crime so that the community can become more wholesome, so that people can go out on the streets feeling safe and free. To allow people to be charged unjustly for crime is to further bitterness and rancor. It encourages crime. And to have people go to prison, guilty or not, is to place them in an institution where there will be ever-greater anger. Their outlooks will harden such that when they return to the streets they'll be more dangerous than ever. If the innocent are defended, and if those with problems can be treated or at least watched through probation, there is some redemption in the system and some hope for improvement."

Despite the community's problems, Hogren is quick to point out that many fine people have come out of Cabrini-Green—some who have risen to great heights professionally and educationally. Nevertheless, there are others, equally talented, whose potential appears to be wasted.

An example of such waste is Terry Hart, recently charged with armed robbery. Chuck had called Terry's mother and she said he was in jail. She didn't know why. "I went to see him in jail on a Saturday morning," says Hogren with a tone of sadness. "He told me he was back on drugs. I had taken him to Gateway House some time ago and he was going to enroll in their rehabilitation center. But he never got around to it. Back into drugs, Terry went out into the suburbs and used a toy gun to hold up a store. It's very sad. His mother is a fine woman; she goes to our church. In fact, I sat next to her yesterday. It's tragic to see him throwing his life away."

Hart is a classic case. He is a small youngster who got into trouble early in life and was one of Chuck's first clients. The first time Hogren dealt with him, Terry had been apprehended for smoking marijuana in the basement of a project building. He received an extended probation since he had been in some minor trouble even before that.

After that, Terry was involved in a number of capers, mainly to support a drug habit which has grown over the years. More recently he was arrested for robbing an eighty-year-old shopkeeper of $50, tying him up and putting a ladder on top of him. Almost all of his crimes have been free of physical harm to the victim; he only tries to get enough money to keep his habit running.

Despite his diminutive stature, Terry is heavily into sports. Because he doesn't have a job, is not well educated, and is not a very good athlete, his self-concept appears to suffer. His need for esteem showed rather markedly in a Young Life basketball game while Terry was on Dave Mack's team. Usually a benchwarmer, Terry finally got into a game. Wonder of wonders, he promptly stole the ball, raced the length of the court, and laid it in the hoop. Mack reports that he's never seen anyone strut the way Terry Hart did—a superstar sailing into an NFL end zone couldn't hold a candle to Terry's performance out in the middle of that court celebrating his athletic accomplishment. It brought down the house with howls of appreciative laughter; the instant celebrity received a standing ovation for his exhibition.

That incident was typical of Hart's need for achievement and recognition. His love for the glamor of sports is unbending. When Chuck visited Terry in jail he asked him what he would like. Terry requested two things: money from his mother and the *Sports Illustrated* magazine to which he subscribes.

Terry Hart is a youngster who could be reached if only he could kick his drug habit. He's actually a rather harmless fellow, not interested in hurting others. According to Hogren, he "doesn't have such a bad set of values and does have a wonderful mother." But Terry Hart is a victim of his own drug habit

229 | DREAMS

and is not able to make it in the community, educationally, occupationally, or athletically. He is one of many.

"I see the needless crimes," laments Hogren, "and the only way to help the victims is to prevent the violence through ministering and effecting change in the city." One of those ministries is justice.

Bill Leslie is very concerned about drugs. "I don't know where it's coming from but I do know that whenever the police have raids in the community the drug supply gets scarcer and, like coffee or anything else, the price goes up. With the price going up you get more crime and more money taken from the poor. Whenever I see the police make a successful raid or see a bunch of kids get arrested, I watch my step and keep vigilant on the street because I know the price is up and the crime will be too.

"Some representatives from the community came over to the church one night and said to Chuck and me that what we were doing at the legal aid clinic was fine, but it resembled the activity of an ambulance parked at the bottom of a hill, picking up already severely injured people. By severely injured people, they meant those on drugs. Although the overwhelming majority of the people Chuck deals with are acquitted and probably most of them are innocent anyway, the others are guilty and nearly all of their crime is drug-related.

"To get a kid off drugs we have very few alternatives. Perhaps the main one is the methadone route. But if a kid doesn't go to school regularly he isn't likely to go to the methadone clinic daily either. Besides, if he misses a day and needs a fix bad, it's all around him. His peers are probably on heroin and the pusher is itching to sell him some. Anyway, the community representatives wanted us to 'repair the dangerous highway, not just run an ambulance service.' They asked us to use our contacts to develop a farm where kids could both kick dope and learn how to work. That way we would have them away from the environment in which they got hooked and in a rehabilitative one. The representatives felt strongly that no kid with a record of drug addiction can survive in the community in which he got hooked. He knows too many of the wrong people.

"For example, Chuck was working with one youth who had four brothers, all addicted to heroin (one was a pusher). There is almost no way for a kid like that to survive here. All you're going to do is get him out of jail two or three times a year or maybe send him to an agency that is unable to deal with him where he really is.

"The community people were pressing for a farm where the kids could learn how to work and where the staff could work with the youth effectively outside the community. In addition, we could have a GED program (a program in which a person can earn the equivalent of a high school diploma) since most of the kids we're talking about are dropouts. We then would help some kids get back into school, obtain vocational training for others who aren't college bound, and use our contacts in Christian circles to place in jobs the kids who are prepared.

"They also suggested that we don't relocate the kids in Chicago but that we use the Christian network to locate them in other cities. A farm like that is a high priority of ours. We'd have to locate it in an area where people would tolerate such a program. We probably would mix the drug rehabilitation program with other church uses, making it more palatable to the community in which it would be located. Maybe we'd never have in excess of ten kids there at one time, but we could really make the thing work and bust this pattern of drugs and crime. Besides, with Chuck's success in negotiating lesser sentences for kids involved in Young Life and other ministries, we know that the courts would cooperate with us.

"As it is, the programs are just not there in the secular community. In one city I know of, there's one paid professional—whether it's a teacher, social worker, or administrator—for every seven children. Now you'd think that with one paid person earning ten or fifteen thousand for every seven kids, something would happen. But basically those people are sitting in offices; they aren't getting out on the street where the kids are. What's worse, the kid has to relate himself to seven or eight different agencies in order to get any help at all. Often he's got to hunt up those agencies by himself and frequently they're not in his neighborhood. What's needed is a network to follow the kid through."

As Bill Leslie drove through the community, his mind floated back to the late sixties. "When the gangs arose, crime picked up and there was a lot of hostility. I can remember kids in the tutoring program coming in with butcher knives, confronting their tutors. I can also recall playing basketball behind the church with some of the kids when all of a sudden they'd see a couple of whites walk down Wells Street. The kids would drop the basketball, go over and rob the passersby. They would take their watches and billfolds back to the court, and then resume playing the game."

Black-white tension was then at its apex. Bill told of incidents in which he would be playing ball with some of the neighborhood youths only to have a black fellow walk by and call the participants "Uncle Toms" for associating with him. The kids would immediately scatter. "We whites in the community were the only whites the blacks knew; therefore, we had to absorb a lot of the tension and hostility," says Bill matter-of-factly.

"Interestingly, the people in the red Cabrini buildings generally feel superior to those in the newer white structures in Green," said Leslie as we drove by the two sets of projects. "They want to have the area termed Cabrini *and* Green. That's a new phenomenon. Now they're even trying to identify each building so that instead of being a resident of Cabrini-Green, you're a resident of such and such a building. There's an effort to build some pride and respect into the individual buildings.

"The community has always been poor, but during the era of the riots about two-thirds of the families had working heads of the household. Now only one of every six families has an employed head. There was higher employment before the influx of poor blacks from the South. Currently in Chicago, just a shade under half of the welfare case load is from the rural South, nearly all from Mississippi and Alabama. In fact, I read in the paper recently that the South is the only area that has experienced a decrease in the number of youths on welfare. In essence, what's happened is that *we* have picked up rural southern poverty. These people are being stacked in high-rises amid the worst forms of destitution.

"This had been a black and Italian community. The blacks who were here deeply resented the influx of the rural southern blacks. I've had many old blacks tell me that the earlier community was one in which people knew and cared about each other. There were better schools and safer streets. Yet many from the South, living in rural poverty, adopted the neon dreams of riches in the city through television, etc., and came up to strike it rich. All they did was trade their rural poverty for urban squalor.

"About the time of the migration the unskilled jobs began drying up or went with the businesses to the suburbs. Some businesses remain on the fringes: the Oscar Mayer corporation is still here and they make the hot dogs sold in Disneyland and all the Marriott Great Americas. There is also Dr. Scholl's, and Montgomery Ward's home office. Ward's has built 68 million dollars' worth of office space here, so they have made their commitment to this community. A few other developments are going up as well. Montgomery Ward's has squawked to the city, too, about the city's commitments to the area in view of Ward's own investment. Mayor Daley had talked them into staying here and they wanted to see what the city would do. At one time Ward's told me they would pay anybody a hundred dollars who could find a secretary for them from the community, they were having such a hard time getting them to come and work there. I thought it might be a good way to raise money for the clinic.

"Unemployment is about as big a problem as any in this community. A lot of the crime and drugs is related to joblessness," says Bill. As a result of the lack of employment, about the only economically successful models the youngsters see are pimps, prostitutes, and pushers. The pimp drives the shiny car, can sit around all day and drink wine, while having the attention of attractive women at any time. He's rich and celebrative and doesn't have to work.

For girls, prostitution is magnetic. Prostitutes have money, nice clothes, a nice apartment, and constant solicitations from men. Though lower profile, the pusher is often the most affluent of all and holds tremendous economic and social power in the community. His power exceeds that of the pimps and prostitutes since he is the source of the drugs on which many of them are hooked. In the absence of many lawyers, doctors, or even community schoolteachers as models, those "three p's" loom influential.

"It seems that on the national level business people are saying we need to run with a 6 to 8 percent unemployment rate," continued Leslie. "Basically those are the unskilled buried at the bottom. Since so many living here are unskilled, the community unemployment rate is absolutely staggering—running somewhere around 50 percent, especially for young males between eighteen and twenty-five. We have worked and worked and there just aren't any jobs for them."

In addition, the lifestyle many Cabrini-Green residents have grown up with has not socialized them for the American job market. For example, 40 percent of the over 500,000 children in the Chicago public schools are on welfare. That means they don't see someone in the family get up and go to work each day. They don't see anyone get up early in the morning and skip breakfast in order to get to work on time. They don't see adults taking aspirin so they can make it to their job even though they're not feeling very well. The greatest lessons in life are "caught, not taught." Part of the family socialization process in the middle class is seeing adults do those things in holding down a job. But these kids never see anybody they know successfully employed; there are simply no models.

"A good bit of federal money comes through the city, especially in the summer, for teen-agers. In the past, there existed in theory an excellent program called the Neighborhood Youth Corps. Basically the program provided that a kid go out and associate himself or herself with a professional and work with that person for forty hours a week. The kid was paid a decent hourly rate. Unfortunately, because there were so many kids to be placed, some professionals were given nine or ten kids instead of one.

"I remember one summer, when we were running a summer day camp for maybe thirty-five community kids, the Neighborhood Youth Corps wanted to give us forty workers. The camp was for junior high kids and the Neighborhood Youth Corps wanted to give us forty high-school workers!

"The kids' skills were limited, so often they simply became your daily shadows for two and a half to three months. Since they were getting that money to supplement a family income of about three thousand a year, you desperately want them to get these jobs, so you take them on. Often, however, the kids wouldn't come in until eleven in the morning—but you would be thankful because that gave you three uninterrupted hours to get some things done. If they didn't come in at all you were really grateful because that gave you a full day. Nevertheless, you knew how desperately they needed the money so you signed their time slips so that they still got paid for the day. That was very common among businessmen in the neighborhood.

"The tragic result of all of this is that when the kid graduates from high school, with actually a sixth-grade education, he gets a job and comes in at eleven in the morning. His employer says, 'Hey, you can't come in at this time of day; if you aren't here by eight in the morning you're not getting paid at all,' and the kid can't believe it. In other cases the kid may come in about six days out of ten and he gets nailed for that. He's developed those patterns in the past when he was rewarded for that kind of behavior. Many of the kids, then, aren't prepared for the job market, so it's simply not enough for us to go out to the suburban churches and find jobs for many of them. If we did, the kid would lose the job; by the time he's lost two or three that way his failure pattern will have been further reinforced and he'll have such a depressed self-image that functioning will be difficult."

Bill Leslie has a dream. "What we have envisioned is to develop our own company," he explains. "It would take some money, although I don't know what the bucks would look like. Anyway, we would create our own business or corporation where we could employ kids for six or seven months and deal with them on all these work issues. We would have them work alongside professionals and in that fashion give them models. There are a number of different possibilities. One is to form a rehabilitation corporation which would rehab some of the old housing around here. We would hire a carpenter and plumber along with a few other people and then spot-pick some of the kids from the community who would come in to help. We could work with them on self-discipline and other things for six months or so and then go to some of the churches in the area where there are business people and ask each for one job a year for our 'graduates.' Knowing what the job would eventually be, we could prepare a kid between eighteen and twenty-five for it. When we felt a kid was ready, we would place him in the job.

"Such a corporation would benefit everyone. It would be productive for the kid and us in the community. It would also help some of the businesses who need to hire more minorities in order to land federal work contracts. This corporation concept is something we feel very keenly about. Of course, neither Chuck nor I can handle it. It would involve some sizable seed money, but once underway it would pretty much pay for itself."

Bill Leslie is interested in follow-through. He feels bad about nonsuccess stories like that of Mack Andrews, the unreconstructed drug addict. Routing him into the Young Life program, the next stop was the GED program at Kennedy-King College. "We didn't follow through enough and neither did they," laments Leslie. "He had to go down and study for four hours a night two or three nights a week when he wasn't really ready for that much self-discipline. He probably needed someone to go with him and get him started. Not having gone to school since he was thirteen, he just wasn't able to make that kind of commitment by himself."

Ever on the upbeat, Leslie adds, "But Andrews is an example of how we're trying to interlace the legal aid clinic with Young Life, educational programming, and spiritual growth. It's also evidence of a young man, even though it didn't succeed, being willing to give it a real shot on his own. He was willing to meet the program halfway."

A question about financing the legal aid clinic stimulated a bit of reflection.* "The clinic started out with a $10,000 foundation grant, followed by lesser amounts to maintain it in the next few years," says Bill. "But before we even had a clinic Chuck already had twenty-eight cases going from his work at the recreation center. Seeing that kind of need I felt we had to become active in pursuing justice in the neighborhood. His law firm objected to his involvement because most of the people couldn't pay and they were eating up a lot of Chuck's time."

Then when Hogren's father died, it appeared that Bill was going to lose even Chuck's part-time efforts if he moved to Florida with his mother. Leslie remembers the series of events well. "They had loaded up the furniture and the van had already left for Florida when his mother died. On the way to the cemetery I broached the subject of his future and the possibility of a legal aid clinic. Chuck agreed to do it for $100 a week. I

---

*The Cabrini-Green Legal Aid Clinic does not charge its clients attorney's fees. Defendants are requested to pay costs—if they are able.

think he was paid less than Gina, who was secretary to both Chuck and Joe White, and she was getting peanuts."

Looking at the big picture, Leslie remarked, "Money has always been a serious problem to the urban church. Financially, there are two ways to look at neighborhood ministry. One is that you won't do anything that your church itself cannot fund; a number of people, some of my dear friends, take that position.

"I've opted for the other view. I felt that our church should carry on everything a normal church would, because I didn't want the members to develop a welfare mentality where people from the outside have to bail you out. I do feel that where your treasure or money is, there is where your heart will be as well. So I wanted us to commit ourselves to making our regular budget. But I also saw us located here right next to a big section of the poor, where a lot of caring was needed in the area of justice and matters of that type, caring which we couldn't afford to carry on as a church. For awhile the separate legal aid budget was about equal to the size of our church budget. So I decided we would accept money from the outside to help fund other programs, particularly caring for the poor.

"I found over four hundred passages in the Bible that deal with the poor and I realized that most of my Christian friends have no relationships with the poor because geographically the poor aren't where they live. Yet all Christians have some responsibility to be obedient to that biblical command. I felt our church had a good track record, so we could put their contributions to good use in this community."

It hasn't been easy. Leslie has learned, over the years, to live without knowing where the next dollar is coming from. "I think it's a little easier for me to live with that feeling than for Chuck or Lynette or Gina," says Bill. "Some exciting things have come about as a result of that uncertainty. Time and time again the Lord has bailed us out at the last minute.

"I remember when the whole 'God is dead' theology came out. To my surprise a number of evangelicals were saying, 'Well, maybe he is. At least he is in my experience because there's nothing going on in me.' Money problems have spared me from that. We have such a history of having our backs to the financial wall, only to have the Lord provide miraculously, that no one can convince me that God is dead.

"Basically, we have operated from the beginning not knowing where the money for the next year and sometimes for the next month was coming from. It has come from a variety of sources. One is through interested people, sometimes from within our church. I remember one wife of a teacher who committed herself to making clothes and macramé hangings, selling them, and then turning the proceeds over to the clinic. Many of the people in the church have given generously. This spring one young woman who worked for a Christian organization and made very little money gave the clinic a thousand-dollar gift. She also sent me a note to pass on to Chuck which said that since the previous September she had prayed for the clinic at least a half hour a day. I told her that I wasn't sure I'd be able to pray that long daily for the clinic, since I didn't know enough to say for that length of time. But that kind of support has kept us going.

"Some of the money has come from 'alumni' of the church. Because we're in an area of the city where there's a lot of transience—few people own their own homes, many of our people are students, and so forth—we knew that many would eventually move away. So we decided to develop an alumni like that of a college, an alumni with a commitment to turf and the poor so that even after they leave, their support will go on.

"We also receive some money from two suburban churches, and through articles appearing in newspapers and Christian magazines, which have stimulated people's interest in justice. We've also had a number of small gifts from individuals who have given very sacrificially."

Despite those fund-raising efforts, the clinic has been on the brink of closing many times. At one point it was running over $10,000 in the red, forcing the church to float a four-figure loan to the clinic. By then the clinic had lapsed so far behind that Chuck went for three months with no salary at all. Then, theoretically, he worked half time. The arrangement provided that he be retained on a half-time basis along with half-time secretarial aid. Of course, for Chuck, in the final analysis about the only reduction was in his pay. Chuck's full-time salary now is $13,000 a year, ludicrously short of what a lawyer in Chicago's Loop makes.

Bill observed that the constant and seemingly over-accumulating deficit acted as a "heavy noose around Chuck and Lynette's necks. They were faced with the monstrous task of defending the community residents by themselves in the absence of almost any support at all. It's miraculous that both of them didn't burn out long ago. When you're that far in the red, it becomes very depressing. You wonder if anyone out there cares about justice for the urban poor at all."

The church hasn't always been in a financial position to help the clinic. But because of Bill's intense commitment to the clinic and a ministry of justice, the church used money given to it for other reasons to ease temporarily the clinic's perilous money crunch. "For obviously ethical reasons, we don't like to do that, even for a short period of time," says Leslie. The alternative, however, seemed even worse.

"In the autumn of '76 we were in deep trouble, so one Sunday in October we took a Fellowship Hour after the morning worship service to talk about the clinic and ask that people pray. To our everlasting amazement, on the following Tuesday we received an unsolicited gift in the mail for $4,000. The check had been written on that same Sunday.

"Now $4,000 may not seem like much to a lot of people, but to us down here in the city that kind of affluence is rare. In fact we were really debating whether to close the clinic or not. We were wondering what God was saying to us: Should we pray more? Should we close? I kept saying No to the latter question because I saw all those verses in the Bible about justice and the poor and I also saw all the injustice around here. Now if we had cleaned up all the injustice or if there were a lot of other people in here doing the same thing we were, then we could easily have eased our way out and said God had brought the whole thing to a halt. But, if anything, there was more injustice going on here, and a greater-than-ever need for that kind of witness."

When you ask Bill Leslie about the needs of the clinic, one of his top priorities is prayer. "There's a tremendous need for prayer. The clinic's whole story is one of constant near-miracles closely related to people's prayers. Prayer is vital," he asserts.

Money has taken on a new dimension. "Hoping to have two full-time lawyers like we did when Dan Van Ness worked here, along with secretarial help and office space, our optimum budget is about $40,000 a year," explains Leslie. "When you're talking about $40,000 that's an awful lot of ten and fifteen dollar gifts. If Chuck or I have to spend our time hustling that money, he isn't going to do much at the clinic and I'm not going to do much ministering. Besides, Chuck isn't a very good fund raiser largely because he doesn't feel comfortable doing it. He can ask for money for somebody else but not for money that will go in part for his salary. When we were talking about $10,000 I could raise that myself, but the whole thing has gotten beyond that. And of course, we have four or five other church programs that demand time as well."

Despite the need for big-money support, Leslie knows that smaller gifts count as well. "I think that within Christian circles now everybody is going after the big bucks and if you can't give at least $5,000 no one takes any time to court you. It almost looks as if inflation has pushed everything up so that 'the widow's mite' is a thing of the past. I don't feel that way; I still think that low-income people need to be involved in this as well—they need a sense of participating in support of justice too."

Sizable effort has been expended in seeking foundation grants and other larger sums. "I've observed that most foundations and businesses will give you money to get started," commented Leslie, "especially if you've got something unique that could be reproduced elsewhere. But no one is interested in providing maintenance money. After you've been operating four or five years, established a solid track record, and are about to reap a lot of what you've sown, money is hard to come by."

The resourceful Leslie is never out of ideas. While continually seeking small gifts as well as foundational and institutional support, Bill sees the legal community in particular as a potential helper. "If a law firm or business could pick up the salaries of our legal aid personnel it would be mutually beneficial. They could get a sizable tax deduction for contributing to the salaries, and their help would literally enable the clinic to turn the corner financially. They could even hire the legal staff as public relations people and then release them to do the clinic's work. In addition, it would help if a law firm were to let our personnel, especially Chuck, use their library for research purposes.

"Another thing that would really help would be to have a business manager or fund raiser for the clinic. That would not only aid us in raising money but would enable us to make better use of Chuck."

The legal aid clinic was the brainchild of Bill Leslie. His dreams are now shared more widely—although the financial ones have not as yet come true. In the meantime, Chuck Hogren works on—standing between blood and justice in Cabrini-Green.

Because of urban renovation, the clinic will soon be moving from the Isham YMCA to a new address in the Cabrini-Green community. For a brochure or further information, it can always be contacted through a permanent address: Cabrini-Green Legal Aid Clinic, % LaSalle St. Church, 1136 N. LaSalle, Chicago, IL 60610.

CABRINI GREEN
little city of blackness

Cabrini Green where I had
emerged from ghetto boy
into ghetto man!

For my eyes had saw the birth
of this little black city that
created a ghetto life span!

Cabrini Green my home where
black families roam the streets
of poverty struggling to survive.
For a mystic passion of love
and unity strike the minds of
our ghetto people for somehow
it seems to had disappear
like we are waiting for a new
time to arrive!

Cabrini Green a place
where love and respect could
become a reality in the Blackness
of each others heart!

For hate shall only be a
word that the past had
engulfed and made it
nonexistence, a reality for
a new ghetto passion
shall start!

Cabrini Green a cry of
poverty fills the air
with a new attitude that
somehow create
the flow of black
ghetto blood!

As Black and beautiful
people become more
aware of what we are
doing to make ourselves
distinct within the Cabrini
Green and everywhere else
where Black life exist in
all the little Black cities
for unity and love for each
other shall forever stop the
evil flood.

By a student from the Cabrini-Green housing project,
painted on the wall of a building at 515 W. Oak St.

APPENDIX 1
Statistical Presentation of the Clinic's Case Load

Cabrini-Green Legal Aid Clinic
1515 North Ogden Avenue   Chicago, Illinois 60610
TEL (312) 266-1345   November 15, 1977

TYPE OF CASE & NUMBER HANDLED

Appeal   1
Legal Advice   41
Domestic Relations   87
Consumer   56
Traffic   34
Employment   14
Landlord/Tenant   28
Public Aid   8
General Information   20
Community Organizations   22
Family   14
Miscellaneous   80
Attempted Murder   1
Resisting Arrest   3
Murder   4
Robbery   13
Armed Robbery   37
Rape   5
Burglary   23
Battery   20
Aggravated Battery   11
Assault   2
Aggravated Assault   11
Disorderly Conduct   7
Drugs   19
Unlawful Use of a Weapon   30
Possession of Stolen Property   2
Theft   49
Forgery   2
Prostitution   3
Sex Offense   4
Criminal Damage to Property   6
Violation of Probation   3

244 | THE RELUCTANT DEFENDER

Shoplifting 2
Defacing a Weapon 1
Unlawful Possession of a Motor Vehicle 1
Mob Action 1
Unlawful Restraint (Kidnapping) 1
Trespassing 2

Statistics
Cabrini-Green Legal Aid Clinic
1973-1977

YEAR	SETTLED	DISMISD	PROB	TIME	PROB W/ CONDITION	ADVICE	REF'D	TOTAL	%
1973	49	31	15	4	3	42	23	167	31%
1974	46	26	7	7	4	21	28	139	26%
1975	39	22	8	1	1	17	21	109	20%
1976	24	9	16	7	5	13	24	98	18%
1977*	19	-0-	3	1	1	-0-	4	28	5%
total	177	88	49	20	14	93	100	541	
	33%	16%	9%	4%	3%	17%	18%		100%

1. Stats do not include 83 Divorces handled by the Clinic
2. Stats do not include 29 currently OPEN cases
3. Stats do not include 15 cases handled by PLS because files are with PLS

*The diminished number of cases in 1977 was due to the Clinic's board placing an almost year-long moratorium on taking new cases, because of lack of funds and assistance for Hogren. The caseload is now increasing once again.

APPENDIX

SETTLED: usually to the client's satisfaction, negotiated settlement, etc.
DISMISD: dismissed, SOL, DWP, acquitted
PROB: probation, supervision
TIME: conviction with prison sentence
PROB w/ condition: probation with the condition that client enter drug, alcohol or psychological treatment.
ADVICE: legal advice, or clients who decide not to continue with action and so withdraw
REF'D: case referred to PD or other attorney usually because of "lack of co-operation" on the client's part; also clients who are not financially eligible for services.

SOL: Stricken Off with Leave to Reinstate (Case is dismissed but can be reopened within 60 days. It rarely is, however.
DWP: Dismissed for Want of Prosecution (Case is dropped because no complaining witness is present.)
PD: Public Defender
PLS: Preventive Legal Services

APPENDIX 2
Population and Income Characteristics of Cabrini-Green*

	Project	Area
Total Population	14,240	26,730
Total Families	3,058	5,164
Total Families Below $4,000 Poverty Level	1,908	1,911
Percent Below Poverty Level	53	37
Median Family Income	$3.895	

PUBLIC HOUSING DEVELOPMENTS
Frances Cabrini Green   1943
Number/Type of bldgs: 55/2-story
Total Units: 581
Population: 1,950
Average Family Size: 3.4
Median Family Income: $3,715

Cabrini Extension   1958
Number/Type of bldgs: 7/7-story midrises
                                 5/10-story midrises
                                 3/19-story midrises

Total Units: 1,896
Population: 6,975
Average Family Size: 3.7
Median Family Income: $3,775

William Green Homes   1962
Number/Type of bldgs: 5/15-story highrises
                                 3/16-story highrises

Total Units: 1,092
Population: 5,220
Average Family Size: 4.8
Median Family Income: $4,425

*Source: Chicago Housing Authority Statistical Summary 1976
U.S. Census 1970

APPENDIX 3
Motion for Pre-Trial Discovery

State of Illinois
County of Cook

In the Circuit Court of Cook County—
County Department—Juvenile Division

PEOPLE OF THE STATE OF ILLINOIS)
                vs.   )JUVENILE NOS.
        Roy Harris
_____)
          Respondents   )

MOTION FOR PRE-TRIAL DISCOVERY
PURSUANT TO ILLINOIS SUPREME COURT RULE 413
TO:

Now come The People of the State of Illinois by BERNARD CAREY, State's Attorney of Cook County, by his Assistant Leonard Spaulding and moves this Honorable Court, pursuant to Illinois Supreme Court Rules 413 (c), 413 (d) and 415 (b) and subject to any limitations set therein, to enter an Order directing the defendant and his attorney or attorneys:

    1. To give written notice to the People of the State of Illinois of any defense, affirmative or non-affirmative, which the defendant intends to assert at any hearing or at trial.

    2. To furnish in writing to the People of the State of Illinois the names and last known addresses of persons the defendant intends to call as witnesses, together with their relevant written or recorded statements, including memoranda reporting or summarizing their oral statements, and any record of prior criminal convictions of such witnesses known to the defendant.

    3. To inform the People of the State of Illinois of, and to permit the inspection and copying or photographing of any reports, results or testimony relative thereto, of physical or mental examinations or of scientific tests, experiments, or comparisons, and any other reports or statements of experts which defense counsel has in his possession or control, including, but not limited to, statements made by the defendant contained in reports, any part of which defense counsel intends to use at a hearing or trial.

    4. To furnish the People of the State of Illinois with any books, papers, documents, photographs, or tangible objects the defendant or his attorney intend to use as evidence or for impeachment at a hearing or trial.

5. To notify the People of the State of Illinois of the existence of any material or information subject to disclosure which is discovered subsequent to compliance with any Orders entered pursuant to Illinois Supreme Court Rules 413 (c) and 413 (d).

BERNARD CAREY
State's Attorney of Cook County
By Leonard Spaulding
Assistant State's Attorney
Juvenile Court, Room 305,
2246 W. Roosevelt Road,
Chicago, Illinois
Telephone 633-2040

APPENDIX 4
Statement of Juveniles Lockhart and Brown
CID   6 HOM/SEX
21 April 1973

This is a joint statement of Martin E. Lockhart M/N 12 Years of 982 N. Hudson Phone 312-642-6498 and Ellis Brown M/N 14 Years of 983 N. Cambridge Phone 312-664-3514 relative to the fatal shooting of Mr. Edgar Richards which occurred on 20 April 1973 at about 9:15 PM at 978 N. Hudson Avenue.

Statement taken at 3801 N. Damen Avenue 3rd Floor Homicide Office 21 April 1973 at 4:40 PM.

Questioned & Typed by Inv. Phillip J. Rollins #39221 CID #6 H/S YO George Royce #49321 area #6 Youth Mr. Louis Lockhart (father of Martin E. Lockhart) of 982 N. Hudson Ave. Phone 642-6498

Q. Martin, will you tell me your full name, age, address and the name and grade of the school you attend?
A. Martin E. Lockhart, 12, 982 N. Hudson, St. Joseph's, the grade is 7th.

Q. Ellis, will you tell me your full name, age, address and the name and grade of the school you attend?
A. Ellis Brown, 14, 983 N. Cambridge, St. Joseph's, 8th grade.

Q. Ellis, did you have occasion to be in the 900 Block of Hudson Ave. on 20 April 1973 at about 9:15 PM?
A. Yeh.

Q. Martin, did you have occasion to be on the 900 Block of N. Hudson Ave. at about 9:15 PM on 20 April 1973?
A. Yeh.

Q. Martin, while you were in the area of the 900 Block of N. Hudson Ave. on 20 April 1973 at about 9:15 PM, did you have an occasion to see anything unusual happen?
A. Yes.

Q. Ellis, you have heard the question which I have just asked to Martin, did you see anything unusual happen at the time?
A. Yeh.

THE RELUCTANT DEFENDER

Q. Martin, will you tell me in your own words what, if anything unusual you observed at the time?
A. I saw a man got shot and I saw the man that got shot driving down the street in a cab. He hit this man named John Feller's car and he kept on going till he hit the pole.

Q. Ellis, did you see a man get shot?
A. Yeh.

Q. Martin, who were you with when you saw this man get shot?
A. Me, Ellis Crown, this girl named Henrietta and her sister and this girl named Charlene Dandridge.

Q. Martin, where were you standing when you saw the man get shot?
A. In front of the girl named Henrietta's house.

Q. Ellis, where were you standing at the time?
A. In front of Henrietta's house.

Q. Martin, have you ever seen the man in the cab before?
A. Nope.

Q. Ellis, have you ever seen the man in the cab before?
A. No.

Q. Martin, did you see who shot the man in the cab?
A. Yep.

Q. Ellis, did you see the man who shot the man in the cab?
A. Yeh.

Q. Martin, will you tell me what you saw at that time?
A. I saw the boy and the man in the cab, they was struggling with each other. Then I heard two shots. Then I ran.

Q. Martin: have you ever seen the boy who was struggling with the cabdriver before last night?
A. Nope.

Q. Ellis, what did you see?
A. I just see the boy. He walked up to the taxicab, he grabbed the cabdriver's hand and they was tussling, the boy stuck his hand into the coat pocket in the inside and then I heard POP, POP, then I run down the street.

Q. Ellis, have you ever seen that boy before?
A. Nope.

Q. Martin, would you be able to recognize this boy if you saw him again?
A. Yep.

Q. Ellis, would you be able to recognize this boy if you saw him again, I am talking about the boy who was tussling with the cabdriver?
A. Yeh.

251 | APPENDIX

Q. Martin, I will now show you a photograph of five (5) male negroes, out of these five men, do you recognize any of them as being the boy who walked up to the cabdriver?
A. Yep.
Q. Martin, I will write the numbers one through five over the heads of these boys from left to right, will you tell me which numbered boy is the one that you saw struggling with the cabdriver?
A. Two.
Q. Ellis, I will show you the same photo, can you tell me which of the numbered boys was the one that you saw tussling with the cabdriver?
A. Two.
Q. Martin, did you see, excuse me, did you hear this boy say anything to the cabdriver?
A. Nope.
Q. Ellis, did you hear this boy say anything to the cabdriver?
A. I heard the boy mumbling.
Q. Martin, when you say that the boy and the cabdriver were struggling, what do you mean?
A. The boy stuck his hands in the car and the cabdriver grabbed the boy's hands.
Q. Ellis, did you see the same thing?
A. Yep.
Q. Martin, how far from the cab were you when you saw the boy struggling with the cabdriver?
A. About 20 feet.
Q. Ellis, how far were you from the cab when you saw the boy tussling with the driver?
A. About 13 feet.
Q. Martin, do you know this boy's name?
A. Nope.
Q. Ellis, do you know this boy's name?
A. Nope.
Q. I will ask both of you boys to sign your name on the back of the photograph from which you have identified the number 2 boy. SO AFFIXED. The back of the photograph was also signed by Mr. Louis Lockhart.

APPENDIX 5
Motion for Substitution of Judges
IN THE CIRCUIT COURT OF COOK COUNTY
COUNTY DEPARTMENT—CRIMINAL DIVISION

PEOPLE OF THE STATE OF)
ILLINOIS)
                                  Plaintiff)
              vs.)
ROY HARRIS)
Defendant)

MOTION FOR SUBSTITUTION OF JUDGES

Your Petitioner, ROY HARRIS, by and through his attorney, CHARLES V. HOGREN, respectfully represents unto this Honorable Court that he is the Defendant in the above entitled cause, now pending before your Honor, one of the Judges of the Circuit Court of Cook County.

    Your Petitioner further represents that he fears that he will not receive a fair and impersonal trial or hearing in said cause if he is tried before the Honorable Judge John Preston before whom the above entitled cause is now pending, because the said Judge is prejudiced against the Defendant herein.

    Your Petitioner further alleges that he fears that he will not receive a fair and impartial trial or hearing before the Honorable Judge Sampson, one of the Judges of this Court, because he is also prejudiced against the Defendant.

    Your Petitioner further alleges that the knowledge of said prejudice did not come to this applicant prior to ten days before filing this petition, but said knowledge came to your Petitioner less than ten days before the making of this application; that said knowledge came to your petitioner on the 1st day of April 1974.

    WHEREFORE, and because of the fact that this Petitioner fears and believes that he will not receive a fair and impartial trial or hearing before the Honorable Judge Preston nor before the Honorable Judge Sampson, he respectfully prays this Court to allow a substitution of Judges, and for an order referring this matter to the Presiding Judge for reassignment.

                                                      Charles V. Hogren
                                                          PETITIONER

253 | APPENDIX

I, Charles V. Hogren, on oath state that I am the Atty. for the Defendant in the above entitled action. The allegations in this motion are true.

             Charles V. Hogren
              for Roy Harris

SIGNED AND SWORN TO
before me this 8 th.
day of April
1974.

_____

NOTARY PUBLIC

CHARLES V. HOGREN
Attorney for Defendant
825 N. Hudson
Chicago, Illinois
266-1345

APPENDIX 6
Classification of Offenses
ILLINOIS REVISED STATUTES 1975 Chapter 38, Sec. 1005
1005-5-1
Classification of Offenses (a) The provisions of this Article shall govern the classification of all offenses for sentencing purposes. (b) Felonies are classified for the purpose of sentencing, as follows:

(1) Murder (as a separate class);
(2) Class 1 felonies;
(3) Class 2 felonies;
(4) Class 3 felonies; and
(5) Class 4 felonies.

(c) Misdemeanors are classified, for the purpose of sentencing, as follows:

(1) Class A Misdemeanors;
(2) Class B Misdemeanors;
(3) Class C Misdemeanors.

(d) Petty offenses and business offenses are not classified.

1005-8-1
Sentence of Imprisonment for Felony (a) A sentence of imprisonment for a felony shall be an indeterminate sentence set by the Court under this section. (b) The maximum term shall be set according to the following limitations:

(1) for murder, the maximum term shall be any term in excess of 14 years;
(2) for a Class 1 felony, the maximum term shall be any term in excess of 4 years;
(3) for a Class 2 felony, the maximum term shall be any term in excess of one year not exceeding 20 years;
(4) for a Class 3 felony, the maximum shall be any term in excess of one year not exceeding 10 years;
(5) for a Class 4 felony, the maximum term shall be any term in excess of one year not exceeding three years.

(c) The minimum term shall be set according to the following limitations:

(1) for murder, the minimum term shall be 14 years unless the court, having regard to the nature and circumstances of the offense and the history and character of the defendant, sets a higher minimum term;

(2) for a Class 1 felony, the minimum term shall be 4 years unless the court, having regard to the nature and circumstances of the offense and the history and character of the defendant, sets a higher minimum term;
(3) for a Class 2 felony, the minimum term shall be one year unless the court, having regard to the nature and circumstances of the offense and the history and character of the defendant, sets a higher minimum term, which shall not be greater than one third, of the maximum term set in that case by the court;
(4) for a Class 3 felony, the minimum term shall be one year unless the court, having regard to the nature and circumstances of the offense and the history and character of the defendant sets a higher minimum term, which shall not be greater than one-third of the maximum term set in that case by the court;
(5) for a Class 4 felony, the minimum term shall be one year in all cases.

(d) The court may reduce or modify, but shall not increase the length of a sentence by order entered not later than 30 days from the date the sentence was imposed. This shall not enlarge the jurisdiction of the court for any other purpose.

(e) Every indeterminate sentence shall include as though written therein a parole term in addition to the term of imprisonment. Subject to earlier termination under section 3-3-8[1], the parole term shall be as follows:
(1) For murder, or a Class 1 felony, 5 years;
(2) For a Class 2 felony or a Class 3 felony, 3 years;
(3) For a Class 4 felony, 2 years.

(f) A defendant who has a previous and unexpired sentence of imprisonment imposed by another state and who after sentence for a crime in Illinois must return to service the unexpired prior sentence may have his sentence by the Illinois court ordered to be concurrent with the prior sentence in the other state and the court may order that any time served on the unexpired portion of the sentence in the other state prior to his return to Illinois shall be credited on his Illinois sentence. The other state shall be furnished with a copy of the order imposing sentence which order shall provide that when the offender is released from confinement of the other state, whether by parole or by termination of the sentence, the offender shall be transferred to the Illinois Department of Corrections. The court shall cause the Department of Corrections to be notified of such sentence at the time of commitment and to be provided with copies of all records regarding the sentence.

Amended by P.A. 78-939, § 1, eff. July 1, 1974

1005-8-3

Sentence of Imprisonment for Misdemeanors (a) A sentence of imprisonment for a misdemeanor shall be for a determinate term

[1]Chapter 38, Sec. 1003-3-8

according to the following limitations:
- (1) for a Class A misdemeanor, for any term less than one year except for violations of section 24-1(a) (4), (5), (6), (8), (10) of the Criminal Code of 1961 which provides for a mandatory minimum penalty of at least one day of imprisonment, not counting the day of arrest in a penal institution other than a penitentiary;
- (2) for a Class B misdemeanor, for not more than 6 months;
- (3) for a Class C misdemeanor, for not more than 30 days.

(b) The good behavioral allowance shall be determined under section 3 of the Misdemeanant Good Behavior Allowance Act.[1]

---

[1] Chapter 75, Sec. 32

APPENDIX 7
Impeachment for a Former Contradictory Sworn Testimony in a Previous Trial

The questioning procedure used in the impeachment process is as follows:

LAWYER: Have you ever made a contradictory statement [to the current one]?

WITNESS: No.

LAWYER: At any time?

WITNESS: No.

LAWYER: At any place?

WITNESS: No.

LAWYER: To any person?

WITNESS: No.

The witness is then reminded of testimony given in a prior court appearance; and of the time, place, and before whom the evidence was taken.

LAWYER: You were sworn to tell the truth on that occasion [the previous court appearance], isn't that right?

WITNESS: Yes.

LAWYER: Was this question asked of you and did you make this answer?

The question and answer from the previous court appearance is then read.

Witness: Yes.

The affirmative answer by the witness to the above question has the effect of impeaching his present contradictory testimony. If, however, the witness answers No to the above question, the court reporter who was present at the previous court appearance is summoned to present his/her notes to the court, demonstrating that the witness did, in fact, respond as alleged.

APPENDIX 8
Motion to Suppress the In-court Identification of the Respondent

STATE OF ILLINOIS)
COUNTY OF COOK) ss.
IN THE CIRCUIT COURT OF COOK COUNTY
COUNTY DEPARTMENT, JUVENILE DIVISION
In the interest of)
CARL JEFFERSON, a minor.) No.

MOTION TO SUPPRESS THE IN-COURT
IDENTIFICATION OF THE RESPONDENT

Now comes the respondent, CARL JEFFERSON, by and through his attorney, CHARLES V. HOGREN, and moves this Honorable Court to enter an order suppressing any testimony at the time of the hearing relating to a certain line-up the respondent participated in, and further suppressing at the time of the hearing the in-court identification of the respondent by the State's witness, and in support of said motion states as follows:

1. The respondent, CARL JEFFERSON, was taken into custody on March 3, 1975, in the vicinity of Lincoln Avenue, south of Belmont, Chicago, Illinois.

2. The respondent was transported to the 19th District police station and at that time was put in a line-up.

3. At the police station the respondent was presented to the identification witness, not in an impartial line-up, but in a one person show-up, where the defendant was presented individually in police custody to the identification witness.

4. The one person show-up took place nearly a month after the alleged offense and was not necessitated by exigent circumstances and was thus unnecessarily suggestive and conducive to irreparable mistaken identity.

5. The identification of the respondent was made in violation of his Constitutional rights under the 6th and 14th Amendments of the Constitution of the United States.

WHEREFORE, the respondent requests this Honorable Court to suppress any testimony at the time of the hearing relating to the above stated line-up and further to suppress at the time of the hearing the in-court identification of the respondent by the State's witness.

                                        CHARLES V. HOGREN

CHARLES V. HOGREN
Attorney for Respondent
1515 N. Ogden, Chicago
266-1345

APPENDIX 9
Psychiatric Report

North Park Clinic, S.C.
650 Busse Highway
Park Ridge, Illinois 60068
June 14, 1976

Mr. Charles V. Hogren
Cabrini Green Legal Aid Clinic
1515 North Ogden Avenue
Chicago, Illinois 60610

Re: Keith Moran

Dear Mr. Hogren:

I have now seen Keith Moran at the Cook County House of Correction and his mother, brother and sister have been seen in my Clinic for background information about the family. These contacts have been sufficient to come to a clinical impression and be able to offer some recommendations. I will not review the details that led to his coming to the House of Correction because what he told me was entirely in conformity with what you had indicated to me. He claims that these acts have only occurred under the influence of alcohol and his mother confirms this. It's possible that he is saying this as an excuse to help to alleviate some of the consequences of his behavior legally but I tended to believe him. I say this because Keith was open in so many areas and I sense no resistance. He was cooperative throughout the entire interview. There are several significant features in his background and in his present situation which I would like to bring to your attention.

He has a very conflictual relationship to his father. His father left the family when Keith was six years old. He has little memory of his father at that time but his resentment of his father continues. He sees his father perhaps a dozen times a year and feels as if nothing happens. He has an ongoing fear that his father will hurt his mother. In some ways an Uncle Jack took his father's place as he grew up. Early in his memories of his mother he has considerable sense of pleasure but in his adolescence he has a lot of painful experiences because he recalls times that his father hit his mother and then his mother's alcoholism was very distressing to him. All of this has resulted in his being rather tied to his mother, despite the fact that his mother is now off of alcohol completely and well rehabilitated. It is certainly self-destructive on Keith's part to use alcohol as he does in view of the difficulty that it has presented in the family picture during all of his life.

I would draw attention, also, to the fact that I think there is some suggestion that Keith may have had minimal brain dysfunction as a child although I cannot corroborate this from a clinical interview. He has had a reading difficulty all of his life and his handwriting is very poor. Also, he only went to his junior year in high school and then dropped out. He felt he didn't like school and didn't do well at it.

There is a well known correlation between minimal brain dysfunction and criminality.

This whole family is sad. They all have the same feelings about the tragedies that have occurred to them but they distinctly do not share them with each other. Even though they all indicate that in some ways father cannot be trusted, on the other hand they all feel that mother has an ambivalent relationship to father. Keith has a deep need to have his mother explore this possibility of being with father and settle it once and for all. I think Keith has very deep needs to protect his mother and that's one of the dynamics behind his self-destruction.

Diagnostically, I see Keith as depressed and also as being alcoholic. I would also raise the question of minimal brain dysfunction in the past and possibly even at the present. The impulsivity under the influence of alcohol is certainly a concern.

My recommendations are that whenever it is feasible Keith should be actively involved in Alcoholics Anonymous and be helped to make a consistent commitment to total abstinence from alcoholic use. Furthermore, family therapy or counseling is very important to further explore their relationship ties to each other, to explore the relationship between father and mother even though they are divorced, and generally to reinforce Keith's potential for adult functioning. I wonder, also, whether an alcohol EEG might be useful to explore the possibility of abnormal brain wave patterns while under the influence of alcohol. This has been frequently reported and certainly abstinence is recommended whether such an EEG were abnormal or not. I have interpreted all of these recommendations to Keith and to his mother and they both are responsive to them.

If there is anything further I can do to be of help to Keith and his family, I'd be very pleased to.

Sincerely yours,

Truman G. Esau, M.D.

APPENDIX 10
Order to Recall and Quash Warrant and to Reinstate Bond

STATE OF ILLINOIS)
COUNTY OF COOK) ss.
IN THE CIRCUIT COURT OF COOK COUNTY
COUNTY DEPARTMENT—CRIMINAL DIVISION

PEOPLE OF THE STATE OF
ILLINOIS,
Plaintiff
vs.
Andrew Arthur
Defendant

MOTION TO VACATE BOND FORFEITURE,
QUASH WARRANT AND SET FOR TRIAL

Now comes ANDREW ARTHUR, by and through his attorney, CHARLES V. HOGREN, and moves this honorable Court to vacate the bond forfeiture entered on March 29, 1977, and to recall and quash any warrant entered herein and to reassign the matter for trial, and in support of this motion the Defendant states as follows:

1. He was present in court on March 29, 1977, at 9:50 A.M.
2. He was informed a Bond Forfeiture had been entered and a warrant issued.
3. He was told by the Assistant State's Attorney to leave the court room since the case had already been called.

WHEREFORE, Defendant prays that the Bond forfeiture be vacated, warrant recalled and quashed and that the matter be reassigned for trial.

                                      CHARLES V. HOGREN

CHARLES V. HOGREN
Cabrini-Green Legal Aid Clinic
1515 N. Ogden Ave.
Chicago, Illinois 60610
266-1345

APPENDIX 11
1977 Annual Report
Financial Statement
Cabrini-Green Legal Aid Clinic

TOTAL INCOME	$31,331.00*
TOTAL EXPENSE	$29,006.00
	$ 2,325.00

ON HAND   LSC—$1663.00
                  OAK—$ 661.00

*reflects $6,450.00 from the Illinois Humane Society

EXPENSE BREAKDOWN

PAYROLL	$23,844.00**
TELEPHONE	$ 939.00
RENT	$ 840.00
BOOKS/ SEMINARS	$ 1,425.00
LEGAL EXPENSES	$ 616.00
(transcripts etc.)	
OFFICE EXPENSE	$ 1,092.00
PETTY CASH	$ 250.00
TOTAL	$29,006.00

**includes consulting fees of $5,000.00

PROPOSED (IDEAL) BUDGET
Cabrini-Green Legal Aid Clinic Phase I

Description	1978	1979	1980	Cumulative
Senior Attorney	$17,500	$20,000	$22,000	$59,500
Consumer Affairs Attorney	14,500	16,000	17,500	48,000
Social Worker	13,500	14,200	15,000	42,700
Paralegal/ Secretary	9,000	10,000	11,500	30,500
Two Law Students	5,000*	5,500	6,000	16,500

APPENDIX

Rent	1,200	1,500	1,800	4,500
Telephone	850	950	1,050	2,850
Office Supplies	600	700	800	2,100
Subscriptions, Books Conferences	2,500	3,250	4,100	9,850
Grand Total	$61,650	$68,100	$75,250	$216,500
Increase in Operating Expenses Over Preceding Year	—	6,450	7,150	
*Currently Funded	$61,650	$61,650	$68,100	